Judy Hall's Book of Psychic Development

Judy Hall

Flying Horse Books

Published in 2014 by
Flying Horse Books
an imprint of
The Wessex Astrologer Ltd
4A Woodside Road
Bournemouth
BH5 2AZ
England

www.wessexastrologer.com

ISBN 9781902405919

A catalogue record of this book is available at The British Library

Cover design by Jonathan Taylor

Contents

Introduction
Re–Visioning and Right Timing

Knowing, or perhaps just feeling and intuiting, that we are connected to each other and to the world in more ways than through our senses is not really new, it is as old as human culture and consciousness.

Ervin Laszlo[1]

Many years ago I was asked to write a book on intuition. The brief was precise. It was to be a rigorous handbook that would appeal to men as well as women, and it had to open with research to back up what I was saying. It couldn't be 'airy fairy or nebulous'. Nothing 'woo–woo' – and it certainly couldn't mention the word psychic. It had to be 'scientific': the very antithesis to intuition in fact. Taking a deep breath and drawing on years of experience of teaching psychic development to many different people from around the world, men and women, I wrote a carefully thought–out course that would stimulate the intuitive right brain and engineer a natural opening up of psychic abilities interwoven with what scientific facts there were available about this most mysterious of senses to keep the analytical left brain engaged. The publisher's design was, however, totally left brain and negated my gently nurtured flow of psychic receptivity. Deeply disappointed with this counter–intuitive approach, I heard a voice whisper in my ear: 'Patience, wait, it will come right'.

The company were taken over shortly after publication, the book vanished into a black hole and, eventually, the rights were rescinded. I was able to expand and re–vision the book in a way which I knew would work with psychic perception, not against it. But something else was missing: the right publisher. Again, the inner voice whispered: 'Wait, it's closer than you think'. Suddenly psychic awareness was acceptable and it was time to send it out to the world for its rebirth. I am so delighted that the wonderfully intuitive Margaret Cahill is once again my publisher especially as she added immensely to the depth of the book with her perceptive questioning and working through the exercises herself.

I've kept the research in, because it makes fascinating reading and helps us to recognise the optimum conditions for intuition to flourish – which is an important part of metaphysics, but for the most part the book relies on what I know works because I – and many of my students – have lived with it every day of my life. But it will be launched into a very different world to the one in which *The Intuition Handbook* began life, a world in which intuition is now used routinely in commerce and is actually taught – rather than being objectively studied – in universities, nursing and business schools. A world where psychic experiences are shown almost daily on television. Where near death or out–of–body experiences, lucid dreaming and the like are now called Exceptional Human Experiences (EHEs) rather than an hallucination. It goes to show how things evolve and how important right timing can be – as is listening to the inner voice of our own true knowing.

This book is a companion to *Good Vibrations: psychic protection, energy enhancement and space clearing*; a vital foundation on which to build psychic abilities. If, when you read Chapter 3 'metaphysical preparations' in this book it feels like déjà vu, you've read it before, that will be because you've read one of my books on psychic protection already. But please persevere, don't think 'I know this already' and put the book back or skip over that section as it has additional information on what Einstein called 'spooky action at a distance'. This book is about metaphysics and developing your psychic awareness but psychic protection is essential groundwork. I have included the section on psychic protection in this book so that you don't have to buy the other volume (although you'll find it indispensible once you have it) and because I consider it to be essential if you are to open up psychically. I would be working against my own deeply held credo if I didn't make sure you were fully grounded and shielded before I showed you the way to open up and shift your awareness to another dimension. I've seen too many casualties of the 'open up and don't bother to shut down' school of metaphysics to want this for my readers. I want you to feel that you are in safe hands as we take this journey into your psychic awareness together, and to know that there are good reasons for everything I suggest that you do. Please, try it and see if it works for you. It did for me.

So, please approach this book quietly, receptively and non–sceptically. Work through it methodically in the order it's written and let it do its work to softly open up an invaluable asset: your psychic sense – a natural faculty that really can change your life. And which will be a source of great joy and playfulness as well as guidance in the years to come.

Remember that to be psychic you don't need to do anything, no striving is required. You simply have to relax and allow a natural function to flow more fully in your life. That, and your common sense, is all you need.

Intuitively yours,

Judy Hall

1
Out of the Blue

At the centre of your being you have the answer.
Lao Tsu

There is nothing new about psychic abilities. They have been used for thousands of years and are part of metaphysics: the science of going beyond the boundaries of consensus science. Psychic awareness is a normal and natural function that can significantly enhance your life. The voice that whispers in your inner ear, the pictures in your mind's eye, the feelings in your gut, the messages from the natural world, your significant dreams: all are facets of your psychic sensitivity and all can be honed so that you make skilful use of your innate abilities.

Intuition is a very important part of 'being psychic'. It tells you when to go ahead and when to hold back, who to trust and who to treat with a little more caution and reveals what lies behind the surface reality. It can indicate what is good for you, your health and well–being, and what is not, and can also greatly enhance your creativity and your business acumen. But it's not all there is to being psychic, as you will discover.

This book helps you to identify how your inner knowing communicates with you, guiding you through that process and developing your psychic ability into a highly skilled, reliable tool and then it takes you beyond that to reach the guidance and psychic connections that go beyond this world. It is a carefully structured course in opening your psychic awareness. Each section is accompanied by practical exercises to help you gain insight into how your psychic abilities work and to tone up and develop that sixth sense.

To get the best out of the book, please work through it in the order you find on the pages. I know the exciting bit – or what you might figure to be the most exciting part – is towards the back but this is because building up your psychic sensitivity is rather like building up a disused muscle. You need to take it gently, learn protection and sensible working techniques and, slowly but surely, stretch yourself and gain control of an ability that can, when untrained, be fickle and unreliable but, when honed, can significantly change your life to bring you to enlightenment.

Awakening to psychic awareness

Vision is the art of seeing things invisible to others

Jonathan Swift

If you have picked up this book you may feel in need of guidance but are unsure where to turn – there are some very sensational books on this topic out there. You may be subtly dissatisfied with your life, knowing there must be more. You may instinctively feel that the answer lies within yourself and yet do not know how to find it. You may want to improve your business or personal life or to maximise your health and well–being. Your goal may be enlightenment or consciousness expansion rather than simply being intuitive. But you need to know how to get there and who to trust along the way.

Developing your psychic abilities may provide the answers you are seeking. Psychic awareness has been used for millennia to guide and enhance life. Ancient peoples used it to know the will of, or to seek the favour of, their gods and divination was practised right across the ancient world. It is still used today to win fortune and indicate solutions.

Developing your psychic awareness enhances every aspect of your life. You can access hidden knowledge, recognise the correct action to take, become more creative, and instinctively do whatever is right for you. It takes you beyond the boundaries of the known world and into a place that is as familiar as the palm of your hand, once you re–attune to it. It also takes you into a deep spiritual connection that can, ultimately, lead you to the enlightenment that arises out of knowing that this world of ours is only a tiny part of a much bigger consciousness.

Being psychic is an innate ability. It involves and yet goes beyond the ordinary five senses to the sixth, metaphysical, sense. It is a function of consciousness. Consciousness is one of the last frontiers awaiting exploration. Whilst science thinks it knows a great deal about how the brain functions – and usually attributes both mind and consciousness to the brain – so far it knows little about intuition and other psychic faculties despite having studied it for over 150 years. This is, however, rapidly changing – and will change even faster as more scientists study the effects of expanded consciousness and Exceptional Human Experiences rather than trying to fathom out how the brain creates such states.

Most people are intuitive. You may have had the experience of hearing the phone ring and knowing who is on the other end, or of suddenly thinking of someone and having them call. You may be prone to hunches or premonitions. You may have had lucid dreams, or out–of–body experiences, or had an inspired flash of creativity in a daydream. This is your psychic ability at work – as is suddenly knowing which horse to back, or which stock is going to rocket in value, or which commodity will be in demand. Businesses such as the futures market, or the stock market, rely heavily on intuition. Intellectual knowledge alone is seldom sufficient, and there is an enormous difference between knowledge and knowing. Indeed, the people who succeed in business are often highly intuitive, not afraid to back a hunch or follow their instincts even when it goes against common sense or the received wisdom of the day.

However, because people are rarely taught to trust their psychic ability, they often repress it and repression does not just mean 'thrusting out of sight'. Repression means obliterating something so thoroughly that you don't know you had it in the first place. You actually lose the memory of having known. You might wonder why we would repress our psychic ability. Well, whilst so called primitive societies have always welcomed psychic abilities as something divinely inspired, more recently in the west at least, it came to be regarded as the devil's work. There was a time not so long ago when to be psychic automatically meant you were persecuted and fear is a powerful shutter–down of intuition and other psychic abilities. Self–doubt can also cause you to misread signs and signals, setting up a sequence of failures. So, if you lose your fear and release your inner prohibitions, raising the shutter, you may find you have been psychic all along. You just didn't recognise it.

A simple heart–opening exercise can make you much more open to being psychic. A coherent heart has been shown to increase your psychic receptivity.

Exercise: Opening your heart

Breathe gently and take your attention to the centre of your chest over your physical heart (put your hand or a Rose Quartz or Managano Calcite crystal here if you wish). As you breathe in, feel the energy opening in your heart like a flower. As you breathe out, feel love suffusing your whole being. (If you have difficulty feeling love, breathe in the energy of a crystal or recall a moment of very positive emotion and let that emotion suffuse you.) As you continue to breathe you will become aware that your heart chakra has three chambers, one over the heart itself, one below and one above. As you breathe and let the love flow through your being, these chambers will align and harmonise, beating in a stable rhythm.

Trusting to Intuition

A classic case of trusting to inner knowing was demonstrated by a costume designer working on a long running television soap opera who felt she needed a break. Friends were horrified that she intended to give up a secure job in an insecure profession. She, however, was not worried. "When I need it, something will turn up out of the blue" she asserted. When she returned from a long holiday in the sun she was immediately offered a much better job. It was on a programme called 'Out of the Blue'.

What is psychic awareness?

You can think of it as a sneak preview, like at the movies.

In.Q.

Your psychic awareness is your sixth sense. It is a voice that speaks from inner stillness. A knowing that goes beyond the confines of your everyday mind. An awareness that relies upon gut feeling rather than brain power or intellectual knowledge, psychic knowing is your mind's perceptions rather than your brain's reasoning. It is the guidance you receive from higher beings as well as your own inner self and the connections you make with the worlds beyond this one. It is complementary to intellect but works in a completely different way. Psychic knowing is instantaneous.

Being psychic exceeds the ordinary five senses. Which is why it is often called the sixth sense, extra sensory perception (ESP) or psi. Everyone has it to some extent, and it can be amplified. Much of it occurs at a subliminal level, and a great deal manifests through imagery and feelings rather than words.

Bypassing the logical and rational mind, and able to operate separately from the brain, psychic awareness is a source of creativity, insight and new perspectives. Functioning at an intuitive level, it takes disparate facts and bits of information, synthesises them and comes up with an answer that goes way beyond those facts. Operating at another level, psychic knowing pulls things 'out of the blue' and moves into the future. It gives answers and insights that cannot be obtained through ordinary channels and operates outside time and space. Many of the great scientists and inventors, such as Einstein, Edison and Leonardo da Vinci deliberately used intuition in the development of their theories.

Metaphysical abilities

People often refer to being psychic as:

- a hunch
- inspiration
- an instinct
- a gut feeling
- tapping into the all–knowing universe
- a feeling in the bones
- a knowing
- an impulse
- ingenious thought
- 'a priori' knowledge
- creative muse
- extra sensory perception
- inner guidance
- a brainwave
- visual thinking
- a lucky guess
- prescience
- vision
- something dropping in
- being in the zone
- communicating with the world beyond

Definitions

Intuition: the immediate knowing or learning of something without the conscious use of reasoning, instantaneous apperception.

Webster's Dictionary

… that aspect of consciousness that allows us to see round corners.

C.G.*Jung*

… the creative advance towards reality.

Roberto Assagioli

[not] something contrary to reason, but something outside of the province of reason.
C.G. *Jung*

... the clothing of divine ideas with the subtlest of form
Judy Jacka

The biocomputer within our own mind.
Jeffrey Mishlove

... to know things as they are.
Frances E. Vaughan

The ability to communicate directly with God.
Dr. Melvin Morse

The primary wisdom is intuition.
Ralf Waldo Emerson

... one of the most important abilities we can cultivate.
Jagdish Parikh

Psychic ability and psychic connections

Intuition lets in the light.
Steve Nation

Many people think that being psychic means standing on a platform, or giving messages to clients via the internet or telephone, but there are other more subtle ways of being psychic. At its most simple, being psychic is having an intuitive hunch or knowing there is something you need to do. A typical example of how it works for me is that I woke up this morning with 'don't forget to put in the alta major chakra opener crystals' reverberating in my head. I was halfway to the computer before I even thought about it. I had indeed forgotten to include them. It is a pefect example of a psychic prod. At its most complex 'being psychic' can involve precognition and space–time travel, unity with the divine and exploration of both inner and outer space, and go way beyond so–called 'normal' methods of communication. We'll explore those as we go through the book.The major psychic abilities are deemed to be:

Intuition: Intuition knows things without having to fathom out the reasoning or the logic, it is a subtle sense that puts disparate pieces of information together and makes a great leap. It is also a subtle sensing that takes place in your body or your heart and then communicates the information to your mind.

Inner Wisdom: Attuning to your own inner wisdom involves stilling the everyday mind and shutting off stimuli from the outer world. In the silence, you access your own knowing. Inner wisdom is often referred to as the voice of the heart or soul.

Telepathy: Intentionally, and sometimes unintentionally, passing thoughts, words, pictures and symbols from one mind to another without verbalisation or visual clues is known as telepathy. Telepathy can operate over vast distances.

Precognition: Moving forward in time to access knowledge about the future is precognitive psychic awareness.

Retrocognition: Moving backwards in time to access knowledge about the past is retrocognitive psychic awareness. This can include past life memories.

Remote Viewing: The ability for consciousness to leave the physical body and travel to another place; bringing back a report of what is seen there is known as journeying, remote viewing or astral travel.

Psychokinesis: The ability to move objects by the power of the mind alone uses psychic abilities.

Clairvoyance: Clairvoyance literally means 'clear sight'. Information is received by way of impressions, thoughts, pictures, symbols. The communication is often with another level of existence such as the spirits of those who have departed. Clairvoyance can, however, involve reading the contents of a sealed envelope and such like.

Clairaudience: Clairaudience means hearing clearly. Information may be received through a distinct voice – often heard behind the ear – or by an idea 'popping' into the mind.

Clairsentience: This subtle gift involves receiving information from a flower or similar object through sensing.

Psychometry: The ability to read the impressions retained by objects or places is known as psychometry.

Channelling: Channelling used to be called trance. A spirit or being who is no longer on earth (or who, it is claimed, is extraterrestrial) communicates through the medium of a living person using their voice box or passes information into their mind. In this book the word kything is used as this includes an interaction between the communicator and the person with whom the communication is made.

Kything: A form of communication in which the information passes mainly through the mind of the recipient from the communicator. This is a two–way process that allows for a question and answer dialogue.

Automatic Writing: In automatic writing it feels as though something outside oneself is doing the writing. Words appear without thought.

Sortes: Asking a question, opening a text at random, putting your finger on the text and reading off the answer.

To the above I would add bodily knowing such as gut feelings, muscle testing and dowsing which all use the body's ability to sense and to know.

How do I know if I'm psychic?

> *A characteristic of intuitions is that they are fleeting and, curiously, very easily forgotten…*
>
> *Robert Assagioli*

If you have had a significant dream or dream in colour, followed a hunch, made a lucky guess, had a feeling in your bones or listened to your heart or the whispered voice of your soul, journeyed out of your body or had a near death experience, your psychic sensitivity has made itself known. Intuition and psychic knowing enables you to take great leaps into the unknown and find the answers you seek. Everyone is intuitive: it is an innate quality of consciousness. Not everyone consciously responds to their psychic knowing or even recognises it, however, but it is there and it can be honed.

Appraising your psychic abilities

Have you ever said:

- I had a gut feeling
- I knew that would happen

- Why didn't I pay attention to that hunch?
- I don't know why, I just know it's so
- I was just thinking about you
- My heart told me it was so

  Or,
- Have you had a near death experience?

Ask yourself:

- Do I follow my heart rather than logic?

If so, your psychic ability is already at work, even if you haven't yet recognised it.

Intuition has long been linked to the voice of the heart and researchers have now established that the heart has its own organised intelligence that accesses information a second or two faster than the brain and this, they suggest, is the basis for psychic knowing. They assert that, whether you are aware of it or not, your heart steers you in directions that it deems is beneficial for you. So it is no wonder that intuitive people say that their heart speaks to them. Researchers have also found that around 80% of people who have had a near death experience, or a great trauma, report becoming more psychic afterwards.[2]

Take time out now to ponder how you respond to your psychic knowing, make the insights you gain the first page of a metaphysical journal (see chapter 2). Writing the answers down clarifies your insights and accesses the things you didn't know you knew. It also helps you to look back and join up the dots as it were, bringing together disparate segments that eventually make an inter–connected whole. Questions to ask yourself:

- When did I last have an intuitive feeling?
- What did it suggest I do?
- Did I act on it?
- What was the result?
- When did I last ignore an intuitive feeling?
- What was the result?
- How did I feel?

You will probably find that acting on your psychic knowing was more productive and successful than ignoring it. If you become aware that you have been having intuitions but ignoring them, then forgive yourself and move on; beating yourself up about it is not conducive to future psychic awareness. Either write the following on a piece of card or in your metaphysical journal, then find an appropriate place to read it out loud:

I forgive myself for all the ways known and unknown that I have ignored my psychic knowing and not acted upon it when it would have been beneficial for me to do so. From this moment on I will allow my psychic knowing to speak to me and will follow its guidance and inspiration, living joyfully and intuitively from an open heart.

There are many ways that people receive psychic impressions and we'll be exploring these throughout the book, but the radio serialisation of a Hilary Mantel novel – whose main character is a psychic – reminded me of how I feel when I receive psychic information. As I switched on the radio (one of the ways in which my intuition communicates with me) Hilary Mantel had her character talk about the tin opener that attacks the top of your head, opens it and then drops a whole lot of stuff in that has to be carefully unscrambled and communicated. I always describe this as 'a Monty Python moment'. I love the animation sequences in *Monty Python* where a 'hand of god' reaches down, tears open the top of a head, drops in a load of junk and then shuts it up again. The expression on the face says it all. That's exactly how I felt when I had my first major past life seeing. The components needed unscrambling over quite a long period of time and I had to keep going back to pieces I had missed or misunderstood. Other people have reported similar sensations such as 'pressure in the head' and others that they have shudders or tingles or a multitude of other signs. So it's important to keep in mind that there is no one way that you will receive psychic communications – and to remember that it may need to be unscrambled first. Similarly, some people see images that may be symbolic or mean something to the recipient and it's vital that you first relay these as they are before attempting to interpret them. 'Wrong' interpretation, not incorrect information, is a major cause of failure. Here's an example of how easy it is to put the wrong interpretation on a message. Susannah recalls:

My youngest son and his girlfriend are leaving for the US this morning, and of course my thoughts have been on them since I left London for Budapest yesterday. I woke up very early, around 4 AM, and had a very strange feeling, close to anxiety but not quite. First I thought it was just my natural 'mother is fretting' mode, but as I was trying to go back to sleep, my body felt overtaken by a presence. I was trying to see if this is a premonition that something bad will happen, and the answer came "no". However the feeling got worse so I finally jumped out of bed, made coffee, and read my emails. There was an email from my older son (who is already in Miami with my mother) saying that my ex–mother in law, who was 98, died yesterday afternoon. I really loved her, even after my divorce we kept in touch, and I think she was trying to make contact with me this morning. I saw her a couple of months ago when she was already bedridden and very weak, but still sharp, and she kept saying she wanted to leave because she had had enough and life no longer gave her joy. This all made me think how we literally have only minutes to accomplish what we are supposed to because it will go in a flash....

Can I develop my psychic ability?

Intuition... can be activated following the general principle that attention and interest foster their manifestations.

Roberto Assagioli

In the same way that you exercise a muscle to build up its strength, your psychic abilities can be strengthened. This is where this book comes in. It is a skilfully structured programme for psychic development that is built on forty five years of practical experience using and teaching metaphysics.

You can begin by paying attention to all the times during the day when your psychic knowing tries to speak to you:

- Watch your body feelings and reactions, catch the moment when your stomach sinks or you feel inexplicably keyed up.
- Be attuned to the impressions you receive, this is psychic knowing at its most subtle and sensitive.
- Notice your first, immediate reaction to someone new.
- Notice when you feel good or bad about something.

What impulses do you have?

- Catch the fleeting thoughts that pass through your mind but seem to come from somewhere else.
- Notice the images that pass through your mind whenever your attention wanders.
- Pay attention as you fall asleep or wake up.
- Ask yourself who is on the phone when it rings.
- Note the signals and signs that the universe sends your way.
- Identify when you go into an ultradion rest phase (see p.47).

Make a promise to yourself to act on your psychic knowings now. And keep a note of how often you are successful. There's nothing like success to breed further success and even your failures can teach you a great deal.

> ***Exercise: What would my life be like when I use my psychic ability?***
> *You can find out what your life would be like with your psychic ability fully functioning by closing your eyes, breathing gently and bringing your awareness away from the outside world and into yourself. Give a big sigh, lift up your shoulders and, as you let them fall, drop into an altered state of consciousness without thinking about it. Ask your inner psychic knowing to show or tell you what life would be like if you worked in partnership together. See how it would flow and weave a harmonious whole. Notice how your body feels.*

Programme your psychic knowing

When the lip is silent, the heart has a hundred tongues

Jalal al–din Rumi

Action follows thought. Energy follows intention. Affirming that you are psychic will make it so. Every morning when you wake up look at yourself in a mirror and say to yourself:

- Every day in every way I am more psychic and aware.

Repeat the statement when you go to bed.

When should I not use psychic abilities?

[the fear is] of being overwhelmed, of disintegrating under a pressure of reality greater than the mind… could possibly bear.

Aldous Huxley

A very long experience in dealing with the downside of being psychic and giving first aid to people who have opened up under less than ideal conditions leads me to suggest that common sense says that you should not practise or open up psychically if:

- you are inexperienced and alone
- you have been warned not to meddle

- you are in an energetically unsafe place
- you instinctively do not trust the people around you
- you have or previously had psychiatric problems
- you are under the influence of drink or drugs (including some prescribed medications such as tranquillisers and anti–depressants)
- you are under psychic attack or ill–wishing
- your chakras are not functioning at optimum level
- you are unwell or low in energy
- you have a spirit attachment or are under undue influence
- you are overly–imaginative and ungrounded
- you are under the powerful influence of a guru or other authoritative figure

Not working when you are ill, physically or mentally, or when your energy is low or when you are under psychic attack or when you instinctively do not trust the people around you are sensible precautions to take. Playing with what you don't understand, and don't know how to handle, is also unwise, as is using some of the so–called 'self help' books and downloads that help you to open up alone, and rarely have sufficient instruction on how to close down safely and completely. Tackling something that a more experienced person won't touch is crass stupidity, especially if you don't then recognise that you have yourself taken on the energy and are passing it on to others.

If your chakras are stuck open or are blocked, then safe working is difficult and attachments are possible. Check them out before starting psychic work (see Chapter 6). Getting yourself checked out by an intuitive healer or joining a development circle under the guidance of an experienced leader is also sensible as is working through this book in the order of the chapters. Following the carefully–structured exercises will help you to open up and close down in the safest way possible, and recognise if you have inadvertently picked up something nasty.

Whilst there are many drugs that can forcibly open up your consciousness or drive you out of your body, such trips can leave a legacy of spontaneous flashbacks and uncontrollable opening up when it is not appropriate to do so and there is little you can then do about the situation. You can 'break open your head' in this way but, in my opinion, it is much better to learn to open up – and close down – with the power of your own mind and the naturally occurring psychic chemicals in your brain.

It is also sensible to avoid drinking when working psychically as, at the very best, your discriminatory faculties are lessened and at the worst suspended, and your boundaries can be loosened so that discarnate spirits slip in. Dr George Ritchie, an early recorder of a near death experience (NDE), described how, after his 'death', he was taken in his spirit body to a pub where he could see many discarnate spirits desperate for a drink who were just waiting for the opportunity to slip into an un– or semi–conscious physical body so they could re–experience the taste of their addiction. They were like hitch–hikers who refuse to leave after having a lift in a comfortable car. They knew that by remaining attached they would have the opportunity to satisfy their craving again – and again. These uninvited squatters can be extremely difficult to clear out afterwards (see 'What to do if things go wrong'). I have seen exactly the same thing at workshops and circles designed to open up awareness but without proper attention being paid to setting out a safe space in which to do so. Not all spirits are malicious or have bad intentions, many are merely lost or desperate to communicate but they need experienced handling.

Working in a safe space is sensible and that can mean not only checking out the space as it is today but also checking out what was on the site previously (See *Good Vibrations* for more assistance on this). Many years ago I was asked to work with a group of young punks who had played with a Ouija board in one of their homes. What they did not know at the time was that it had formerly been a police station and the room they were in was where the cells had been. A spirit communicated saying he had been a prisoner in the cells and had hung himself there. It was impossible for them to move the spirit on and the room became a centre for extreme poltergeist activity. As one of the group had to sleep in there, it was a situation fraught with difficulty. Research in the local paper archives showed that a suicide had indeed taken place there many years previously. They asked me to move the spirit on, which I did, and then taught them safe working and psychic opening up. The young man went on to become an excellent healer and never forgot his hard–learned lesson about basic protection.

How you feel about a place on first entry is probably your best indication, if you get an unexpected cold shiver, leave it alone. Similarly if you feel tired or as though you are walking through treacle, start to yawn or feel hyped up or depressed for no reason, don't work psychically unless the space has been properly checked out and, if necessary, cleared (see *Good Vibrations*.)

Is there anything I need to know before I start?

> *Many people do not realise that all around us there are unseen vibrations, imperceptible emanations and subtle energy fields.*
>
> *Judy Hall,* Good Vibrations

There most certainly is. You need to be in control of your psychic sensitivity, not allowing your psychic abilities to overwhelm you at any time of the day or night. It is essential to learn how to close down and shut yourself off from your psychic sensitivities whenever you are in an unsafe environment or when unwanted guests in the form of mischievous spirits come to call. Being ungrounded and wide open all the time is like being a psychic lighthouse. It attracts spirits with whom contact is most unwise. Also knowing your guides and having your psychic gateways open and functioning is essential which is why chapter 3 starts with practical psychic protection, opening and closing tools. Please, whatever else you do, read this chapter and familiarise yourself with the exercise before moving on. (Please also read 'What to do if anything goes wrong' in Chapter 17). It will help you whether you are working alone or helping someone else.)

How do psychic abilities communicate?

> *The intuitive mind tells the thinking mind where to look next. I wake up in the morning wondering what my intuition will toss up to me like gifts from the sea.*
>
> *Jonas Salk*

Research carried out in the sixties showed that at least half of spontaneous extrasensory perception experiences occurred during dreams, and in 1970 it was concluded that 70 percent of such cases involved imagery of one kind or another. Imagery is the language of psychic connection. Because images are constantly passing through our minds, the trick is to recognise those that have a message for us.

The ancients' answer to the question 'how does psychic ability speak' would be 'through the gods, signs and signals'. They assumed that everything in the natural world was a communicating whole that spoke to them. So, if they saw a flock of geese fly overhead, it was an omen that signalled something was about to happen. All they had to do was be alert – and take appropriate evasive action if necessary. Other signs were seen in the stars – from which astrology was born – and a complex system of divination developed, much of which is still used today.

There is, however, no one right way to access psychic knowing. One person will 'hear an inner voice', another will 'see a mind picture', whilst a third will 'feel it' or 'get a sense about it' and yet another will 'just know', someone else will 'get it in the gut' or 'feel it in my heart' or 'get the impression' while yet another person will take notice of the stag that stands quietly observing them, tosses its head and veers back into the trees or majestically steps out in front of their car.

If your psychic awareness functions through your body, it is kinaesthetic (see Receiving information p.17). Kinaesthetic awareness covers sensing with your hands, feelings in your bones, gut feelings, tingles, shudders, head prickling or the hairs on your arms standing up. It is what makes dowsing work. Minute twitches in your muscles translate into a pendulum swinging, a rod moving or your finger sticking. You may also have a different kind of feeling, something that involves 'just knowing'. You aren't quite sure how you came to know, but you do indeed know.

Psychic sensitivity can function at a mental or psychic level. If it is mental, a thought that is not yours floats into your head answering a question, or giving the information you need. If it is psychic, you may clearly hear a voice speaking to you, or you may get a mind picture projected onto an inner screen. Psychic awareness may come when you write without thinking first, or when you enter a creative reverie or dream state. By trying out the different methods, you can develop a range of psychic skills appropriate to a variety of situations. Psychic knowing is a valuable tool. It may even save your life.

Are there any signs to watch out for that I am psychically attuned?

Yes, your intuition does have a way of making you pay attention – once you recognise that it's a signal that your psychic sensitivity is trying to communicate. And there are definite sensations that occur when you are attuned. Typical signs and feelings are:

- Shudders like buckets of cold water going down your back
- The top or one side of your head tingling
- A tap on your shoulder
- Sudden pressure in your head
- A feeling that a string attached to the top of your head is pulling you up
- An adrenaline rush
- A sense of alignment, as though your body and some other subtle self have come together and landed in a still, calm place

- Hairs standing up
- Gurgles and rumblings from your gut
- Eyes going out of focus
- Ears hearing swishing or buzzing noises or actual words

We'll be exploring more of these as we journey through the book.

Is psychic knowing always accurate?

Sadly information received psychically isn't always one hundred percent correct for a variety of reasons, but you can improve your hit rate. Untutored psychic awareness can be coloured by wishful thinking, desire for a particular outcome, misinterpretation of images and intervention by the ego, especially the desire to impress, or by self–doubt, and is not therefore an accurate process, which is why psychic sensitivity needs to be honed and developed to make it more reliable – and common sense needs to be your constant companion as you walk the metaphysical path.

Receiving information

> *The state of awareness of visions is not one in which we are either remembering or perceiving. It is rather a level of consciousness at which we experience visions within ourselves.*
>
> *Oscar Kokoschka*

Psychic information is received through the physical body or the subtle senses in various ways:

- Hearing (aural)
- Seeing (visual)
- Sensing (kinaesthetic)
- Feeling (kinaesthetic)
- Knowing (kinaesthetic)
- Smelling (kinaesthetic–sensate)
- Muscles or skin (kinaesthetic–sensate)

Which mode do you use?

There is a vast difference between looking and seeing.
Ernest W. Watson

There are three main modes of perception through which we experience the world:

- our eyes, the visual mode
- our ears, the auditory mode
- our senses, the sensate or kinaesthetic mode, which includes our body feelings, smell and taste

These modes govern the way in which your psychic awareness functions and knowing which mode you use will facilitate opening your psychic connection and increasing your perceptions. Most people use a combination of two or more modes and the more modes that are open the more acute your psychic sensitivity becomes. It is perfectly possible to strengthen your weaker modes and so open your psychic abilities even wider but you may need to balance the modes so that one doesn't overwhelm the subtle signals you would otherwise receive via a different mode. When you are working through the exercises in this book, try deliberately switching modes by focusing your attention on the inner eye or ear, your senses or your body.

Visual people are stimulated by patterns, colour, images, gestures and body language. They find it easy to visualise and tend to think in pictures and to have vivid, techni–colour dreams. If you allow your eyes to go slightly out of focus and 'see' from the corner of your eye, you are visual. If you use phrases like 'I don't quite see what you mean' then you are probably using the visual mode to process information. You can enhance your psychic sensitivity through the use of vivid imagery, mandalas, crystal mirrors and quiet observation. Try seeing from the corner of your eye or on an inner screen.

Auditory people are powerfully affected by words, sounds and music. If you find yourself asking someone to 'could you repeat that' or 'I didn't quite catch that', you probably use the auditory mode to process information. If you close your eyes and listen when you want to concentrate, or tilt your head to one side with a particular ear forward, you are auditory (the ear you point forward will be your dominant, psychic ear). If you feel uplifted by a swell of music, your psychic awareness can be enhanced by chanting, mantras, background music, and focused sounds such as a Tibetan bowl or cymbals but sounds that are too loud could shut out your inner ear. I cannot work against background noise or a babble of voices as I find it interferes with the energy of what I'm sensing.

Kinaesthetic–Sensate people are strongly affected by smell, touch, gesture and sensation. I strongly suspect that sensate people have a particularly large number of active mirror neurons in their brain (see p.152). If you make touch statements like 'I can't quite get a grip on that' or body–orientated observations such as 'my gut tells me' you are using the kinaesthetic mode to process information. Similarly if you make statements like 'I'm feeling a little blue today' you are sense–orientated. If your body feels like a receiver that shivers or quivers or experiences nausea or excitement in the gut in response to places or people, then your psychic awareness will be enhanced (or smothered) by incense or perfumes, by tracing symbols or making ritual gestures and body movement such as dance, walking or tai chi, or massage with scented oils over the third eye. 'Seeing' can be facilitated by drawing, maybe with your non–dominant hand or by shuffling cards and laying a spread out or by casting the runes and so on.

Smell and psychic awareness

The olfactory sense is often overlooked in psychic sensing and yet it is a powerful and evocative form of communication. As metaphysical abilities develop it is common for certain aromas to be perceived even though they are not present in the physical world. Incense often wafts through the air or perfumes such as lavender or rose suffuse your immediate environment. Smells that belong to a certain location can alert your attention to events occurring there, even if you are many miles away. Foul odours can be a warning or a signal that all is not well. Psychic sensitivity can be enhanced by burning suitable fragrances or joss sticks, and some oils such as sandalwood and frankincense have been prized over millennia for their consciousness–lifting effects and, equally, it can be suppressed by strong artificial perfumes.

What facilitates psychic awareness?

> *Imagination is more important than knowledge.*
> *Albert Einstein*

Practical experience tells me that getting out of your own way is the first thing that assists psychic awareness. If you learn to stand aside placidly, putting aside wishful thinking, prejudice, hopes and expectations, and allow your psychic abilities to make themselves known in their own way, you stand the best chance of developing your own inner awareness and listening to the signs and signals all around and within you – your body might be talking to you right now, but are you listening? Are you still trying to figure things out with your head? If so, stop the mind chatter and listen to the still voice from within yourself. If you can clear your mind of the clutter and chatter, take time to sit down quietly and contemplate your navel, and remember to ask for guidance, you will be on your way. Then, it's a case of asking the right kind of questions instead of constantly questioning. After that, trust is the quickest way to get your psychic knowing moving.

Scientific research has, however, shown that altered states of consciousness and deep relaxation help psychic awareness to function efficiently, as does emotional empathy – it is difficult but not impossible to be telepathic with someone you dislike for instance. The mind needs to be slightly displaced, disengaged from the everyday. You need to move from functional perception into psychic perception – a much older and more natural way of perceiving the world. In laboratory tests dreaming, hypnosis, reverie and meditation have been proved to be conducive to psi and psychic abilities. A survey of research in 1976 showed that experiments performed with the subject in an altered state had a 56% success rate compared to a chance expectation of only 5%. Exactly what shamans and spiritual masters have known for thousands of years! More recent research has given further confirmation and brain scanning has pinpointed some of the more useful techniques.

Aspiring spiritual seekers in the East were taught how to enter a state of consciousness in which there was no clear boundary around oneself and in which sensory input was at a minimum. They sought the elusive goal of 'no mind', but one of the side effects was an increase in extra sensory perception and visionary experiences – although Buddhist monks, for instance, were taught to devalue such psychic states and move beyond them into the more highly valued enlightened states. In the Americas and elsewhere, shamans underwent profound initiations in which they died to their old self and emerged into unity with the natural world which spoke to them in myriad ways through its various parts, but always as part of a wholeness.

Western mystics are familiar with the same state. In the thirteenth century, Meister Eckhart wrote: "I assert that in heaven all is in all and all is one and all is ours… Thus spirit is in spirit." For him the goal of religion was to realise the 'God–within' and once this union was achieved, there were no boundaries.

With a little application, you too can utilise altered states of consciousness to access your psychic awareness. Learning to relax is a crucial first step and as you work through this book you will gradually build up other skills such as visualisation and sensing subtle signals.

Relaxation is a little like self–hypnosis. Many of the exercises in this book take you into a state similar to light hypnosis – which means you enter an altered and heightened state of awareness to facilitate the working of your psychic knowing. Behavioural psychologists have proved time and time again that if an action is reinforced, it becomes habitual. So, exercising your psychic awareness strengthens it. The more you listen to your inner voice or open your third eye, the more often you reach out to access higher levels of consciousness, the more psychic you will become.

As shamans have always known, repetitious sounds or movements help you to change your awareness. Dance, chanting, rhythmic breathing and massage have all been traditionally used. In addition, consciousness–raising agents such as incense, oils and certain hallucinogenic substances can play a powerful part in enhancing psychic awareness, although you certainly do not need drugs to achieve a transcendental or altered state of consciousness. More recently, researchers have found that a sustained positive emotional state, in other words feeling good, is also conducive to psychic insight.

Enhancing psychic awareness

Major components are:

- Muscle relaxation
- Reduced sensory input
- Cortical arousal (that is, the subject remains attentive)
- Spontaneous mental processes, especially imagery
- A goal or a need to communicate
- Staying present in the moment
- Sustained emotional well–being
- A calm, cleared headed and focused approach
- Rest phase of the Ultradon cycle

Research has shown that there are ten crucial factors that enhance psychic awareness:

- An open mind
- Belief
- Desire
- Focused intention
- Expectation

- A positive attitude
- The ability to move out of everyday awareness
- Trust
- Common sense
- Willingness to take risks

An open mind: Keeping an open mind is essential but this does not mean being gullible. If you explore your psychic abilities with a cynical and critical attitude, you will not get far, nor will you if you accept everything and anything uncritically. Intuition is a subjective state and, if you try to remain objective during experiments you will not access the subliminal perceptions on which intuition is based. A closed mind shuts out intuition and, even if your intuition starts screaming at you, you won't hear it. An open mind looks at the evidence, assesses it dispassionately, and accepts or rejects it on the basis of what is. Academic researchers in the past have tended to say that they must remain skeptical (the American spelling of sceptical) but I always write this as septical – it literally poisons the mind's ability to access or assess the metaphysical realms

Belief: Whether or not you believe in psychic awareness will affect whether your inner knowing can function. If you don't believe in psychic abilities, for you that innate skill will not exist. Psychic knowing, which is a delicate and sensitive force, disappears under the weight of doubt and disbelief. When you first explore psychic ability, you are in something of a Catch 22 situation. If you have not experienced it for yourself, someone else telling you will almost certainly not lead to belief. You need to have the experience. But, even if you do have the experience, you may try to explain it away. Most people who have one or two unexplained things in their life are apt to say: "But it could all be my imagination". Yes, it could. But if such things prove themselves over and over again to be true and reliable, it might be more sensible to start believing in them. If you believe you are psychic, you will find something magical happens. Your inner knowing will be so pleased it has caught your attention at last, it will work extra hard on your behalf.

Desire: Desire is a powerful force and an excellent motivator. You must want or desire an outcome. If you are indifferent as to whether you succeed or not, your psychic awareness will be dulled (but beware trying too hard). However, having once desired the connection, you must then let it go, as emotional investment in the outcome actually inhibits psychic awareness.

Intention: Similarly you need to have the intention that you will succeed. Intention is what shamans have used in their work for thousands of years. It focuses the will and sets things in motion. If you hold an intent strongly and clearly, it will manifest. Intention has to be pure, that is it must not be contaminated by an emotional investment or a hidden agenda.

Expectation: If you are to fully utilise your psychic ability, you must expect that it will work. Doubts poison psychic knowing. An expectation that you will quickly master an exercise, having positive thoughts and attitudes, allows your psychic knowing to flourish. The expectation that you will receive an answer sets receiving that answer in motion. You may need a little patience, but the answer will come. Once again, expectation is different from having an emotional investment or hidden agenda over the outcome.

A positive attitude: If you constantly undermine yourself by believing that you are not good enough, not capable enough, too stupid and so on, you will consistently fail. If you have negative thoughts, you will manifest what you most fear. On the other hand, positive thoughts and attitudes can overcome the most difficult handicap. As a child, Albert Einstein was dyslexic and had problems with his speech. He initially flunked the entrance exam for college and, when he finally graduated, he could only find a dead–end job in the Swiss patents office. However, he overcame these problems and was later regarded as a genius. In 1905, at the age of 27, he published his theory of relativity – which had come to him in a five second flash of intuition but it took ten years to decode the implications. Maintaining a positive attitude enhances your psychic awareness.

The ability to move out of everyday awareness: Psychic sensitivity functions best in a state of heightened awareness and low sensory input. This is achieved by withdrawing your awareness from the outside world and bringing attention into your self to contact the source of your knowing. Optimum conditions for heightened awareness are created by stimulating combinated alpha and theta waves in the brain, a signal that you are relaxed and in a receptive state. The optimum alpha wave is in the range of 7 to 14hz. This occurs most easily during the rest phase of the ultradian cycle (see p.47) when the right brain is more active.

Trust: You need to trust yourself, the guidance you receive and the process. However, this trust is not a naïve, gullible state where you take everything you are given and assume that it is absolute truth. You also need to use your common sense and ability to discriminate.

Common sense: Some people believe that psychic sensitivity is the antithesis of common sense. But this is not true. Your common sense will help you to keep your feet on the ground

– and some people's 'common sense' is actually extremely psychic. But too much common sense can be a handicap. It can lead to questioning everything and accepting nothing that does not follow the known laws of logic or science. However, applying your common sense to whatever your intuition urges you to do can be a useful process. If you get into the habit of checking things out with an open mind whilst still trusting the process, your common sense will be harnessed to your psychic awareness instead of creating mental conflict.

A willingness to take risks: Speaking from your psychic knowing, certainly in the initial stages, may feel threatening, especially if you lack confidence in yourself. The willingness to take a risk is vital if you are to expand your psychic awareness. Without that ability, you may never begin the exercises. And, if you are working with a group, the ability to take a risk – especially the risk of not getting it right first time – is of paramount importance.

To the above should perhaps be added strong emotions or traumatic situations. While I would certainly not recommend inducing one voluntarily, the vast majority of people who undergo an NDE experience a profound shift of consciousness afterwards and find, as I did, their metaphysical abilities greatly enhanced. They know that there are other dimensions and that consciousness can exist outside the physical body. People often find themselves capable of great feats during emergencies and may say that they heard a voice directing them or saw a figure beckoning. It is as though they reconnect into an older way of knowing, one with which our ancestors would have been all too familiar. This is why a drum beat or rhythmic chanting can also stimulate psychic abilities as it reaches the oldest part of the mind. However, having an emotional investment in being right is not the same as having an emotional stimulation that opens your sensitivity.

The latest research suggests that a coherent heart with a smooth rhythm and an ordered, regular beat is also conducive to psychic awareness – a state that is found during sustained positive emotions. The researchers claim that psychophysiological training and biofeedback can enhance intuition and synchronize heart and brain: inducing a state that athletes refer to as 'being in the zone', a condition in which you have heightened perception and optimum physiological functioning. It is very similar to the state of consciousness brought about by an ancient Buddhist practise of heart meditation:

Exercise: Heart Meditation

Breathe slowly and gently, taking your breath deeply into your belly for several breaths. When your breathing has settled into a regular pattern:

Take your attention into your heart, feel its beat, its rhythm. Feel the tides of the blood swishing through.

Breathe into your heart for a count of five, hold for five and then breathe out for five. Repeat for ten breaths. Notice how your heartbeat stabilises and slows.

Now feel love in your heart, bring to mind someone you love very much and hold that feeling of love for them and for yourself within your heart. Let that love flow out all around you.

Increasing empathy

You can also increase your psychic awareness if you are reading for or with another person by:

- breathing in harmony with them
- mirroring their language
- reflecting their gestures

as this increases the empathic and intuitive connection between you.

What acts against psychic awareness?

> *Before working with the Oracle, it is important to know that your mental and emotional state at the time you use it will affect the outcome.*
>
> *Philip and Stephanie Carr–Gomm*[3]

Both day to day experience and scientific research has shown that certain things adversely affect your ability to be psychic:

- Pressure to perform – either from within or an outside source
- Trying too hard – an overwhelming desire to get it right
- Attempting to replicate results
- Preconceptions and fixed beliefs
- Cynicism and scepticism
- Wishful thinking and subconscious desires

- Projection
- Expecting your psychic ability to work in the same way as someone else's
- Your emotional or mental state
- A desire to please

Pressure to perform: As researchers have established, pressure to perform blocks intuition. Being expected to give results every time is counter productive and constantly being asked to give readings or advice quickly drains all but the most experienced psychic.

Trying too hard: Experience has shown that a relaxed receptive state is best for psychic functioning, so trying to force things and concentrating too hard works against psychic ability. If you can be laid–back about it, your psychic knowing will have a much easier time communicating with you.

Attempting to replicate results: Psychic awareness tends by its very nature to be random and fleeting, so trying to get the same result over and over again is not conducive to psychic ability functioning at its best. Whilst statisticians like replication, the metaphysical world is much more fluid.

Preconceptions: All too often someone sees what they expect to see – conditioning from the past producing a preconceived image that may be far from true. If you assume you know the answer before you start, your psychic knowing can't get a look in. Ingrained expectations can mean that you see what you want to see and disregard the rest. No matter how strong the signals, you will not be sensitive to them if you are looking for a particular thing or expecting it to be a specific way and no other. The same applies if you are given a somewhat cryptic reply – you will interpret it according to your preconception, which may be incorrect. The preconception of 'not being able to do it' will also block psychic awareness, as will cynicism and scepticism. Equally, if you are a pessimistic person who always expects the worst, your 'psychic knowing' will focus on the negative rather than positive outcome and you will 'see' disaster and not recognise opportunity. Equally, if you are an optimistic person, you may see success ahead but might overlook pitfalls in the path that could be skilfully negotiated with the aid of a more realistic viewpoint.

Cynicism and scepticism: All too often the idea of keeping an open mind turns into being cynical about psi abilities, but there are also professional skeptics who look for a rational answer to everything. The late Professor Alan Bennett, who extensively tested the British healer and psi exponent Matthew Manning and who instigated one of the first university parapsychological testing centres in Britain, told me that he could tell by the laboratory results which researcher had administered the tests. If the researcher was cynical the results were never as good as those in tests which were applied by a researcher who was sympathetic to the idea, he stated.[4] This was not to suggest any form of cheating or connivance went on. He was strongly of the opinion that the minds of the researcher and the subject meshed when there was empathy and that enhanced the possibility of significant results.

Wishful thinking and subconscious desires: The subconscious mind is a very powerful entity. If you secretly want a particular answer, you will probably get it no matter what method you use to access your psychic awareness. This is particularly so when using body–based methods such as dowsing or gut feelings but it can affect card spreads, telepathy and kything too.

Projection: Projection occurs when someone attributes feelings, abilities and qualities which belong within themselves to 'out there' in the world or to another person. This may be something unpalatable that the soul cannot own as mine or it may be unrecognised strengths which are then attributed to someone else. People who constantly expect doom and gloom or deviousness in the world will see exactly that – and will frequently project it onto another person. So, for instance, if someone has a problem with money and harbours resentment of those who do well, they may 'psychically' feel that someone is money–grabbing and too success–orientated although this may be a fallacy concocted from their own negative projections. Equally someone who is timid and lacks confidence in their own ability may project onto someone else their own inner gifts and yet not recognise them in themselves. A flawed perspective results and psychic knowing is stymied.

Expecting your psychic ability to work in the same way as someone else: Psychic abilities aren't standardised: Everyone accesses their psychic sensitivity in a slightly different way. What works for your friend probably won't work for you. Being alert to the signals your psychic awareness sends you necessitates tuning into your own inner self and listening to your own voice.

Your emotional and mental state: If you are stressed, anxious, distraught, angry or distracted, your focus gets lost. Also your emotional and mental state is likely to affect how you formulate your questions and how you interpret and respond to the answer you receive. So being calm and centred enhances psychic awareness, being scattered and unfocused, emotional or distraught does not.

The desire to please: Whether you are just beginning to open up your psychic abilities and want to please your teacher or the others in your group or whether you are an experienced psychic who is giving readings, the desire to please your sitter can overwhelm your psychic sensitivity. Unconsciously or otherwise you subtly meld what you sense or see into something pleasing to the other person. You may also work when you are not in the right state to do so out of a desire to please. Never underestimate the destructive power of people pleasing.

Getting out of the way

> *Always try to keep your mind blank when you ask the question, even if you are 100% certain you know the answer.*
>
> *Wilma Davidson*[5]

One of the most effective things you can do to enhance your psychic awareness and to avoid pitfalls is to get out of the way. If you take away your desire to succeed, stop striving to do, remove your need to know, expunge your expectation that things will happen a certain way, and rise above a need to please, your psychic abilities will work from a much clearer place. You also need to recognise when an ideal, or your dearest wish, is being projected into a scenario so that you can remove yourself and see what it means for the person you are reading for – even if this is yourself. So, say for instance you are doing a psychic reading for someone – or for yourself – and you see exactly the cottage you have always wanted for yourself. Rather than describing that particular cottage to the person in front of you, or to yourself, it is much better to say: 'I see you finding your ideal home'. They can then put their own picture in place. Only if they cannot accept or understand the picture should you then seek further clarification but always offer your interpretation in the spirit of 'how do you respond to this' rather than insisting: 'it must be so because I say so'.

2
The Metaphysical Journal

Detailed study of and reflection on intuitive experiences proves invaluable in the discovery process.

Bill Taggart [6]

You can develop your psychic faculty by keeping a metaphysical journal. A journal is vital if you are to gain full benefit from this book and learn to access your psychic abilities in the most efficient and appropriate way possible, as it keeps track of how your psychic connection communicates with you.

If you get into the habit of recording your experiences, especially those odd synchronicities and little nudges throughout the day, you will have a useful tool for developing your psychic awareness. It is only when you look back and link up disparate incidents that you can discern patterns and 'wholes'. Relying on memory is unwise as it is easy to overlook small details that add up to a big picture. When you begin working metaphysically information often comes in 'pieces'. You may need several sessions to put them together into a coherent whole.

By recording everything that happens, you also begin to pick up signals. The greater part of psychic communication occurs at the subliminal level. It is easy to miss the cues. If you record or write down what you 'saw' or 'heard', paying attention at the same time to how your body feels as you review the experience, you may pick up details that you did not notice the first time round.

You may get body signals in the form of tingles, twitches or jerks, hair standing on end, strange facial expressions, and sensations or smells. The graphic twitches and jerks that can accompany the opening up of psychic awareness usually indicate that you are a kinaesthetic person. Your body is responding to signals that your mind cannot yet make conscious. If you allow the process to happen naturally, you will become conscious of what your body is saying to you, especially if you write freely in your journal at the same time or record your thoughts.

Some signals are subtle. It took me months to realise that the touch on my shoulder as a meditation session began was actually a gatekeeper saying: "I'm here". I had been expecting to 'see' a gatekeeper, not feel him and only picked up the signal when I consulted my journal. Similarly, a discarnate guide indicated his presence by a prickling on my scalp. That was over forty five years ago and I now take it for granted that they are there when I need them, I do not require signals. They, and other aspects of my psychic connection, do what I call a 'straight through job'. Words flow out of my fingers as I type, or out of my mouth as I talk. I am often surprised, but rarely dismayed. I have learnt to trust my psychic abilities. It is essential to record sessions like this because they seem to bypass the memory cells. Clients often tell me that it was remarkable that I had said such and such on the taped reading I prepared for them. I have no memory of having done so. (I could not and would not want, in any case, to hold onto all the information that passes through me in this way.) Writing at random without pause or censoring, for five or ten minutes after meditation is another way to develop psychic ability through your journal.

Keeping a journal

> *A deeper level of self–knowledge creates an energy reservoir that is capable of producing a desired outcome almost instantly by directing one's desire and intention.*
>
> *Source unknown*

Select a book that you keep especially for the purpose or open a separate folder on your computer, phone or tablet. Write in the present tense: 'I am seeing…' 'There is …' As you write, you may find yourself recalling something that happened in a meditation or exercise but which you did not consciously remember until you began writing. This is part of the reason for recording your experiences. Or, you may find that new information comes. Let it.

Always date and time each entry and state whether it was an exercise, a dream, a psychic feeling and so on. Timing events may pinpoint a period of the day or month when you are more receptive as there are certain parts of the bioenergetic and endocrine cycles that are particularly conducive to psychic perception (if you are menstruating try recording the day of your cycle, if you are post–menopausal record the day of the moon's cycle). If you have developed the habit of monitoring the ultradian cycle note note which phase you are in (see Timing pp.49, 81). You can also add any unusual features with regard to mood, moon, weather, and so on that may have had a bearing. Thunderstorms, for instances, hype some people up and make them supersensitive while other people feel doomful and depressed by storms. Eclipses and full moons are times when, traditionally, the veils between the worlds are thin but other people find new moon a productive time to meditate.

Your journal can also be used to note down any random thoughts, impressions, perceptions and 'good ideas' that you have at any time. This is an excellent practice to adopt. Only about two percent of the population keep a journal, but virtually all 'geniuses' are within that percentage. It ensures that you overlook nothing, and reinforces your psychic ability.

Make a note of any action you take about an intuition, whether you understood it completely, and whether it was successful. Carry your journal with you so that you will always be able to record these moments as they occur. The more you keep a record, the more useful thoughts you will receive. Responding to subtle awareness reinforces that awareness.

Research has shown that using a structured format for your journal can further enhance your understanding. The structured format can be used at the time of writing or applied for analysis and evaluation afterwards. One classic structure is to record who, what, when, where, why and how, but the College of Business at Florida International University has developed a seven point recording system with subdivisions that I have tailored to your psychic development. It can be expanded upon so as to enable you to cooperate fully with your psychic awareness. Record and analyse everything, especially your 'failures' as you will often learn more from these than your successes.

Timing

- Phase of the moon
- Menstrual cycle if you have one
- Period of the ultradian rhythm (active or resting)

The experience

- Type: passing thought, dream, visualisation, meditation, external sign or signal, sortes or cledon etc.
- What was occurring just prior to the experience – assists in discovering triggers or signals that alert you to an intuitive event or receptive state
- What occurred at the time – as full a description as possible

- What occurred just after the experience – assists in sustaining and amplifying the experience – 'capturing the moment' – and drawing it back to awareness

The context

- When it occurred – precise time and date, during sleep, daydreaming, meditation etc.
- Where it occurred physically – surroundings and companions, anything unusual, strange sensations present
- Where it occurred mentally – state of mind at the time
- When it was recognised – how long did it take to recognise it as a psychic experience: immediate, minutes, days, weeks?
- Invoked or out of the blue – was it the result of a deliberate invocation of psychic ability?

Any distractions

- What else was going on around you?
- Physical tensions and stress
- Joyful expectation
- Mental clutter
- Obsessive thoughts
- Focus on a person or hope
- Fears felt
- Desires felt

The message

- Type – personal, professional, other
- Form:
    - Sensation – bodily or otherwise
    - Emotion
    - Thought
    - Images
    - Sound

Static picture
Apparition or presence
'Dropped in'

Source

- Mind, body, higher self, guide, seemingly random, etc.
- Internal self or external source
- Conscious/subconscious/supraconscious (higher consciousness)
- Internal/external (subjective/objective)
- Apparently rational/clearly psychic

The information

- Strength
- Clarity
- Accuracy
- Element of surprise

Your evaluation

- How true or false was the intuition
- Was it objective or subjective, based on wishful thinking etc.
- Degree of intentionality
- Usefulness of information
- Benefits derived
- Personal or professional learning gained

This process of evaluation and analysis is both valuable and essential – as is that you use your common sense. Do not immediately act on what an intuition says – or on what you *think* it says, the message may be subtle and need further clarification or you may be making an unwarranted assumption. When you first begin, remember that you are still learning and need to test out the information. Is it coming from the highest possible source and for your highest good? (Even when you are experienced it is still a good idea to test it out, do not become complacent as the ego or wishful thinking is quick to slip in.) If you have any doubt, put it aside. Have a mental filing cabinet into which such things go – or flag it in your journal with a special coloured tag. Periodically take the information out and see if it fits in with anything else you've received.

Reviewing your journal after three months or so will show that you have made enormous strides forward in your psychic perception:

- You see that you now 'catch' an intuition as it happens rather than recognising it sometime afterwards
- You instinctively move into psychic mode when appropriate
- You pay attention to what your psychic awareness is trying to communicate
- You have recognised the conditions that maximise your psychic abilities
- You have learned to trust those intuitions that are true and distinguish those that are wishful thinking

The inner conversation

Being prepared to receive what thought is not prepared to think is what deserves the name of thinking.

Jean–Francois Lyotard

There is another way in which to work with your metaphysical journal, this is to have a dialogue with your psychic knowing. It is extremely helpful for clarifying reactions and feelings that might be trying to tell you something important. Say for instance your teenage offspring or your best friend comes home with a new friend and you suddenly feel deeply uneasy, or have such a powerful reaction against them that you wish to bundle him or her out of the door immediately and forbid your child/friend to ever see them again. Write to your psychic awareness, or a guide, in your journal.

Exercise: Writing to your psychic awareness

Set out how you felt and ask why, what lay behind that reaction? Was it jealousy, a memory being triggered, something that hasn't taken place yet? Then write the reply from your psychic awareness or guide and continue questioning and writing your fears and 'but what if's' until you find peace within yourself.

In our example, part of that peace may come from finding a way forward that enables you to monitor the friendship in a way that will keep you alert to any harm, but it may also be that you have to learn to trust your child or your friend's psychic awareness too and allow the friendship to proceed without interference.

3
Metaphysical Preparations

Please read this section even if you have read *Good Vibrations* as it contains vital information specific to metaphysical working

Your place of enchantment may look quite ordinary to the outer eye.
Diane Skafte [7]

Having a safe space in which to work and being well protected is essential if you are to open your psychic awareness fully, especially in the initial stages. It marks out your boundaries, gives you a space into which to withdraw your attention and enhances your trust in the process. But your space doesn't have to be anywhere special or a particular location: it is within and around you and can be protected with a simple visualisation, something you can easily learn. Learning to distinguish what is a safe space from somewhere unsafe is also part of the unfolding process. Modern shamans who have learned from wise elders of tribes often speak of how the shamans know if a place is welcoming, appropriate for a ritual or somewhere to be avoided at all costs.

Before you start

We need to be willing to let our intuition guide us, and be willing to follow that guidance directly and fearlessly.
Shakti Gawain

Set your intent

Setting an intention sets the scene. It focuses your consciousness and alerts awareness. Your intention can be as simple as: 'I sense psychic information clearly and unambiguously' or 'today my psychic sensitivity works at its optimum power', or it can be geared towards an unfolding process: 'today I learn more about my psychic abilities and the way I gather signals from the universe'. Or you may choose to have the intention to learn more about working with your chosen divination tool. Taking a few moments to hold that intention in your mind starts the process and your psychic awareness will do the rest.

Some people like to begin a psychic development exercise or divination by inviting a sacred presence in to guide and guard the session: in other words, by making an invocation **(see p.39)**. Traditionally, an invocation asked the gods or goddesses to be present and show favour to the enterprise. Such invocations have been used for thousands of years and are a way of setting intention. You can call on your guardian angel or a power animal or other guide. Uttering an invocation can completely change your space, bringing a sacredness to metaphysical work or divination that reaches out and claims you. It is as though the god speaks through you: your psychic connection uses you instead of the other way round. This is when true psychic knowing becomes a natural part of your being.

Creating a safe space

If you keep a positive energy field around yourself, negativity cannot penetrate and your energy will stay high.

Judy Hall [8]

Creating a safe space can easily be achieved through visualisation (there's more about visualisation later in this chapter if you'd like to know more before you start), especially when enhanced with a crystal. The Purple Pyramid Meditation below can be used to protect a room or a building during metaphysical work or meditation. You can leave a virtual pyramid in place permanently around your home, but it can also be used whenever you feel the need of protection – some people add wheels to their pyramid to make a mobile shelter that accompanies them wherever they go.

If you have difficulty visualising, use your hands to physically mark out the space by drawing it in the air, and place an actual amethyst pyramid in the centre, or make a paper pyramid and paint it purple – a three–dimensional model with a base is ideal. Kinaesthetic people find that movement is the best way for them to create safe space. In which case, walk the sides of the pyramid on the floor and use your arms to go to the apex, or run your hands over the sides and base of an amethyst pyramid telling yourself that it is surrounding and encompassing you and then place it where it will remind you of your safe space.

Exercise in Visualisation: the Purple Pyramid

Sit quietly and comfortably, breathing gently. Close your eyes and look up to the space above and between your eyebrows.

Imagine that you are sitting in the middle of a purple pyramid. It is made of amethyst crystal and has a floor under your feet and four sides that meet above your head.

Trace the outline of the pyramid with your mind or your hands, and see clearly it in your mind's eye or follow its contours with your hands. Fill the inside with purple light to transmute any negativity and fill your space with light. Allow the light to revitalize the space within the pyramid. Amethyst is both protective and uplifting. Sitting in this pyramid will take you to the highest vibration possible whilst keeping you safe.

When the pyramid is strong, let it expand to encompass the room in which you are sitting or the whole building.

Slowly bring your attention back into your body and be aware that you and the room, or house, are now protected by the purple pyramid. Take your attention down to your feet and re–earth yourself by picturing a cord going from the centre of each foot deep down into the earth, joining and passing through the base of the pyramid. If you need your pyramid to be mobile, put wheels on each corner so that it moves with you.

Checking out a space

It almost seemed as though the place didn't want them there.
Diane Skafte

Perhaps you've had the experience of walking into a place and feeling a cold shiver run down your spine, a slightly nauseous feeling settle in the pit of your stomach, a headache quickly develops and your feet begin to move uneasily as though wanting to run away but it feels like walking through treacle. I feel such a body–response in haunted houses and dungeons, but I also had it on an idyllic beach on a remote Greek island that seemed to be saying 'go away, go away'. I did. My companion didn't and he got stung by a jellyfish but there was something deeper about the warning than that. It was as though the actual land was resentful, full of pain and anger. Later I found out that it was a place where survivors of a shipwreck during battle had been slaughtered as they came ashore.

It may not be anything that dramatic when I feel those body–responses. It may be that the place is on a rather nasty geopathic stress line or right in the beam of a powerful telecommunications aerial. It can also happen in a strange hotel room when I'm picking up the energy of everyone who ever slept in the bed, especially those who were deeply troubled. (As a matter of course I use Clear2Light space clearing essence for cleansing a hotel room or any bed before sleeping in it.) Such symptoms may indicate that there is work needed, but if you are new to metaphysical work it is wise not to meddle until you've been properly trained. But you can use such a response to get out of there fast or to put yourself into a protective bubble. You just need to train yourself to be aware of your own signals that all is not harmonious around you.

Exercise: Scanning your space

As you enter a space practise checking in with your body to see if all is well. Deliberately scan around you with your attention noticing how your body feels and whether there are cold or 'dead' patches of energy and whether you pick up any feelings that are not yours. You will quickly come to recognise your own signals that all is not well.

If the space does not feel good, picture it filling with bright white light as an emergency 'first aid' fix. If you can leave, do so. If not, pop yourself in a purple pyramid and ask for help to clear the energies. (You may find crystals such as smoky quartz very helpful for this and Petaltone Z14 essence is excellent for a rapid clearing.)

Inviting sacred presence

Uttering an invocation changes the atmosphere in the room completely.
Diane Skafte

In ancient times divination was never practised without invoking the presence of the gods, it was a sacred process. Your psychic awareness can be considerably highlighted by inviting this sacred presence, whether you call it deity, the gods, angels, divine light, power animals, the directions, your higher self or a daimon (a Greek term for a guide or mentor) into your life. It is particularly effective before making any kind of divinatory reading but an invocation can also be helpful before undertaking any of the exercises in this book. It takes you into an oracular space in which higher awareness is joining with your own interior patterns and instructing you even in your sleep. It is what I would call the interface of your inner knowing with greater knowing.

This is a space that needs to be approached with reverence and joy, not pomposity or indifference. An invocation from your heart is sufficient. It does not need to be showy, simply sincere. Everyone finds their own invocation based on their beliefs and what works for them but a useful general example would be:

- *I call in divine light and ask that my higher self will be with me, linking me to the guidance of universal love and all that is. May all my guides and helpers be with me for my highest good.*

Or you could call in Archangel Michael and his warriors to protect you and lend his power during your work. A shamanic invocation, which would be carried out facing each direction, could be:

- *I call in the power of the South and the element of water, the nourishment of the plant people and the guidance and protection of the power animals of the South.*
- *I call in the power of the West and the element of earth, the wisdom of the stone people and the allies of the West.*
- *I call in the power of the North and the element of air, the cleansing of the rushing wind and the allies of the North.*
- *I call in the power of the East and the energising fire element, the spirits of the ancestors and the power animals of the East.*
- *I call in the Above, the creative power of Father Sun, and I call in the Below, the nurturing care of the Earth Mother. I stand in the place of All That Is.*
- *Grandmother and Grandfather Bear be with me and guide me in my journey today and for all time.*

If you have opened a sacred space by invoking a presence, remember to thank that being when the session is over and to close the session. Gratitude and blessings enhance your psychic abilities and bring about further blessings. Traditionally closing was done by stamping a foot upon the ground three times and all the exercises in this book have a close down, but an end to a session can also be signalled by gathering up your divination tools and putting them away.

Closing down

Yes I know we haven't covered opening up yet, but you might do that inadvertently and closing down is one of the most essential tools for metaphysical working of any kind. This is the quick way – we'll explore more advanced ways of shielding yourself later.

Exercise: Shielding

When you want to close down after visualisation or meditation, picture shields closing over your third eye or cover the top of your head or your third eye with your hand. This acts as a signal that the visualisation is ended.

Then take your attention to your feet, make contact with the earth and stand up and move around.

This works equally well if you find yourself in detrimental energies or if an unwanted visitor tries to come to call.

In an emergency, stamp your foot three times to close the psychic gates.

The grounding cord

The next step is to strengthen the grounding cord that holds you in incarnation and keeps you in touch with your body and the earth plane. This cord is flexible and does not hamper your movement but it does help you to settle your consciousness back into your body when meditation or exercises are complete and it can help to 'reel you back in' during an out–of–body experience or if you feel floaty at any time. Being fully grounded is one of the best methods of protection.

Exercise: Grounding cord

Stand or sit with your feet firmly on the floor and take your attention down to your feet. Close your eyes.

Picture a cord growing from the centre bottom of each of your feet, rather like a root. They pass into the centre of the earth chakra about a foot beneath your feet where the two strands unite. The cord goes deep down into the centre of the earth. It is flexible and allows you to move around, but it holds you firmly in incarnation.

When you feel firmly grounded within your physical body, open your eyes and bring your attention fully back into the room.

Psychic protection

We are surrounded by a host of unseen vibrations, a field of invisible energies, many of which can subtly affect our sense of well–being – and our ability to protect ourselves psychically.

Judy Hall

One of the most efficient ways of ensuring that there is no downside to your psychic awareness is to practise psychic protection. A healthy aura naturally acts as a protection during metaphysical work. The aura is often known as the 'energy body' or biomagnetic sheath because of its vital and energetic appearance (see p.92). A strong aura is essential for health and well–being at the physical, emotional, mental, spiritual and psychic levels. If there are 'holes' or weak spots, energy can penetrate, or be drawn out from, your force–field and this will need healing. In an emergency, you can gain instant protection by imagining that the outside edge of your aura has crystallised – turned into a light refracting crystal coating that neutralizes anything untoward. One of the first ways I was taught to protect myself was to mentally jump into a bright shiny dustbin and slam down the lid (the disadvantage is you cannot see what is going on) or to put on a spacesuit. Your attitude also affects how effectively protected you are. Fear attracts fear so stay upbeat. Fortunately learning some basic protection techniques greatly enhances your protection. The companion volume to this book, *Good Vibrations: psychic protection, energy enhancement and space clearing*, goes into this in detail but I have included the basics in this chapter so you can get started.

➢ **Banish fear**: The first rule of protection when working with psychic awareness is to banish fear. Metaphysics teaches that like attracts like and fear attracts undesirable entities and energies. If you have no fear, you will not need protection. If you have learnt to protect yourself, you have no need to fear. Working only at the highest possible vibration automatically protects you – as does practising discernment and discrimination.

➢ **Apply common sense**: The second rule of psychic protection is to retain your common sense. So much that passes for 'psychic guidance', 'kything' (channelling) and the like is at best rubbish and at worst misleading and sometimes downright dangerous. It comes from working at the lower astral levels closest to earth or through your own subconscious mind or ego rather than accessing your higher self and the soul guidance that it offers. If your psychic sensitivity or inner voice ever seems to be suggesting that you should harm yourself or others in any way whatsoever it is safe to assume that this is not coming from a good space nor is it for your highest good. We all have inner figures that sabotage us and there are beings on other planes of existence that, unfortunately, delight in misleading the gullible.

So, it is essential to know where your guidance is coming from, to ensure that you can close down at will, and to be able to filter out anything undesirable. Practice and discernment together with appropriate exercises and tools make protection an instinctive act. Working at the highest possible level in a safe and protected space ensures that you will receive only wise council. Wearing Black Tourmaline constantly protects you.

Instant protection

For instant protection, you can create a barrier of light around you and a shield to neutralize negative energies. You also need a filter, something that will screen out the rubbish. If you practise the following exercises until they are automatic, protection will be there immediately you need it.

Exercise: The psychic shield

Picture yourself entirely surrounded and enclosed by light. (You may find it easiest to start with a light over your head and bring this down around your body, working towards your feet). Make sure that the light bubble goes under your feet and seals itself there. In one hand, visualise a silver shield that pulsates with light. Placing this shield between yourself and anything doubtful or dangerous will neutralise the energy.

You can also 'crystallise' the outer edges of the bubble for additional protection.

Or,

Visualise yourself standing inside a large, hollow, crystal that is filled with light.

[If you are kinaesthetic, use your hands to outline your aura and feel it surrounded by light or use a candle flame or torch, allow it to crystallise.]

Exercise: The filter

Picture yourself entirely surrounded by a silver space suit. This space suit has a communication panel on the front that has been programmed to only let truth communicate with you. If you press the green button on the panel, you will be able to hear – and see – what is being communicated to you in truth. If you do not hear or see anything, you will know that what was being communicated to you can be disregarded.

[If you are kinaesthetic, touch your hand to your chest, just below your throat. As you touch this place, say out loud 'I now touch the place of truth, everything I hear or sense will be truth'.]

If at any time you become aware that what you are hearing is negative and damaging, you can press a red button to immediately cut off and end the communication.

When you no longer need the filter, take your space suit off and put it away safely until you need it again. Remember to close your third eye shield and to check on your grounding cord and earth chakra (see p.40).

I wear a Labradorite or Shungite crystal or use Healer's Gold to create an interface with a built–in filter. Having asked the crystal to work for me in this way, whenever I put it on it automatically seals my aura and enhances my perception. It is invaluable to me in my work.

Gatekeepers and psychic gateways

> *In addition to guardian angels, guides and helpers, we all have a doorkeeper whose job it is to protect us... they guard our psychic doorway and allow only helpful energies to enter.*
>
> *Wilma Davidson* [9]

In the esoteric view, everyone has a gatekeeper, who may be male, female or of indeterminate gender, or an animal or bird. Metaphysically speaking, your gatekeeper is someone with whom you have travelled through aeons of time and whom you can totally trust, part of your greater soul group. But if you don't believe that there is anything outside this present life, you can look on your gatekeeper as part of your psyche. Even when you can't sense your gatekeeper around you, one will be there for you. You just need to trust.

Your gatekeeper has control of the gateways to your psychic mind. Located around your head, these psychic gateways allow a flow of energy between the physical and subtle levels of being. They are what enable you to make journeys out of your body and to pick up psychic communications. If your psychic gateways open and close at your will, they can prevent anything untoward happening to you during meditation or altered states of consciousness. If a gateway is stuck open you could suffer from psychic invasion, attachment, and the like.

If you have used recreational or prescribed psychotropic drugs and have experienced 'flashbacks' or uncontrolled altered states of awareness, you may have blown your gateways and should not undertake the exercises in this book until the gateways have been healed. Traditional Chinese Acupuncture can help with this condition or a very useful combination of crystals for creating an 'airlock' for a gateway that has been stuck open is a Selenite wand, with Chlorite Quartz and then Stibnite crossed over the top in an X shape. Place over the psychic gateway and ask that the gateway be brought back into balanced functioning and that your gatekeeper will only allow through that which is beneficial for your highest good (wash your hands after handling Stibnite and remember to cleanse the crystals regularly). The X shape is the ancient St Andrews cross which symbolises the joining of above and below, heaven and earth – although I only discovered this after I had intuitively created the portal during a workshop. Some specialist essences can also help but it is wise to seek the guidance of an experienced practitioner to find exactly the right one for you (see www.petaltone.co.uk).

Getting to know your gatekeeper is one of the best ways to feel safe during any metaphysical work. When you trust your gatekeeper, you focus your intention on the work you are doing. Gatekeepers are often to be sensed standing behind you but they may make themselves known in other ways. You may experience a tingling on your scalp, a feeling of hands on your shoulders, sense a cloak or arms wrapped around you, or become aware of a particular perfume for instance. There are hints on how to visualise later in this chapter but give this exercise a try first to see how you do without any coaching.

Exercise: Meeting your gatekeeper

Settle yourself quietly in a chair in a place where you will be undisturbed. Let your physical body relax and settle. Breathe gently and bring your attention into yourself. If you have any thoughts that do not belong to this work, let them drift past. Do not focus on them.

Take your attention to the top of your head and allow yourself to mentally reach up to the highest possible level. You may feel that you are being pulled up by a piece of string attached to the top of your head. If your head spins, take your attention down to the base of your spine and open the energy centre there. Then take your mind back up to the top of your head and around your shoulders.

When you have reached up to the highest possible vibration, ask your gatekeeper make him or herself known to you.

Watch out for any unexplained feelings in or around your body – tingling, touch, movement of air, etc. You may receive a mind picture of your gatekeeper or have a sense of someone with you. You may also see a colour or feel hot or cold. Just allow your gatekeeper to communicate with you without forcing anything, simply be receptive to meeting now or some time in the future.

Spend as long as you need getting comfortable with your gatekeeper. You may need to agree on a few ground rules for protecting your psychic gateways. If so, negotiate these until you are satisfied that your aims and those of your gatekeeper coincide. Ask your gatekeeper to show you where your psychic gateways are (usually over the chakras). Check them out. Practise by visualising them open and then closed.

If you become aware that your psychic gateways are stuck open, and anyone can access you or move in to influence you, ask your gatekeeper to help you bring these gateways back under your conscious control. When you have completed the exercise, shut your psychic gateways and ensure your grounding cord is in place going deep down into the earth. Then slowly bring your attention back into the room.

If you don't see or feel anything at this point, don't worry. It doesn't mean that your gatekeeper isn't there. It may take some time to contact your gatekeeper – or your guide when we come on to that. This is a skill you are developing and the communication has to grow between you – and you may need time to discover exactly how your gatekeeper is going to make its presence known. It's like tuning one of those old fashioned radio sets in, you turn the dial and at first hear nothing, then static comes in and a few scrambled words. Finally, if the aerial is in the right place, it becomes clear. But sometimes you need to move the aerial around several times until you find the right spot. Your psychic antenna is like that radio aerial, your sensitivity needs tuning in and you will develop that as you move through the book. Sometimes the signal of contact is not what we are expecting. As I've already said, it took me months to realise that the lightest of touches on my shoulder meant that someone was with me. Be patient with yourself and trust that the process will unfold. In the meantime, as long as you feel safe and protected, you can affirm that your gatekeeper is there without you having to see or sense anything. So long as you do the appropriate protection in your mind and ensure that you are in a safe space before starting an exercise, and then close down at the end, you will be protected and the contact will gradually strengthen.

A word of caution

You need to feel safe during your psychic opening up. A guide or a gatekeeper will understand this and will introduce themselves to you in an appropriate manner. But there are pushy entities out there who are just looking for someone to influence, not always for the highest good, or they desire particular experiences that they enjoyed while they were in a body – such as drink or drugs. So checking out who is around you is a sensible precaution especially in the initial stages. You are entitled to feel safe when doing this work.

- Do not allow unknown entities into your energy field especially when channelling, kything or meditating.

Questioning the spirits, your guide or your intuition and using your common sense is a vital component of sensible psychic working. No matter how experienced you become, if you are unsure of who is trying to communicate, or sense an alien presence that makes you feel uneasy, close your psychic gateways until you are sure that this is a benign presence. Always check out who wants to work with you. Beings who are there for your highest good will never object if you are cautious. They will take the time to get to know you, and for you to know them, making you feel safe and trusting. Indications of a benign presence tend to be intense feelings of love surrounding you, or beautiful colours or aromas around you. Indications of an 'alien' entity tend to be a distinct uneasiness, horrible smells or whirling sensations in your head and destructive thoughts that are not 'yours'. If you feel the latter, simply jump into your mental dustbin or spacesuit (see p.98) and protect yourself until the entity leaves. You may be called to do spirit release work when you have fully developed your abilities, but, for now, leave well alone.

Relaxation and visualisation

> *Relaxation exercises can be divided into two broad categories: those for the body and those for the mind. Body–centred exercises also have an effect on the mind.*
>
> *James Tighe* [10]

Relaxation will greatly assist all the exercises in this book and it has been proved to facilitate opening psychic abilities. Practise the following exercise until you can relax quickly and easily whenever you do an exercise. Ensure that you will not be disturbed and that you are comfortable and sufficiently warm without getting too hot.

Exercise: Relaxation

Settle yourself down in a comfortable place where you will not be disturbed. Breathe gently and easily focusing on your breath for ten breaths. As you breathe out let go any tension you may be feeling. Pause. And then breathe in a sense of quiet peace. Slowly raise and lower your eyelids ten times, allow your eyes to remain closed. Your eyelids will feel relaxed and pleasantly heavy.

Raise your eyebrows high and stretch your whole face. Relax and let go. Let the relaxed feeling from your eyelids travel slowly up your forehead and across your scalp, and through all your facial muscles. Smile as widely as you can, move your jaw from side to side, and allow your face to relax.

Now lift your shoulders up to your ears and let go. Allow the relaxed feeling to flow on down through your body. Take a big breath and sigh out any tension you may be feeling. Let your chest and back relax and soften.

Clench your fists and let them relax on your thighs. Allow the sense of relaxation that is passing through your body to go down your arms. Any tension that is left will drip out of your fingertips and trickle down to the earth.

Pull your belly in, breathing deeply. Let all your breath out and count to ten. Allow your lower back and abdomen to feel warm and relaxed.

Let the feeling of relaxation go on down through your thighs and knees, flowing down your legs to your feet. Raise and lower your feet and let your calf muscles be soft and loose. Scrunch your toes up and let them relax. If there is any tension left in your body, allow this to drain out of your feet.

You will now be feeling comfortably warm and peaceful. Spend a few moments enjoying this feeling of total relaxation. You will remain mentally alert but physically relaxed

When you have finished your relaxation, bring your attention back into your surroundings. Place your feet firmly on the floor and slowly sit up straight. Be aware of your connection with the earth. Get up and move around.

Remember to enter a state of quiet but alert relaxation before attempting any of the exercises in this book.

Time for intuition

During the ultradian rest response, your body goes into an intuitive mode. You are more receptive to impressions from your unconscious.

Ernest Rossi [11]

When keeping your metaphysical journal (see Chapter 2) you will undoubtedly find that there are times during the day or the month when, initially, it seems easier to move into an altered state of consciousness, visualise and relax. The moon has a bearing on this, as does the female menstrual cycle, but there is another cycle that you can take advantage of: the ultradian. The ultradian cycle has a profound affect on which hemisphere of the brain is active during a one and a half to two hour cycle throughout the twenty four hour circadian rhythm period. An essential part of biological organization, ultradian rhythms time the cellular processes in your body and are essential if the electrical, endocrine and behavioural systems are to function efficiently. A disrupted ultradian rhythm leads to insomnia, mood swings and physiological and psychological dis–ease so getting in touch with your ultradian rhythm can be good news for your well–being. In the comparatively brief, less than two hour, ultradian cycle, high activity is followed by a twenty minute 'low' or resting period in which your parasympathetic nervous system is activated and your intuitive right brain is switched on. Your neurophysiological system realigns itself and you are more likely to be able to relax and slip into an altered state of awareness. This is the time when 'aha' moments and out of the blue insights occur. It can be a period of intense creativity. It is the ideal time to employ self–healing techniques, to meditate or practise the exercises in this book. You can identify it by:

- Difficulty in concentrating
- The outside world 'disappears'
- The internal world becomes more vivid
- Exceedingly short attention span
- Mental fuzziness
- Low energy and fatigue
- Day dreams and sleepiness
- An urge to take a break from what you are doing
- Desperate desire for a cup of coffee, chocolate or a cigarette
- Yawning and sighing
- Irritability, discomfort and fleeting depression
- Prickling or unfocused eyes, buzzing ears
- An inability to hear or understand what is said to you the first time around
- Increased use of your hands if you find it difficult to explain something
- Increased visual imagery if you are writing or talking

Take advantage of this natural rhythm by taking time out from your daily activity. Remove yourself from all external distractions. Breathe deeply and slowly, let yourself fall into a reverie (similar to the hypnagogic state as you fall asleep or wake), and simply observe what your mind is doing for ten to twenty minutes. Don't try to focus, ask questions or concentrate. Simply be with what is. (You can formulate a question first and the answer will spontaneously emerge during your resting period.) Afterwards record your experience in your metaphysical journal. When you return to your daily activity you will be considerably energized and highly creative.

Visualisation and affirmation

What the mind of man can conceive and believe, it can achieve.
Napoleon Hill

Many of the exercises in this book start with guided visualisation. Visualisation uses your mind's eye. It involves seeing pictures as though projected on a screen, which may be inside your head or a few feet in front of you. Visualisation is a form of visual thinking. As belief is such an important part of all psychic awareness, worrying that you wont see anything is counter–productive; affirm to yourself 'I can see, my inner eye is open although my psychic sensitivity may work non–visually'. Believe it and it will happen.

In most people, these images go on all the time but are screened out. You can quickly learn to tune in. However, if you are not a visual person, and not everyone is, you can use your hands to help you in exercises by tracing shapes in the air or feelings objects. Visualisation images can be helped, however, by looking up to your inner screen. This is located between and slightly above your eyebrows (the site of the metaphysical third eye). The act of raising your eyes triggers alpha waves and the visual part of the brain – which is useful whenever you are working with your psychic awareness as it helps you to enter a relaxed state and to picture things. If you do this with your eyes closed, it enhances the images you want to access in guided visualisation. If you want to change a scene, look down to your toes with your eyes closed, look up to your screen again and the picture will have changed.

Visualisation and creative reverie are extremely effective ways to access your unconscious mind – the part of you that knows and that is connected into a greater whole. The unconscious mind is where enormous wisdom is stored and it contains knowledge that you have never actually learned.

Relative visualisation

Handicapped by a lack of language skills in his early years, Albert Einstein learned to access a stream of imagery instead. As he grew older, he let this image stream run freely whilst he observed its content. By imagining a train travelling at the speed of light, for example, and observing what he saw in his mind, he was able to formulate his complex theory of relativity – which arose out his own psychic rather than intellectual processes.

How to visualise

If you have eyes to see it, the whole world around you simply reflects your inner mind.
Chuck Spezzano [12]

Struggling to visualise is counterproductive. The more you can relax and the more you can withdraw from the sensory input of the outside world, the more easily images will form. Always choose a place that is free from distractions and where the light is not too bright. Switch off your phone because there is nothing so irritating as an image beginning to focus and the ringing of the phone shattering it. If you find that there is a repetitive noise in the outer world, incorporate this into your visualisation, telling yourself that each time you hear it, you will relax more deeply.

When you begin practising visualisation, try not to get too hung up on the details. Colours and directions are easily transposed because you are using a part of your brain that is not concerned with such details. Do not assume that you have got something wrong because the instructions say something else. It is your psychic knowing that you are accessing, not mine. If you get a picture or an impression that is different to what an exercise says, work with that. It is an excellent sign that your psychic knowing is communicating with you!

Exercise: In Your Mind's Eye

To prove to yourself that you can use your mind's eye for visualisation, ask a friend to read this list to you slowly at first and getting faster. Notice – or ask your friend to notice – where your eyes move as you picture each item:

Close your eyes and picture the following:

A bright yellow ball — *A bright red square*
An orange triangle — *A glass table*
A chair — *A table and 6 chairs*
Your childhood home — *Your first school*
Your desk — *Your favourite teacher*
Your child — *A place that fills you with horror*
Your mother — *Your great–great grandmother*
Your partner — *Your great–great grandchild*
The surface of Saturn — *The centre of the earth*
Your favourite smell — *The worst smell ever*

Very few people find this exercise impossible. A little challenging in parts perhaps but imagination fills in the blanks, especially where it takes you into the past or the future. In visualisation, active imagination acts as a vehicle for psychic awareness. Notice too whether your other senses come into play. Do you smell your un–favourite place, does your nose wrinkle when you think about it, for instance? Even though you can't see the worst smell ever, your nose will recall it. The more you can engage all the senses, the more real the experience will be.

Your favourite place

Having proved to yourself that you can visualise, close your eyes for the following exercise. You can have a friend read it to you if that helps you to focus:

Excercise: Your favourite place

Close your eyes and breathe gently. Slowly bring your attention into yourself and allow the outside world to fade away. If you hear noises, let them fade away. If you have thoughts, let them pass on by. Let your mind be quiet and calm.

Now take yourself to your favourite place. Picture it, see the colours. Feel yourself there, notice its textures, smell the smell of the place, hear its sounds. Feel the temperature, the air on your skin, the ground beneath your feet. Enjoy this space. Rest and relax here, allow it to revitalise you. Let it bring you to a point of inner stillness.

When you are ready to leave, open your eyes. Feel your connection to the earth beneath you. Stand up and move around.

The place to which you go will be the starting point for some of the guided journeys you will take as you work your way through this book.

Confirming visualisation

Visualisation does not depend on seeing images clearly. Many people say they cannot visualise and yet they react strongly, especially on a physical level, to visualisation exercises because they are sensing rather than using a visual mode. Brain scans show that people who are visualising have exactly the same brain activity as they would if they were actually hearing or seeing something. When they imagine a picture, the visual cortex lights up. When they imagine a sound, the auditory cortex becomes active.

If you want to check whether you are visualising or not, try the following exercise. **Do not look at it until you are ready to do the exercise**. If possible have someone else read it to you while you sit with closed eyes. But if not, actively read the exercise, involving your feelings, making the movements, and really trying to picture it. If you get a physical reaction, you are visualising!

Exercise: Eating a pear

Sit comfortably. Now imagine that you are holding a ripe, greeny–yellow and juicy pear in your left hand. Feel its weight, its coolness and smooth roundness. Take it up to your nose and sniff it. In your right hand, you hold a knife. With this knife, peel the top of the pear. Then cut yourself a slice. You will feel the juice oozing out and smell the aroma of freshly peeled pear. Lift it to your mouth. As you take a bite, you realise that it is a cooking pear, extremely sour and sharp, that pulls the moisture from your mouth and puckers your skin.

Practise visualising a new food every day for a week and your visualisation skills will come on in leaps and bounds.

You may have found that you had a physical reaction and your mouth puckered from the sour taste as you did that exercise. If it did, you are visualising even if you may not have actually been able to picture the pear. With more practice, images will form but allow your senses to inform you along with the images.

Try the exercise again substituting your favourite food, and then the food you dislike most. Allow yourself to smell it, taste it, feel its texture as well as see it. If you don't like avocado for example it feels slimy to the tongue and smells like rotten eggs.

Aids to visualisation

Crystals are extremely useful for inducing visualisation. If you place an Auralite 23, Prehnite, Azurite with Malachite, Selenite, Rhomboid Calcite, Apophyllite pyramid or Golden Labradorite crystal on your third eye, visualisation becomes much sharper.

- Certain scents were traditionally used to enhance psychic connection. We can no longer find ancient Egyptian blue lotus perfume, but you will be able to obtain rose or frankincense oil to rub into your third eye or joss sticks to burn. Experiment until you find one that transports you into an altered state simply by inhaling. Gazing into a scented candle may assist.

- Another aid is to remove all outside stimuli. Draw the curtains to exclude bright light (although you don't need pitch darkness). Cover yourself completely in a cloak or blanket, put cotton wool into your ears, use headphones, or use one of those eyeshades that airlines hand out on long flights. This helps you withdraw your attention deep into yourself and to create an inner screen on which to see.

Music and the mind

Journey back through time on the wings of sound
Stephen Halpern, Initiation

Music can help images to form. Music that has been specially written for visualisation or meditation is preferable as it assists your brain to slip into the alpha and theta wave states that creates the optimum conditions for visualisation and psychic awareness. Such music is often slow and soothing. However, it has been found that extremely complex music and progressive jazz both stimulate images but not necessarily psychic awareness.

Music has a powerful effect on behaviour. Researchers at Ben–Gurion University in Israel have confirmed earlier findings by the RAC in England. They proved that drivers who listen to fast dance music or complex classical music such as opera, whilst driving, are twice as likely to have an accident. They have shown that music above sixty beats a minute, or with many notes and a crescendo–diminuendo – rising and falling – pattern, increases your heart rate and blood pressure – which is antagonistic to relaxation. On the other hand, music with less than sixty beats a minute actually lowers the heart rate and induces relaxation.

Visualisation or '*seeing*'?

I believe that we are a vibration of our inner and outer consciousness ... It is tapping into that which is our challenge.
Lucy Setters

There is a difference between deliberately visualising or bringing to mind an image, and true psychic sight. In psychic sight, the image tends to appear spontaneously as a vision. However, in clairvoyance ('clear–sight') the image is deliberately invoked by inviting the spirit to appear. In such sensing, or receiving an impression, an image may or may not form visually but will still be there in a different form, you just need to identify how it is making itself known to you (see the different modes on perception on p.18) Seeing, sensing and clairvoyance may be subjective, that is the image appears within your head, or objective, it is outside your head literally in front of your eyes. An objective image can be mistaken for a person who is present, for example, or you may see swirling mists of colour around you rather than behind your eyes. This difference between objective and subjective is beautifully epitomised in the writings of the Spanish mystic St. Teresa of Avila, as is the reality of the whole experience.

> *I saw an angel close by me on my left side in bodily form. This I am not accustomed to see unless very rarely. Though I have visions of angels frequently, yet I see them only by an intellectual vision...*
>
> *He was not large but small of stature and most beautiful – his face burning as if he were one of the highest angels, who seem to be all of fire... I saw in his hand a long spear of gold, and at the iron's point there seemed to be a little fire. He appeared to me to be thrusting it at times into my heart and to pierce my very entrails, when he drew it out, he seemed to draw them out also and to leave me all on fire with a great love of God. The pain was so great that it made me moan and yet so surpassing was the sweetness of this excessive pain that I could not wish to be rid of it. The soul is satisfied now with nothing less than God. The pain is not bodily, but spiritual though the body has its share of it, even a large one. It is a caressing of love so sweet which now takes place between the soul and God, that I pray God of his goodness to make him experience it who may think I am lying.*

If you have difficulty seeing on an inner screen, projecting the picture or the seeing objectively out in front of you can make it easier to both visualise and to see. To do this, place your hand at arm's length in front of you. This is your screen. Close your eyes and let the pictures form on this screen as though you were at the movies or watching television.

Meeting a guide or wise teacher

> *For now I saw that it was not light but a man who had entered the room, or rather, a man made out of light, though this seemed no more possible to my mind than the incredible intensity of the brightness that made up his form.*
>
> George Ritchie [13]

The following exercise, as others in this chapter, also appears in *Good Vibrations* but it is an essential stage of psychic development and so I have included it here for those who have not read that book. But, even if you have, please take time to check out your connection to your guide as it is an essential part of psychic work – although it may take time for the contact to develop. At first you may not see an identifiable person or animal. Some people never actually see, they simply get a sense of someone with them or a particular smell alerts them. For some people it's like having a continuous head–chat going on with their guide, for others it just happens occasionally or under specific circumstances. As I have said elsewhere, for a long time all I felt was a hand on my shoulder and a sense of a cloak being wrapped around me. Eventually I came to realise that this was my guide. Then I progressed to finding myself speaking or writing something that didn't come from my own mind. What I call a straight through job. Nowadays I rarely 'see' my guide and simply have to open my mouth to speak or start typing to get a connection going. I often look at the page, or listen to myself, and think 'where did that come from?' Fortunately I have learned to trust that process or I wouldn't get any books written.

A guide or wise teacher assists hugely with your metaphysical understanding. Wise teachers come in many guises. Inner or outer figures, they may appear as people, animals or otherworldly beings – and may change form. During one of my workshops, a woman 'saw' a Jesus–like figure as she waited for her wise teacher. "Oh no", she thought, "I don't think I can be good enough to have you for a guide." "Is this better?" he asked as he transformed his robe into sweater and jeans. She found him much easier to relate to and her self–doubt abated.

Wise teachers may be with you for a lifetime or during a specific task. If you have something to do that you find difficult, you can request that a wise teacher be sent to assist. This can be useful if you have to navigate around a strange place or somewhere you do not speak the language for instance, but there are wise teachers that have advanced business acumen and others who offer innovative solutions or necessary skills.

Sometimes people find that the 'wise teacher' who appears in the following visualisation is someone they would rather not have assisting them. One woman, for instance, found that her mother–in–law arrived in her visualisation. She had been a controlling figure when alive and the woman's heart sank at the thought of further control. So, she thanked her mother–in–law but explained that for the tasks over which she needed guidance someone with more specialised knowledge would be appropriate, and added that she did not want to stand in the way of her mother–in–law's progress on the other side. Her mother–in–law was perfectly happy to leave the guiding to what she described as a 'higher being'.

Exercise: Meeting a wise teacher or guide

Relax and take yourself into your favourite place. Ask that a wise teacher or guide will come to you. Be expectant but not insistent. Have patience. Take time to walk around enjoying this beautiful space and the feeling of joyful anticipation this meeting invokes. As you walk around, you will become aware that someone is coming towards you. This is your wise teacher who will act as your guide. Take all the time you need to get acquainted.

When it is time to leave, thank your wise teacher or guide for being there and arrange a call signal in case you need to get in touch. Your wise teacher will probably give you a recognition signal for future occasions.

Then bring your attention back into the room, get up and walk around to reconnect to everyday awareness.

***If you are kinaesthetic or aural rather than visual**, your wise teacher or guide will probably make its presence known by touch, smell, words, impressions, or an instinctive **knowing**.*

Do not be afraid to test your guide until you are sure that this is a wise being you can completely trust and who has your highest good at heart. Question, question and question again. A truly wise being will never be annoyed at being asked to clarify and confirm.

Receiving a message from your guide

Once you have established a firm and trustworthy connection with your guide you can begin to receive messages to assist your everyday life or your spiritual development.

Exercise: Receiving a message

Send out a thought asking your guide to communicate with you. (If you have a call sign, use that.)
Imagine a ladder of light going out of the top of your head to meet your guide.
Set out your question or the information you require.
Sit quietly and listen for the reply.
When you have finished, thank your guide, withdraw the ladder of light back into the top of your head. Make a note of what you were told. Get up and move around.

If at any time you receive the call sign or signal that your guide is present, sit down and repeat the process to access the information your guide has for you. However, always ensure that it is an appropriate moment to be receiving the information. If not, ask your guide to return later. In time you will be able to receive the message instantly without impinging on what you are doing at the time.

Meditation

Within every single one of us lies well upon well of spiritual peace untapped, of spiritual intelligence untouched.

Dr Paul Bruton

Regular meditation is an excellent way to expand your psychic awareness. The type of meditation that does this is not one that concentrates on a mantra or on the breath. You don't want to empty your mind or ignore stray but meaningful thoughts that pass through. That form of meditation takes you beyond the place where images form and psychic awareness expands. Psychic meditation uses imagery but if you don't see pictures, let yourself feel and smell your favourite place all around you or open your inner ear to the hidden voice that whispers in the background, or have the impression that you are there. What you are seeking is a quiet mind, an inner point of stillness, and a blank screen on which your psychic sensitivity can write, rather than an empty mind. Appropriate music can be extremely useful in helping you to relax and put aside thoughts of the day as it puts your mind into the right space.

It is traditional to sit with a straight back for meditation, with your feet on the floor and your hands resting lightly on your thighs, or in the lotus position: legs crossed and feet up on your thighs if you can manage this but many of us can't. Having your feet on the floor helps you when you want to end the meditation. If you find another position more comfortable adopt it. It is more important to be fully relaxed and free from distractions than to sit in the 'right' pose.

It is also traditional to meditate at the same time every day but again it is more important to actually do the meditation each day rather than stick rigidly to a particular time. You may find that you can quieten your mind more easily in the morning than the evening, or vice versa, in which case time your meditation accordingly.

Always chose a time when you will not be disturbed – take the phone off the hook or switch off your mobile. Allow yourself five or ten minutes when you begin, gradually lengthening it to fifteen or twenty minutes.

Initially you will probably find that many trivial thoughts pass through your mind. If this is the case don't try to stop them, let them pass on through. In time the 'thoughts' that you have will be your psychic awareness communicating with you. You may 'see' them as pictures in your mind's eye, 'hear' them as an inner or outer voice speaking to you, or 'feel' them without knowing quite how it happened. All of these are equally valid ways, nothing is right or wrong. You have to find the way for you.

Calming the mind

> *Clarity, insight or understanding are only possible when thought is in abeyance, when the mind is still. Then only can you see very clearly, then you can say you have understood.. then you have direct perception.*
>
> *Krishnamurti*

Research has shown that psychic awareness functions best when outside stimulus is reduced but the mind remains attentive. A still mind has always been the goal of eastern meditation practices. To achieve this absence of thought, concentration on the breath is often used: sitting quietly and observing the gentle sensation of the breath entering your nostrils, passing down into your lungs, and moving out again. This can be a useful way of moving out of everyday awareness into stillness. With practice, it only takes a few moments to calm the mind and it is an exercise that can be performed anywhere. If you let your eyes go softly out of focus at the same time, sensory input is considerably reduced and you enter a state of attentive expectation. If you find that 'mind chatter' is a problem, try placing a blue Selenite or Rhomboid Calcite crystal on your third eye.

Exercise: Psychic meditation

Settle yourself comfortably and close your eyes. Raise and lower your shoulders and as they drop allow any tension you are feeling to fall away.

Take your attention to the base of your spine. You have an energy point here that, when open, will stop you drifting away. You may feel it rotating like a wheel or sense energy pulsing there. If you feel yourself 'floating' or drifting too far away from contact with your body, take your attention to this point and it will bring you back. It is helpful to feel a root going from this point deep down into the earth to anchor you.

Begin by asking that your energies be raised to the highest possible level and that any guidance you receive comes from the highest source.

Establish a gentle rhythm of breathing with the out breath slightly longer than the in breath. Pause between each in and out breath.

Slowly bring your attention into yourself and allow the outside world to fade away. If you do hear noises, do not be disturbed by them. If you have thoughts, let them pass on by. Let your mind be quiet and calm.

Now take yourself to your favourite place. Picture it, see the colours. Feel yourself there, notice its textures, smell the smell of the place, hear its sounds. Feel the temperature, the air on your skin, the ground beneath your feet. Enjoy this space. Rest and relax here, allow it to revitalise you. Let it bring you to a point of inner stillness.

If anything else happens, note it but do not focus on it for too long. Allow your mind to remain quiet and peaceful. If you drift off into inappropriate thoughts, gently bring yourself back to your favourite place but be open to the possibility of your intuition communicating with you.

When you are ready to return, slowly become away of your body sitting in the chair and of your feet on the floor. Picture a cord going from your feet down into the centre of the earth, gently and flexibly holding you in your body. Close a shutter over your third eye (see chakra shields).

Another way of calming the mind is to contemplate an image (see below). Mandalas have been used for this purpose for thousands of years. They bring you to the same point is stillness, the space in which you can hear your inner voice.

Entering a meditative state with ease

When you go into meditation you enter an alpha brain wave state and then move into theta. Remaining attentive and retaining some beta (the alert, everyday brain state) brainwaves helps you to process and remember the information. If you find difficulty in entering a meditative state play music that has been specially written to enhance meditation. Music appeals to the right hemisphere of your brain, the side that is psychic and meditation–orientated. The following exercises (which are also in *Good Vibrations*) help you to slip into a meditative state quickly. See which one is the most effective for you and introduce it at the start of the exercises.

Exercise: The golden circle

Close your eyes and look up the point above and between your eyebrows, focusing on your third eye. You will find a small golden ball here. It is turning slowly. As you watch, it spins faster and faster moving into your skull. It moves in a great flat circle all around the inside of your skull, level with your third eye. It is moving so fast that all you can see is a golden circle spinning inside your head, like a halo that has dropped down around your brain. When it slows down, it settles at a point exactly in the centre of the circle. This is your point of stillness.

[If you lose that point of stillness, go back to the circle and let it settle in the middle again.]

Exercise: Pointillion

Close your eyes and look up to the inner screen above and between your eyebrows. Using large black dots, write your full name on the screen, followed by the word RELAX also in dots. Then rub it off. Repeat. [This puts you into alpha waves.]

Exercise: The ball of light

Close your eyes and look up to the point above and between your eyebrows. Now take your awareness out a few feet in front of you. There is a ball of light here, like those used in discos. As it turns it flashes coloured lights out from the many facets on its shiny surface. Watch it turn, spinning faster and faster with the light flashing and sparkling, more and more light spinning off it, until it suddenly stops and leaves you in a peaceful space.

Face or eye clearing

A disembodied eye, invisible, incorporeal, seeing but not seen.
R. Gordon Wasson

Strange things can happen when you begin to meditate or to open your psychic connection. If you consciously take your vibrations up to their highest levels before you begin meditation, and keep the energy centre at the base of your spine open to help you ground the experience, you should experience little difficulty. However, it is quite common for colours, eyes or faces to zoom in when you start to meditate and some of these faces can be unpleasant. Initially, allow them to be there, don't focus too hard and don't be frightened. As time goes on these may resolve themselves into guides, in which case you will be able to communicate with them.

Faces or eyes most often appear from four sources: your psychic awareness, your unconscious mind, thought forms created by other people or yourself, and the dimensions close to the earth on which 'lost' or malicious souls may become trapped. If you are unfortunate enough to attract the unwanted attention of the souls who hang around the earth and you don't feel competent to move them on, you can use the power of your mind to 'rub them out' using a light wand (see 'What to do when things go wrong' p.235) or a bucket of old–fashioned whitewash (and wear a black tourmaline for protection). These techniques also work for thought forms or faces that arise out of your own mind.

With practice you will soon reach a level where these faces or eyes no longer bother you.

Notwithstanding, such faces or eyes, and the animals or 'part faces' that may appear during meditation, may be gifts in disguise. If you can slow the faces down – they often move very quickly – and check them out from within your safe space, you may find that they are not as frightening as they appear. You may be able to communicate with them. Guides or other helpers such as power animals often initially present themselves in this way. Whilst it can be disconcerting to see a disembodied eye, the whole face may gradually be discerned.

Opening your physical eyes and putting your hand over your third eye to deliberately close the third eye should stop faces or eyes intruding. If the faces continue to bother you, or seem to be asking you for something, it would be wise to find someone who is experienced in such matters to help you deal with them.

Hearing with the inner voice, seeing with the mind's eye

> *[An oracle] addresses itself to those thinkers who are compelled by an inner voice to go into the depths of all things, and remains incomprehensible to those who stop at the external meaning of words.*
>
> O. *Wirth*

Opening the inner sense organs and listening to the intuition of the heart and the inner voice is the key to intuitive living. It is not only during meditation that your psychic awareness will speak to you. At every moment, it is necessary to be attuned to the whispered inner voice or subtle clues glimpsed by the mind's eye. You will get into the habit of recognising psychic signals. It is a matter of bringing them into focus, of paying attention. As Dr Paul Brunton explained:

> *Such signs and tokens are shown us by the soul but they are often misunderstood or simply not noticed. They come quietly, as quietly as the sun steals into a darkened world, so quietly that [you are] likely to dismiss them as useless fantasies, meaningless thoughts or unimportant imaginings.*

The classic method of introspective enquiry that he and many occult schools taught is still effective today and only takes a minute or two of your time. At moments throughout the day, suddenly stop what you are doing, breathe gently and bring your attention quietly into yourself. Drop into the resulting silence a question, and wait with patient expectation for the answer to arise intuitively. Typical questions to ask are:

- Who is doing this?
- Who is feeling this emotion?
- Who is thinking these thoughts?
- Who is speaking these words?

This breaks the illusion that the outer person is all there is, and focuses you into your inner being:

> *The practice of suddenly observing oneself, one's desires, moods and actions, is especially valuable because it tends to separate the thoughts and desires from the sense of selfhood that normally inheres in them, and thus tends to keep consciousness from being everlastingly drowned in the sea of five physical senses.* [14]

Practised regularly, this introspective enquiry moves you out of intellectual and emotional sensing, and into psychic *knowing*. You no longer strive to achieve but rather seek to allow. The voice of the psychic self will speak.

To open the inner eye and ear

During meditation, or when commencing a visualisation, it is common to see an eye opening at your third eye (above and between your eyebrows) or feel your ear pulsating – usually one ear, often the left, rather than both. This can facilitate your inner eye and ear opening. Before doing the inner eye exercise it is helpful to use a technique from the Emotional Freedom Technique to switch from functional, everyday perception to psychic, primary perception:

Exercise: Open inner eye and inner ear

With your eyes open, look up to the left as high and far as you can without moving your head, then switch to the right, then look down as low to your right as possible again without moving your head and then switch to the left, reverse the process. Now make big sweeping circles with your eyes, and then a tiny circle. Now rotate your eyes the other way. Close your eyes and repeat twice more.

Exercise: To open the inner eye

With your eyes open or closed, whichever feels most comfortable, look up to your inner screen, the place where your third eye lies between and slightly above the place between your eyebrows. Now move your attention forward about a foot. Picture an eye opening before you. Place this open eye on your third eye, absorb it so that it passes through the skull and lodges behind your third eye.

Exercise: To open the inner ear

Tap gently with the fingers of both hands just behind your ears moving along the bony ridge until your hands meet above your spine, and then tap back to your ears again. Then tap the little hollows in front of your ear slightly below the corner of your eyebrow and where your ear joins your head. Feel how the blood pulses in this spot. Hear it swishing and sighing.

Feel your ear pulsating with half–heard sound. Move this pulsation back behind your physical ear and hear how the sound clarifies itself.

If you are non–visual: *hold an Ammolite crystal or Ammonite fossil behind your ear or a shell to your ear. Listen quietly and allow the inner voice to speak through it.*

Framing questions

I have answered three questions and that is enough
Lewis Carroll

Asking questions is a necessary part of psychic development. After all, if you don't know what you want to know or to ask questions clearly, how will those who are trying to communicate know what you wish to understand or the guidance required? This is particularly so if you are using divination tools. The type of question and the way that you frame it will to a large extent determine how helpful an intuitive reply is. You also need to identify the appropriate method for receiving answers to specific questions (see Divination Tools) – and to frame the question concisely and precisely.

- Closed questions are ones that have a yes or no – or sometimes maybe – answer but open questions allow for further exploration.
- Closed questions demand rigid yes or no answers – but psychic awareness and divination tools rarely give straight yes or no replies.

  - Open questions create a space for the unseen to become visible, for something new to manifest.
  - Open questions illuminate choices, bring out potential, and highlight hidden resistance or self–sabotage.
  - Open questions *allow* and *facilitate*.

Guidance is difficult to obtain from a closed question. 'Fuzzy questions' that ramble and could have several answers are also hard to answer. Be succinct. But, if you make your question too simple, it may defeat itself. Too complex and you may have to stretch the answer to fit. Ask too many questions and the oracle refuses to answer. It is better to take questions in manageable chunks and to do a reading in several parts with an appropriate divination tool. If you are trying to answer a complex psychological question, you need a method that points with great accuracy to the lifescripts underlying events (try Chuck Spezzano's *Enlightenment Pack*) and for soul questions one that tunes into your lifepath (such as my *Crystal Wisdom Oracle*). If you want a simple answer, dowsing a circle of possibilities can give answers such as 'Hold back' or 'Go for it'.

Asking questions such as: 'Why did he do that?' or 'Will she marry me?' put the focus on the other person. Such questions not only block insights into your own self but are easily misinterpreted as you project your own inner reasoning, wishful thinking or excuses which then come back as an answer from 'out there'. Also, you cannot control or be responsible for someone else's behaviour and choices. This is why psychic connections or readings which rely on someone else doing what the reading says they will do invariably disappoint.

Opening to answers

My soul now belonged to another mystery, and everything else paled in its light.
Diane Skafte

Oracular answers were notoriously ambiguous. When Croesus asked the Delphic oracle if he should make war on the Persians, he was told he would overthrow a great empire. So he went to war. But it was his empire that fell.

When you receive an answer, you need to remain open to possibilities. An answer that seems to indicate one thing, may actually point to something different – like the reply Croesus received from the Delphic Oracle. So, for instance, a woman's aunt was very ill. She had already made the 400 mile round trip to visit her several times. The hospital rang again saying her aunt had deteriorated. Wanting to be with her aunt when she died, the woman asked for a sign to show her whether it would be appropriate to go. Opening a book at random, there was one sentence on the page:

There really is nothing left to do.

She interpreted this to mean she should make the journey immediately – that is, in her emotionally sensitive state, she thought it was saying there was nothing else to do but to go. She rang the hospital to say she was on her way only to be told her aunt had died as she was reading the sign. There really was nothing left to do.

Answers can be interpreted at different levels. If you asked if you were pregnant, for example, you could receive the answer: 'Yes'. This reply could, however, relate not to physical pregnancy but to the fact that you were pregnant in the sense that something was being gestated within you – a new possibility, the germ of an idea, a creative project and so on. You would give birth in due time, but it would not be to a child.

When using your psychic sensitivity, try to avoid the kind of question that combines an either or scenario or you may become confused as to which part of the question is being responded to. 'Should I do so and so or should I do this and that' is best avoided. Examine two possibilities through two separate questions. It is also wise to avoid asking too many questions one after the other, especially if you are, at heart, only trying to get the answer you would wish for.

For clear questions and answers, focus on yourself rather than another person. Ask precise, open questions – and not too many of those – and seek understanding and clarity rather than rigid answers. Write your questions down. Ponder on them. Take time to ensure that they are correctly phrased. Then ask your psychic sensitivity or divination tool. And ponder the reply when you receive it, allowing time for its full meaning to percolate through into your conscious awareness. Don't be too quick to jump to conclusions, look for the subtle and hidden meaning.

Useful Questions

Please give me insight into … … [be precise]
How can I move forward?
What lies behind this situation?
What can I learn from this?
How is the past affecting the present?
Please clarify this situation for me. [Set out the situation first]
Please show me how to resolve this situation.
What do I need to know about ….. [name the person or situation]
What is needed to heal this situation?
Please reveal what is hidden from me in this situation
Please give me guidance as to whether I should …… [be precise]
Would this be a good course of action for me?
What would be the result of this action? [Specify]
What would be the result of embarking on this relationship?
What do I need to know today?

Selecting the right tool to answer a question

Some oracles use what appears to be random chance, others are more scientifically based.
Judi Hall What's my future?

Your psychic awareness can be focused through various divination tools to answer questions, some of which will be more suitable than others for particular types of question and also for how your own psychic awareness functions (see Divination Tools). As you work through this book you will find which tools best assist you in accordance with how your psychic abilities function. But it is helpful to consider at what level your question is operating and what lies behind it.

The question: 'Will I find the right relationship soon?' for instance could be asked at several levels. You may simply want a 'yes/no' answer. In which case, especially if you are kinaesthetic, dowsing could be sufficient. A crystal oracle could also have something to say or a card spread if you are visual. A tarot or rune reading could set out the timing and any obstacles in your path.

But, the question could be emotional or psychological. Some of the newer tarot packs or specially designed self–awareness systems would be appropriate. These would tell you the inner changes you need to put in place to attract exactly the right relationship. They would also pinpoint the emotional basis on which you asked the question in the first place – does it arise out of the need simply to fill a hole in your life, to make yourself feel wanted or complete, or does it arise out of a desire for a life–enhancing partnership? By choosing your metaphysical tool carefully, you will receive the most enlightening answer for your deepest intention.

Appropriate tools for you will also depend on which mode functions best for your psychic perception of the world and whether you are kinaesthetic or visual (see Body Awareness).

Crystals and essences for psychic connection

Each crystal is unique, carrying its own particular theme and frequency.
Stephanie Harrison and Barbara Kleiner

Crystals have been used to enhance psychic abilities for thousands of years. Gazing into a crystal ball sets your rational mind free and focuses your psychic awareness. Crystals can put you in touch with your own inner guidance, or attune you to guides and your higher self.

Crystals to enhance psychic abilities

Your psychic abilities can be developed and heightened by holding one of the following crystals to your third eye for a few moments daily or by meditating with the crystal in place. This is particularly useful when you begin scrying or when you are seeking guidance. You can also meditate by gazing into a crystal's depths. Wearing crystal earrings can also heighten your psychic abilities.

Stimulating psychic awareness: Amethyst, Bytownite (Yellow Labradorite), Amazonite, Ametrine, Ametrine Apophyllite, Aqua Aura, Azeztulite, Azurite with Malachite, Celestite, Herkimer Diamond, Kyanite. Lavender Smithsonite, Lapis Lazuli, Moonstone, Petalite, Phantom Quartz, Star Sapphire, Selenite, Smoky Quartz, Sodalite, Yellow Calcite, Anandalite.
To close off mind chatter: Auralite 23, Blue Selenite, Rhomboid Selenite or Calcite.
To induce dreaming: Amethyst, Selenite, Blue Howlite, Bloodstone, Celestite, Charoite, Rhodocrosite or Moonstone, Diaspore.

Cleansing and dedicating your crystals

Before using any crystal for scrying or other purposes, it must be cleansed and dedicated, and then cleansed again after use as crystals easily pick up negative energies.

I personally prefer to use purpose–made crystal cleansing essences for cleaning and reenergising my crystals as these work at a subtle etheric level in addition to the purely physical, but traditionally crystals are cleansed under running water and recharged with the power of the sun as long as they are not friable or layered – in which case place them in brown rice overnight. It is possible to use 'divine breath' to cleanse crystals and many shamans blow on their crystals. However, if you have attachments or influences that are not beneficial to your welfare, these may be blown into the crystals or the energy contaminated and it is sensible to only use this method if you are absolutely sure you have no untoward influences operating.

Dedicating your crystal with intent

Before a crystal can work for you it needs to be attuned, energised and dedicated to manifest your intention. If you don't tell the crystal what you need and attune it to your particular energies, how can it help to protect your or manifest what you want?

So, first of all, spend time formulating your intention very precisely. Ask yourself: do you want to use it to enhance and support your psychic perceptions or are you using it to receive an answer? Will the effect be personal or for a group?

When you have formulated your intention, put it into a simple sentence. For example:

Exercise: Dedicating a crystal

I dedicate this crystal to enhance and support my psychic abilities at all times for the highest good of myself and all those on whom my psychic awareness is focused.

To dedicate the crystal, hold it in your hands for a few moments and focus your attention into the crystal. Feel the crystal attuning to your vibes. Ask that the crystal will work for your highest good and then say your sentence out loud.

Deprogramming a crystal

As has been seen, crystals hold thoughts and intentions. Which means that if you have been gifted a crystal, whatever the giver envisioned or intended for you will be programmed into the crystal. The deepest intention someone has may be unconscious and unacknowledged – and far from what they thought they were putting into your crystal. It is therefore sensible to thoroughly deprogram a crystal and put your own intention into it before use.

There may also be times when a crystal has been dedicated for one particular use and is no longer required for that purpose. This does not mean its usefulness is over. Far from it, it will undoubtedly have other work to do and another purpose to carry out. The crystal should, however, be deprogrammed and rededicated before reuse.

Exercise: To deprogramme a crystal

Hold the crystal in your hands for a few moments, thanking it for doing its work and for holding the intention and purpose it has had. Explain to the crystal that this part of its work is now over and ask the crystal to dismantle the programme it has been carrying. See bright white light beaming into the crystal to help it to deprogram, cleanse and recharge. Wash the crystal in Clear2Light or other cleansing spray or place it under running water. Put the crystal out into sunlight for a few hours if possible. The crystal may need a rest period to rebuild its energies before being rededicated to a new purpose.

If you are not visual*: Cleanse the crystal with Clear2Light, place it under running water or into brown rice, and then into sunlight. Then place the crystal on a Brandenberg Quartz (or clear quartz cluster) and ask that it be returned to its original pure programme and purpose. Leave overnight. Then remove the crystal and allow it to rest before being rededicated.*

Essences for crystal work

Whilst there are many essences to help you be more psychically sensitive, the one essence that I personally feel most assists with psychic development is Petaltone Power Shield. This essence seals the outer edges of your aura whilst still allowing your psychic sensitivity to function. It creates an interface between your energy field and that of someone else, or between one mind and another. Working at this interface facilitates clear, uncontaminated communication between the higher selves and soul consciousness of each person whether they happen to be in incarnation or not. In other words, it also works when communicating with discarnate spirits. Petaltone Greenway cleanses and activates your psychic gateways.

Another invaluable essence is Petaltone Plant Ally which contains a live plant spirit. This wondrous little essence *being* can be requested to work with you in all manner of ways – and may suggest some you haven't thought of. I apply it to many of my crystals for both healing and divination work whether they are done at a distance or one to one. It improves focus, clears and centres energy and ensures that whatever is done will be for the highest good of all.

4
Divination Tools

No one can be absolutely sure of the future, but we can support people to make the best of their present choices and opportunities so that the future can be as health and happy as possible.
David Lawson, Psychic Potential

Divination tools can kickstart your psychic development as they utilise your particular visual or kinaesthetic strengths (see pp.15–18, 115ff). Remember to connect to your guide before beginning a reading.

Divination is one of the most ancient practices known to man. Several thousand years ago men and women in Mesopotamia and Egypt were buried with sets of stones which archaeologists have established were used for the purpose of divination. All over the ancient world, livers were examined and dice cast. The stars were consulted and oracles honoured. In all divination there is a core activity: accessing knowledge beyond everyday reality. To do this many tools are used: stars, cards, dice, crystals, sticks and stones to name but a few. They may appear to have nothing to do with each other, but most have their roots in a past tradition. What is common to all methods of divination is the use of insight or psychic sensitivity to gain information that would not otherwise be accessible.

While you are learning to work with divination tools, always give your psychic insight an opportunity to supply the answer by quietly contemplating the spread or cast for a few minutes before you turn to look up the meaning. This gives your insight a chance to develop. and the knowledge of your chosen divination tool to grow.

What is divination?

For I dipt into the future, far as human eye could see
Saw the Vision of the world, and all the wonder that would be
Saw the heavens fill with commerce, argosies of magic sails
Pilots of the purple twilight, dropping down with costly bales
Heard the heavens fill with shouting, and there rain'd a ghastly dew
From the nations airy navies grappling in the central blue
Alfred Lord Tennyson 1809–1892

Divination is ascertaining the future through insight or psychic ability. In the poem quoted above, Tennyson foresees war in the skies, even though he is writing in 1842, seventy years before planes, bombs and chemical warfare became a reality. Yet he saw 'costly bales' and 'ghastly dew' carried by airy navies. His poetic muse took him forward into the future. Divination offers guidance, it does not tell you what to do. It points to choices and possibilities. Oracles can warn of impending events and show you a way to steer through these, but an oracle cannot show you how to avoid them totally. Used wisely, oracles help you to know yourself.

The word Oracle means 'to pray' or to 'speak'. Oracles are intermediaries between the gods and humankind so an oracle is a divine communication. Divination tools provide a focus for extra–sensory perception. The images used are archetypes, evocative symbols that speak to the psychic mind. Divination is often seen as fortune telling a fixed and pre–ordained future. However, there has always been a split between 'fate' and 'freewill'. In ancient eyes, it was the will of the divine but it could change at any moment. This was why offerings were made to propitiate the gods, especially before consulting the Oracle. However, oracles were not always crystal clear in what they said, nor were they always interpreted correctly. A Scythian prince asked how he would die and received the answer that a *mus* (mouse) would cause his death. He immediately had his house fumigated and forbade anyone called Mus to enter. However, he died from an infected muscle in his arm. The oracle–interpreter – and the Prince – had overlooked the fact that a *mus* was also a muscle.

Fate versus freewill

Fate says that everything is pre–ordained. Each person has a plan laid down for them from which they cannot deviate. So, the Roman chronicler Plutarch in his biography of Julius Caesar tells us that:

> *...a certain soothsayer forewarned him of a great danger which threatened him on the Ides of March and that when the day was come, as he was going to the senate–house, Caesar called to the soothsayer and said, laughing: "The Ides of March are come", to which the soothsayer answered: "Yes, but they are not yet gone."*

And, of course, by the end of the day Julius Caesar was dead. This was seen as his fate. There are those that say, however, that had he heeded the warning, he could have avoided that fate.

Freewill says that everyone has the power of directing their own actions voluntarily. It offers opportunities for growth and change. The choices you make, the decisions you avoid, carve out your destiny.

Although these two approaches seem mutually incompatible, they can be reconciled. There is a path marked out – by yourself or your god. Some would call this karma (the result of past actions) or fate or even destiny. How you approach this path depends on how you exercise your free will. Whether you blindly follow the dictates of fate or seek to grow wiser through choices you make as you develop your psychic abilities and evolve your soul.

The art of divination

Since the future is not yet uncoiled in time, there is no way to unravel it fully in the present. We can only get a feeling for its shape through dreams, revelation, divination, and other oracular means.

Diane Skafte

Over the entrance to the Oracle at Delphi was carved "Know Thyself". Whilst many modern day oracles and divination tools act as intermediary between you and your fate, they can also help you to know yourself better. If you understand the hidden parts of your nature, the fears and desires that subconsciously drive you, then you have more control over your future. And, you will be able to use your psychic ability much more clearly if you know yourself.

Since time immemorial humankind has been using divination to answer pressing questions, to seek a way forward, to ascertain the will of the gods and to seek favour and fortune. Divination tools act as a focus for your psychic ability. They help you to empty your mind of everything but the situation you are asking about. There are literally hundreds of tarot packs, oracles and divination aids. Whilst initially you will probably follow your chosen system rigidly, and may need to consult books of meaning, with practise the symbols come to have a personal meaning for you. This is when your psychic ability really takes off and the more you can allow your own meaning to rise up, the better your divination is. It is always worth using your psychic insight first before seeking the consensual meaning. Whenever you lay out a spread, let your attention wander over the cards or the runes or other tool and note what thoughts and psychic perceptions come into your mind. These will have the strongest personal meaning for you.

Choosing a divination system

First make up your mind, then consult the oracles
Mao Tse

You can choose your divination tool in one of three ways. The first is to use a system that has already caught your eye, such as a specific Tarot pack. If you are strongly drawn towards a particular illustration or symbol, the system will work for you. Secondly, you can carefully formulate your question and then look to see whether it is a straight–forward 'predictive' question – such as: "Will I get the job?" or whether it has emotional, psychological or spiritual significance. This helps you to choose a divination tool, as does ascertaining how your psychic ability functions and choosing your tool accordingly (see Which mode do you use? p.18).

A divination tool that is in harmony with the way your psychic ability functions will clearly be the most effective. If you are kinaesthetic, handling and laying out sticks, cards or runes is tactile and sets up optimum conditions for your psychic awareness. If you are visual, it will be symbols and patterns that speak to you and you may enjoy cards and the like. If your psychic faculty is auditory, you may hear an inner voice speak to you as you lay out cards or cast the I Ching. If you have a logical, analytical mind, you will find that a divination tool such as numerology or astrology satisfies your need for order.

The easiest way to purchase your divination tool is to go to a store that offers a range of possibilities. Take a look at cards, Runes and the I Ching. Read a numerology book. See what resonates with you. Browse through an illustrated divination book and note which images catch your eye. Get together a group of your friends to buy a few tools and try them out. Then it's simply a matter of practice, practice, practice. The more you use your psychic ability the better it will be. If you get into the habit of breathing in harmony with your client it will assist you, as will sitting the way they sit and making the same gestures. This mirroring increases your empathy and harnesses your bodily intuition to your psychic powers.

Getting to know your divination tool

All information is available to us at some level depending on our attunement.
Dawn Robins

You can read a book about your favoured oracle and use 'head learning'. Or, you can use your oracle in a 'getting to know you, getting to know me' way that involves all the senses, body awareness and emotional intuition The more you understand the oracle, the more depth you will receive when using it and the more it will become one with your psychic ability. So, if you practise with your divination tool, choosing one card or symbol to work with for a few days at a time and meditating on it to allow the meaning to rise up into your consciousness, when you come to do a reading you will see a much wider possibility than if you only look the meaning up in a book. There are many different methods for working with your oracle, and they are comprehensively covered in specialist books dealing with those subjects as are the meanings. When choosing a method, relate it to your question. It is a waste of effort to ask a 'when' question of a method that does not give timings or a 'why' question of a tool that does not go deeply into the background of a situation in addition to what will happen in the future.

Dedicating and programming tools

> *Some experts recommend somewhat precious and esoteric handling for your Tarot deck, but such care is mostly common sense.*
>
> *Caitlin Matthews*, Celtic Wisdom

No matter which tools you select to enhance your psychic sensitivity, they will be easier to use and will speak more truly if you take the time to dedicate and program them. They also need cleansing after handling as they will pickup the vibes of the reading. Keep them wrapped in a silk scarf or wooden box when not in use to prevent them picking up further vibrations.

Exercise: To cleanse a divination tool

Using a smudge stick, pass the divination tool through the smoke. If you do not have a smudge stick, you can use the light from a candle or imagine divine breath blowing across them. Or, keep a large Carnelian with the pack to cleanse and energise it.

Exercise: To dedicate a divination tool

Hold the divination tool in your hands. Say out loud:

"I dedicate this tool to the highest good of all who consult it and declare that it will speak only truth and light."

Divination systems

The Crystal Wisdom Oracle

Having written so much about divination, I was immensely pleased when, publication of this book having been fortuitiously delayed, I was asked to create a crystal divination pack. I didn't want to simply create a pack where a few crystals were thrown onto a board to give answers. Instead I wanted to draw on the power of crystals to connect with the querant's soul for guidance. The *Crystal Wisdom Oracle* was born. Illustrated with superb crystal photographs that radiate the very essence of the stones, this crystal oracle deck is designed to help you know yourself. To guide you on your lifepath. To explore past, present and future influences. It draws on crystals used for divination and healing for thousands of years and introduces new, high vibration stones to expand your consciousness and access multidimensions. The cards can also be used to bring well–being to your body. The photographs perfectly encapsulate the energies and can be used for healing instead of the actual crystals. These cards are suitable no matter what mode of sensing you use. The *Crystal Wisdom Oracle* is ideal for 'touchy feely' people who enjoy the act of shuffling and laying out the cards and also for those who enjoy a visual feast, as well as people who sense energy as the cards embody the energy of the crystals. You can lay them out and read the meanings from the book enclosed with the pack at several different levels, or you can trust to your own intuition.

Crystals have frequencies ranging from earthy and dense to the highest, finest vibration. To reflect this, the *Crystal Wisdom* cards are divided into four Vibration suites: Earthy, Healing, Cosmic and Integration. As might be expected, Earthy crystals tend to work well at the material level of being: the physical body and the world around you while exceptionally high vibration Cosmic ones work at the level of the soul and open your intuition. Healing Vibrations assist you in understanding the effect of your mind and your soul's needs on your body, showing how to return to a state of well–being. But there are crystals that bridge the material and subtle multidimensional worlds. These are Integration crystals and their job is to step down higher frequencies so that downloads of celestial wisdom are received here on earth and to step up your vibrations so that you can integrate the guidance.

This wide spectrum gives subtle layers of meaning to answers you receive so when assessing a crystal card consider where in your life it functions best. It is possible to select only cards that operate in one dimension but using all cards accesses all factors surrounding your questions. The cards, which incorporate timings and chakras, are laid out into lattices based on the internal shape of a crystal. As so often happens with oracles, the answers may seem obscure at first and need contemplation to reveal the depth of the answer.

Crystal scrying

A crystal provides a gateway into the future – or the past. It has the effect of focusing the mind, letting it move beyond ordinary consciousness.
Judy Hall, Crystal User's Handbook

Scrying means looking to the future and scrying can reveal what is to come. The accuracy of the vision depends on the skill of the seer. If the answer to a definite question is sought or greater insight needed into your life, then divining gems or crystal cards may be more effective than a crystal ball. Any transparent crystal or cluster can be used. Quartz, Amethyst, Beryl and Obsidian have traditionally been used but Apophyllite gives excellent results. A crystal with internal planes and flaws helps your inner eye to see images within it. It is important that you keep the crystal specifically for the purpose, and do not allow other people to handle it unless you are reading for them as the crystal will pick up vibrations and impressions. When not in use, it is usual to keep your crystal wrapped in a cloth.

If it is the first time you have used your scrying crystal, it should be cleansed and dedicated so that it will always speak true. (Remember to cleanse your crystal periodically, especially after reading for someone else.)

Exercise: Reading the crystal

Settle down where you will not be disturbed. You may like to use candlelight to create a soft atmosphere. If you have a specific question, formulate this beforehand and keep it in your mind. Hold the crystal in your hands or put it on a small table in front of you if it is too heavy to hold. Gaze at the crystal but do not try to see anything at this stage. Let your eyes go out of focus, they need to be gentle if your inner eye is to open. Breathe quietly, setting up a natural rhythm.

As your eyes loosen, allow them to explore the crystal. You may see mist forming in the crystal's depths. When the mist clears, it will form images or you may see scenes as though a film is running deep in the crystal. You may see a symbol that is static or that moves and changes as you watch. Pictures may also form in your mind rather than in the crystal. If you see a symbol, ask if it is positive or negative. Positive images tend to be bright, negative images to be dimmer and darker.

If you are kinaesthetic, you may get feelings or body sensations. Pay attention to these as they will be the answer you are receiving from the crystal.

Tarot

> *The tarot exerts a mysterious allure. Its accessible history is a tantalizing blend of slender facts and romantic speculation, while its symbols continue to have a powerful impact on everyone who sees them.*
>
> *Jane Lyle*, The Renaissance Tarot

Tarot is a complex system of divination. Its meaning is deep and subtle. The cards can be read at a superficial level for 'fortune telling' but they can also offer powerful insights into the forces operating both in your life and within your self. This is an excellent tool if you respond to symbolism and allow the images to speak to you. The images on Tarot cards incorporate archetypes (universal symbols) that speak across all cultures and times. Images such as The Lovers are fairly obvious as to their interpretation – relationships – but cards such as Death are often misunderstood. This is the card of endings and major changes or, when reversed, stagnation. It rarely portends an actual death.

Tarot cards are excellent for people who resonate with imagery and symbolism but they also appeal to those who like 'touchy, feely' sensations. The act of shuffling and laying out the cards is kinaesthetic. There are a number of layouts that can be used for general or more specialised information and the sheer number of packs available means that almost everyone will find a pack that appeals. Tarot is best initially interpreted with the assistance of several good books, you will then instinctively know which interpretations resonate with you and reading the cards will become intuitive and expand into a deeper meaning.

Cartomancy

> *The oldest theory behind cartomancy is that a mystic power of Fate guides the shuffling and dealing of the cards, so the resulting layout will yield a meaningful message when properly interpreted*
>
> *Barbara Walker*

You do not have to purchase a special Tarot pack. Ordinary playing cards can be used for divination as they arose out of the Tarot. The Tarot suits of cups, wands, pentacles and swords evolved into hearts, clubs, diamonds and spades. Of the Major Arkana (or trump) cards, only the Fool remains. He became the Joker. Diamonds relate to money and the material world whilst Hearts, as the name suggests, deals with emotion, romance and relationships. Clubs indicate prestige, influence and enterprise whilst Spades, which are traditionally associated with conflict and misfortune, can give a timely warning.

As with the Tarot, playing cards represent particular traits, personalities and areas of life. They can be used to investigate the future, or to explore the influences operating in your life – some of which may not yet have come to your attention. They may also show someone who is passing into or out of your life.

Numerology

The idea of vibration, described by number, is central to numerology.
Paul Rodrigo

The Greek mathematician Pythagoras taught that number was the essence of all things. Each number had a specific and unique resonance. He believed that if you understood a person's number, you held the key to his psyche and his soul. Numbers reveal an eternal pattern. There are several systems of numerology. On–going nine year cycles favour different areas of life. Attuning to your cycle enables you to maximise your potential.

Numerology is an excellent system for logical people. Precise patterns and progressions create the number whilst incorporating psychic sensitivity to elucidate nuances of meaning. Due to the precise cycles of numerology, it is a useful method of timing events or unfolding changes.

I Ching

It is my firm conviction that anyone who really assimilates the essence of the Book of Changes will be enriched thereby in experience and in true understanding of life.
Richard Wilhelm

The I Ching, or *Book of Changes* is an extremely ancient oracle. Said to describe heaven, earth and all that happens within them, it is based on the idea that everything is in flux and motion. The traditional method of consulting the I Ching uses forty nine yarrow stalks, revealing sixty four possible hexagrams. Nowadays, many people use coins to produce those same hexagrams. It is possible that psychokinesis is involved in the fall of the stalks or coins and it is a useful tool if you are intellectually–orientated as it is a very logical system.

The I Ching is extremely good at pinpointing moments of change and showing how to make the most of them. It makes visible what lies behind the façade of everyday life and can help with timing events. The pattern of the I Ching hexagrams stimulates insights and perceptions moving you beyond the surface meaning. They appeal to people who are visual and those who prefer to touch as the ritual of using the I Ching mellows and focuses consciousness through an orderly set of movements. To use the I Ching successfully you need a book with all the hexagrams and full interpretations but see I Ching Timing p.82.

Runes

Each Rune is a pictorial representation of a particular natural mood or condition
John Tremaine, Casting the Runes

The word rune means 'secret writing' and the symbols are imbued with magical power. It is extremely easy to make a set of runes for yourself, flat polished stones or crystals, clay or wood make an excellent base and the symbols can be inscribed with a permanent marker pen or scalpel. Runes are an excellent tool if you are kinaesthetic as you will quickly come to know the meaning through your fingertips.

Runecraft began several thousand years ago in Scandinavia. Symbols were carved on rocks to represent birds, animals and such like. The word Rune means 'secret writing' and the letters were full of magical power. Runic practice incorporated materials from the natural world. Such materials were believed to be imbued with sacred energy and runecraft is woven into folklore through the ancient Sagas. Runes were dedicated to the God Odin, associated with healing, travel, communication and divination. Mythology tells us that, searching for enlightenment, Odin hung himself upside down on Yggdrasil, the World Tree, impaled upon his own spear for nine days. As he gazed at the ground, Rune stones hidden among the roots of the tree revealed themselves.

Sitting quietly with the runes helps you to go deep inside yourself. Most have a double meaning depending on whether they are upright or reversed. They can describe positive and negative influences operating in your life and highlight hidden factors that will create your future, and show you choices you face. Runes point out how you can overcome negativity and make a constructive choice for the future. Selecting three runes shows past, present and future influences and outcomes. Picking one at random will reveal your innermost fears and desires. They map the path of spiritual initiation, and can help you to make positive choices for the future. Runes are a particularly tactile experience when made of natural materials – wood or stone. Placed in a bag, one or more will 'stick' to your fingers. These are the runes for you.

Throwing the die

I have set my life upon a cast
And I will stand the hazard of the die
Shakespeare, Richard III

It can be argued that throwing the dice is one of the most ancient of all systems of divination, and lots were cast to allot property – as when Christ's robe was given to a soldier. The saying 'the die is cast' comes from the use of dice, or die, for divination or to indicate fate or the will of the gods. Dice give a simplistic answer to a question, unless the complex question and answer method is used. They are pure fortune telling rather than offering true insight into a situation but you can hone your psychic sensitivity by trying to predict the fall of the die – or even to influence its fall.

Chiromancy

The soul of man is in his hand.
Complete Book of the Occult and Fortune Telling

Chiromancy, or palmistry looks to the lines on the hands to read fate, fortune and character. It maps out your life span, your relationships and your health. The lines can tell you a great deal about your temperament and the possible course of your life but it is emphasised that free will and making the best use of your potential can overcome even the most pessimistic of hands.

The lines on the palm 'speak' to a visual person, providing a map that can be read as easily as a book. If you are a kinaesthetic person, you may find that chiromancy brings out your natural psychic awareness. As you hold a person's hand, you will tune into their energies. The lines on the palm merely confirm what you intuit.

Timing

Ascertaining timing can be one of the trickiest parts of using your psychic ability as linear time as we know it does not really exist. Psychic time is circuitous and circular, curling back in on itself and weaving out into the future rather like a net of time rather than a linear time line. It is imbued with possibilities and dependent on responses to previous actions or future choices. Fortunately there are several methods that assist:

I Ching Time

The Chinese use a lunar year. Each month has five hexagrams and each hexagram governs six days so each line on the hexagram governs a day. In addition, there are four hexagrams that govern three–month periods. Without a Chinese calendar to ascertain the first day of the Chinese New Year it can be difficult to ascertain precise timing but an approximate calculation can be arrived at by aligning February with the first month of the Chinese year, March with the second and so on.

Date	Hexagram no. six day period					3 month
First month (February)	11	5	17	35	40	51
Second month (March)	34	16	6	18	45	51
Third month (April)	43	56	7	8	9	51
Fourth month (May)	1	14	37	48	31	20
Fifth month (June)	44	50	55	59	10	20
Sixth month (July)	33	32	60	13	41	20
Seventh month (August)	12	57	49	26	22	58
Eighth month (September)	30	54	25	36	47	58
Ninth month (October)	23	52	63	21	28	58
Tenth month (November)	2	64	39	27	61	29
Eleventh month (December)	24	3	15	38	46	29
Twelfth month (January)	19	62	4	42	53	29

Tarot Time

With the Tarot, the suits can correspond to seasons. Whilst it is not always possible to accurately time an event, the cards can give you some indication. The timing spread below is one method, another is to use the twos, threes and fours from the Minor Arkana to represent months:

Exercise: Timing spread

Count off thirteen cards from the top of the deck, stopping if the two, three or four of any of the suits appears. This is the answer. If none of the cards appears, count off another thirteen cards. If a timing card still does not appear the question may still be undecided and any reply you receive is likely to be unreliable or there may be a delay in the outcome.

Suit	**2**	**3**	**4**
Swords	March	April	May
Wands	June	July	August
Cups	September	October	November
Pentacles	December	January	February

(*Jane Lyle*, Renaissance Tarot)

Pendulum Time

Pendulums can be used to ask 'when' questions. They can establish dates and ages. Draw a half moon on a piece of paper. Mark 0 at one end and 10 at the other. Hold the pendulum at the centre of the half moon. The pendulum will swing towards the correct number. If you want to work with numbers higher than ten, ask the pendulum if it is greater than 10, 20, 30 etc. Use the half moon numbers to refine the answer.

Runic Time

If you need a timing, or wish to look at the year ahead, laying out the Runes like a clock gives you twelve months of the year. Pull twelve stones from the bag and lay out in a circle, starting from the current month. Each Rune indicates a specific 'theme' for that month.

Crystal Time

Each of the *Crystal Wisdom Oracle* cards has a timing attached that can be used to answer 'when' questions.

5
The Metaphysics of Psychic Awareness

What lies before us and what lies behind us are small matters compared to what lies within us. And when we bring what is within out into the world, miracles happen.
Henry David Thoreau

The metaphysical world interpenetrates but goes far beyond the physical world and the five senses of the physical body. Encompassing what has been known as extra-sensory perception, it could be called supraphysical or supraconscious. I tend to call it expanded consciousness or All That Is. In the metaphysical view of the world, psychic awareness is part of a natural process that encompasses all that is. This metaphysical world is subjective, inner centred and private and yet connected to everything else. As V.S. Ramachandran explains, it is the antithesis of how physics views the world as physics eliminates the subjective "I" who experiences the world. In the eyes of the scientist 'there are no colours, only wavelengths; no frequency, only pitch; no warmth or cold, only kinetic activity of molecules; no subject "self" or I, only neural activity'. He reflects on an ancient and fundamental dichotomy between how science and metaphysics view the world: 'Yet to me, my "I" is everything. It's as if only one tiny corner of the space-time manifold is "illuminated" by the searchlight of my consciousness'.[15]

Ramachandran goes on to discuss the idea, set out in the ancient Uphanishads, that 'we are all merely many reflections in a hall of mirrors of a single cosmic reality' pointing out that the dissolution of a sense of separate "I" and "self v. other" separation is the goal of many eastern religions. Ramachandran contends that the identity of your conscious experience (including your "I") depends on the *information content* of your brain and that this data includes ancestral and personal memories and the cultural milieu in which you function. It also, according to Ramachandran, depends on how the "empathy neurons" in your brain function. What he dubs "Dalai Lama neurons", something we will meet in Chapter 9 when we look at how the brain mediates psychic experience.

The metaphysical view of the world

One's soul is a reverberation of the universe
Oscar Kokoschka

In the metaphysical view of the world, everything is interconnected. Whether it be the Buddhist concept of mind, Hindu Brahman, Sufi *nur*, esoteric Spirit or the Web of Life, the shamanic dark sea of awareness or All That Is, or the notion of pure consciousness, there is a subtle substance that interpenetrates matter and is present in the innermost self and the furthest reaches of the universe. Indeed, *it is the universe* in all its forms and dimensions. And it *is* the human soul, or mind or individual consciousness – which metaphysics considers an illusion of separateness.

In metaphysics, there is no division between individual awareness and universal consciousness. In a shamanic journey, I was told that interstellar dust was consciousness and consciousness was interstellar dust, and our bodies are interstellar dust and therefore consciousness, and consciousness is our body. Out at the edge of the universe where interstellar dust is bringing new creations into life, it was totally obvious, and I was able to bring the sensation back to my body. It is as though there is a universal neural net linking each and every part of everything. It is through this interconnection, or consciousness, that psychic abilities function. This view crosses cultural boundaries and is in itself universal:

Consciousness creates reality
Amit Goswami

Mind is the universal seed
Saraha's Treasury of Songs

Consciousness is the source of all things and of all conceptions. It is a sea ringed about with visions.
Oscar Kokoscha

[In the Islamic view] intuition is ... revelation through a mysterious faculty different from mind; yet it comes through mindless mind. The knowledge which intuition obtains comes as a result of a mysterious identification of the consciousness with the unseen worlds. These worlds are made up of luminous matter called nur, existing in sheaths within sheaths, nurun ala nur. Man is connected with all these worlds.
M.H. Abdi

In the view of metaphysics, it is our five everyday senses that create an illusion of separateness and the perception of the functional reality of the world as we know it but the true reality is something very different:

> *The sorcerers of ancient Mexico saw that the universe at large is composed of energy fields in the form of luminous filaments... They also saw those energy fields arrange themselves into currents of luminous fibers, streams that are constant, perennial forces in the universe...These energy fields are converted into sensory data, and the sensory data is then interpreted and perceived as the world we know... What turns the luminous fibers into sensory data is the dark sea of awareness.*
>
> *Carlos Castaneda*

> *The solidity of the material world has proved illusory: it can be resolved into particles and energy. In certain circumstances the particles themselves dissolve into energy of radiation, and this label proclaims our inability to say any more. We only think the material world is solid and coloured and extensive in space and time because of the sort of special senses and minds which we possess. These select for us the qualities of the world we know.*
>
> *Raynor C. Johnson*

Mystics of all ages and persuasions have penetrated the illusion of separateness and moved into wholeness that poets so eloquently express:

> *Today I am the North wind on the wing*
> *And the wide roaring of the clamorous sea*
> *And the huge heaven's calm immensity*
>
> *Rumi (trans. Sir Cecil Spring-Rice)*

> *In the higher realms of true Suchness*
> *There is neither self nor other*
> *When direct identification is sought*
> *We can only say, Not two.*
> *One in All,*
> *All in One.*
>
> The Heart Sutra

One instant I, an instant knew
As God knows it. And it and you
I, above Time, oh, blind! Could see
In witless immortality

Rupert Brooke

Gone is the sense of a separate, finite self, with its individual gains and losses, its personal hopes and fears, and in its place comes the experience of the One Atman, abiding in all beings, of all beings as eddies in that all-pervading ocean of bliss.

Sri Krishna Prem

There are in His universe no fences between the 'natural' and 'supernatural' worlds; everything is a part of the creative Play of God, and therefore – even in its humblest details – capable of revealing the Player's mind.

Evelyn Underhill

To be psychic you do not need to be a mystic, but it certainly helps. You do not need to believe in God, the divine, universal energy and so on, but the more you develop your psychic connections the more you will be aware that there is such an energy underpinning and uniting all the dimensions of consciousness. Some people call this God, others unity consciousness, the source, Spirit or the divine. Psychic awareness almost inevitably leads to spiritual awareness and psychic sensitivity is a by-product of spiritual connection (which has nothing at all to do with religious belief). As the Sufi poet Jalal al-Din Rumi puts it:

Like a mirror my soul displays secrets; I am able not to speak, but I am unable not to know.

For Rumi the only worthwhile journey was the inward one into the greater self:

And you ..., choose to journey into yourself, like a ruby-mine be receptive to a print from the sunbeams.
Make a journey out of self into self ... for by such a journey earth became a mine of gold.

The more attuned you can become to the greater reality, the more connections you open to pure consciousness or the divine, the greater awareness you will have of the web of life that connects and interpenetrates everything:

Genius results from the miraculous fusion of the human race and the creative universe.

Sir Earnest Hall

The physicist David Bohm had a mystic's eye when he said:

Matter is frozen light.

Many of the eastern philosophies, such as the early Hindu Vedas assert that creation is a divine dream. The poet Keats reflects Christianity's view when he asserts that we are part of 'God's long immortal dream'. Author Michael Talbot quotes the Kalahari bushmen who say: "The dream is dreaming itself." And he points out that it does not matter who is dreaming, it is all part of the whole and states that 'the universe is sustained by an act of such stupendous and ineffable creativity that it simply cannot be reduced to such terms.' Sri Aurobindo, a mystic by profession, paraphrased the theosophist Madame Blavatsky when he suggested:

> *If you are embarrassed by the word 'spirit' think of spirit as the subtlest form of matter. But, if you are not embarrassed by the word spirit, you can think of matter as the densest form of spirit.*

So, the metaphysical world is spiritual. Unfortunately, as I've said before, when scientists look at psychic abilities they want something testable and repeatable. Something rational and reliable. A tangible, recordable effect. Nothing nebulous like 'spirit' or impressions. But psychic awareness isn't like that and nor is the metaphysical world. It is fleeting, irrational, and, for the most part, non-testable because it entails acting in the moment not being a laboratory rat. I've had three near death experiences and know beyond a shadow of a doubt that my consciousness functions apart from my physical body and that I will survive death. I know I can communicate mind to mind. It has happened to me ever since I was a small child. I grew up with it as an unquestioned part of my life. I have lived with past life memories and 'knowing' facts about people that I apparently couldn't possibly know. For me, psychic connection is a way of life. It may not be replicable and repeatable and sometimes I may interpret it incorrectly, but it is the best guide I have.

Psychic awareness is spirit. It is consciousness. When you touch the place that T.S. Eliot described as 'the intersection of the timeless with time' you reach the source of psychic connection. That intersection is the place where psychic sensitivity dwells and spills its wisdom into awareness for those who can hear it.

Consciousness

The intellect has little to do on the road to discovery. There comes a leap in consciousness, call it intuition or what you will, and the solution comes to you, and you don't know how or why.
Albert Einstein

Since I began researching this book consciousness studies have become academically and medically acceptable and innovative technology is rapidly catching up. Princeton University has a global consciousness project based on the notion that 'When human consciousness becomes coherent and synchronized, the behavior of random systems may change' (http://noosphere.princeton.edu/.) There is even a 'collective consciousness app' for your phone that assists you to join consciousness experiments (http://www.huffingtonpost.com/gregory-weinkauf/no-longer-science-fiction_1_b_4688935.html) and the internet is rife with tools to expand or harness your consciousness. But, as David J. Chalmers of the Department of Philosophy at the University of California reminds us:

Consciousness poses the most baffling problems in the science of the mind. There is nothing that we know more intimately than conscious experience, but there is nothing that is harder to explain. All sorts of mental phenomena have yielded to scientific investigation in recent years, but consciousness has stubbornly resisted. Many have tried to explain it, but the explanations always seem to fall short of the target. (http://www.imprint.co.uk/chalmers.html).

To my mind, that's because many researches are trying to reduce consciousness to something mechanical and physiological (the brain) rather than looking at the experience of consciousness, although that is, thankfully, changing.

Neuroscientists debate endlessly about consciousness and mind. Most see it as a function or by-product of the brain. Professor Susan Greenfield of Oxford University sums up the scientific viewpoint when she says:

Consciousness gives purpose to our existence. It is an inner world that meshes with the external one but is always distinct.

For her, as for so many scientists, consciousness is the product of 'transient assemblies of different populations of neurons' in the brain and depends on different arousal states. However, ground-breaking research has now established that all the cells of the body are interpenetrated by consciousness. Rather than spaces between the particles that make up the cell, there is awareness. This means that cells can act independently of the brain and the body-mind can have its own awareness, an awareness that often precedes that of the brain by a few seconds. And individual consciousness can unite with other consciousnesses, or with the greater consciousness. EEG studies and MRI scans have confirmed, for instance, a correlation of activity between the frequencies of paired brains such as that of healer and receiver of healing, a telepathic sender and a receiver, a past life regression therapist and the regressee, an effect which is enhanced by empathetic rapport, and the EEG frequencies of a meditation group have been shown to come into entrainment during meditation. [16]

Professor Charles Honorton summed up the essential dilemma between brain, mind and consciousness, asking whether mind 'emerges' out of or represents some 'inner' dimension of physical states or whether mind is an independent entity that interacts with but is not reducible to physical states.

Metaphysicians, however, know consciousness and mind in a much wider form. To them consciousness is immanent within the universe, it is never distinct or separate. Multi-dimensional and cohesive, consciousness is summed up by James Herbert in his novel *Others*:

> *Consciousness is the thing between atoms and molecules and particles, the unseen glue that holds everything together... it's consciousness, which is energy, that binds the patterns and forms shapes, matter.*

Mystic Depak Chopra puts it another way:

> *Cosmic consciousness tells us that there is one thing – consciousness itself – that underlies the appearance of separate creatures with separate minds. Seeing yourself as separate is a mistake. We don't make this mistake when someone shows us a diamond. Although the jewel looks separate, we know that one element, carbon, is common to all diamonds, that atoms are common to all the elements in the periodic table, and that quarks and other subatomic particles are common to all atoms. In the same way, even though one person is climbing Mt. Everest and another is asleep in bed in Rangoon, all experiences have mind in common, and mind rests upon a field of consciousness that permeates the universe.' (http://www.huffingtonpost.com/deepak-chopra/what-is-cosmic-consciousn_1_b_4674373.html)*

If consciousness is one, and separateness is an illusion, there is no barrier to intuition concerning 'another person'. Psychic sensitivity tunes into that part of consciousness that is manifesting through a different physical body and reads its energy vibrations. What is interesting, however, is that to do this, psychic awareness moves out of time (in test after test, telepaths noted down the next card in the sequence not the card that was being sent, for instance). It goes beyond the illusion of past, present and future into the eternal now. Metaphysicians instinctively by-pass time – and space. The exact mechanics may remain something of a mystery, but once you move outside time and space the reality of that experience will convince you of its validity.

Moving out of time

A moment's insight is sometimes worth a life's experiences.
Oliver Wendell Holmes

Essentially, in our limited state of everyday awareness, we live on a time line that goes from the past through the present and onto the future. The time line is what we use to make sense of our experiences here on earth. Step off that line, and you are into timelessness, the eternal *Now.*

Exercise: stand outside time

Draw a chalk line on the floor or use a piece of string.
Stand in the middle of the line in the 'present' position.
Look 'back' behind you to the past. Walk into it and notice what images come to you.
Look 'forward' in front of you to the future. Walk into it and notice what images come to you.
Close your eyes and step off the line into timelessness.
How does it feel?

You have the option as to whether you step back on the line or choose to live in the eternal now. Remember to write up your experience in your metaphysical journal, it will hold many clues to how and why you have been experiencing life on a daily basis.

6
The Metaphysical Body

Please read this section even if you have read *Good Vibrations* as it contains information specific to metaphysical working

The body is connected by sensory perception to a field of energy that enfolds the information we attribute to intuition. [17]
Heartmath Institute

In the West, we are used to regarding our body as 'all of a piece', flesh that is separate and unique with its edges neatly defined by skin, but the East and metaphysics have long seen the physical body as linking to and interpenetrating with subtle energy fields that extend far beyond the physical. It is these subtle bodies that receive information psychically and convey it to the body before the mind has time to focus.

The aura

All living things have an aura – an energy field that surrounds the body… which we cannot detect with our physical senses but only using our inner awareness. [18]
Sue and Simon Lilly

Metaphysically speaking, psychic awareness works in conjunction with the aura, or biomagentic envelope, that forms a subtle energy shield around the physical body. It is visible to psychics as a shifting, interweaving field of coloured light and can be captured by a kirlian camera. Disturbances in the aura reflect dis–ease that may be physical, emotional, mental or spiritual in origin. Conversely, physical, emotional and mental symptoms may reflect imbalances in it.

Science is now confirming the existence of the aura. A machine has been developed that can read the energetic imprint of a body, or a handprint, in a room for several hours after the occupant has left, and can distinguish how many occupants there were. What is extremely significant, as it backs up what psychics have been saying for millennia, is that, according to its inventor, each individual energetic imprint is as different as a fingerprint or

DNA (and could be used as forensic evidence in the future).[19] Science is also demonstrating the aura's ability to hold and convey emotional information. It has been established that the heart has its own energetic system that creates a measurable, rhythmically pulsating field that can be measured several feet out from the body and which mediates bioelectromagnetic communication both within and outside the body and which can convey information to the brain. This field changes in response to positive or negative emotions.[20] What is most exciting – and significant for how psychic awareness functions – is that this energetic heart–field is perceived by other people's brains, which can entrain with it (that is, come into alignment and synchronise the brain waves), and appears to be capable of affecting water, cells and DNA. The suggestion is that:

> *People may be able to affect their environment in ways not previously understood and such 'energetic' interactions may be prominently influenced by our emotions. Growing evidence also suggests energetic interactions involving the heart may underlie intuition and important aspects of human consciousness.* [21]

Auras are extremely sensitive and extensive, and can intermingle with other people's energy fields to the extent where you can pick up their emotional and physical state; for instance, you can easily pick up a headache from someone this way. The mental aura holds thought impressions and ingrained patterns, but these layers are not separate. They interweave through, and affect, each other. Fortunately there are ways to combat this without shutting off your psychic sensitivity.

It is possible, but not desirable, for someone else to draw energy from your aura, which leaves you feeling depleted. Or for you to drain energy from them, which will leave you feeling exhilarated and them exhausted.

Getting into the habit of monitoring your aura not only protects you, but it also alerts you to unconscious psychic communications you may have been receiving.

Seeing the aura is a psychic skill that many people have without knowing it. If you tell someone they are looking a little down today, you are probably unconsciously reading their bioenergy field. If you instinctively avoid someone, you may have sensed something unpleasant in their energy field. Troubled auras look 'down', 'grey' or 'dark'. Emotions such as anger or resentment tend to show up as swirling clouds of dark red, jealousy and envy as bottle green. Illness shows up as a murky patch over the part of the body affected. You may have caught glimpses of someone's aura as a halo of white or coloured light. You can, of course, learn to consciously 'see' this energy field.

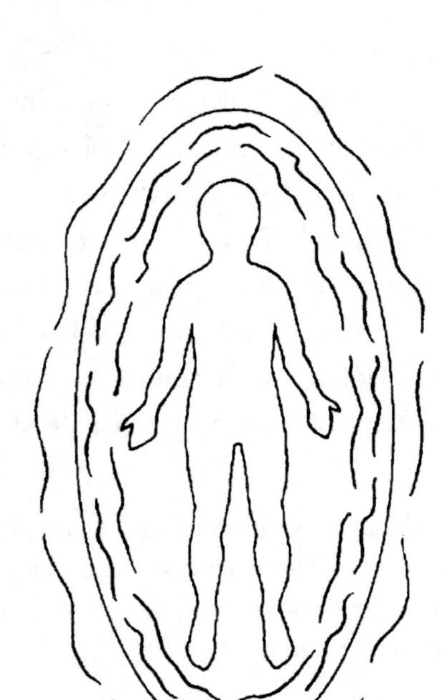

Seeing or sensing the aura

Paradoxically, you see an energy field when you are not really looking. It is best seen against a white background in muted not too bright light.

Exercise: Seeing or sensing the aura

Ask the person whose aura you wish to see to stand against a suitable light colour background.

Letting your eyes half close and go out of focus, and looking out of the corner of your eye, allow your eyes to drift slightly to the side of the person and around their head. (If you blink and try to focus, the images fade.)

You will perceive a light fanning out around the body.

With practice you will be able to see the colours extending out from the body.

You may also be able to sense an energy field when you brush up against someone, either by feeling the energy prickling up against your body or sensing it with your mind. With a little practice, it is possible to do this at will but remember that you must have permission to do this as otherwise it is intruding into someone else's psychic space and that is unethical and abusive. **You also need to keep them out of your space (see pp.39, 240).**

Monitoring the aura

Monitoring your aura helps to protect your energy and ensures that you will not leak energy or allow subtle intrusion into your energy body. Practise the monitoring exercise below once or twice a day until you can sense your aura by mentally scanning your body. You will then know instinctively if your energy starts to drain or if something tries to invade your energy field, and will automatically seal it. The exercise can be performed sitting if you prefer and with your eyes open or closed whichever feels more appropriate.

Exercise: Monitoring the aura

Stand so that you can reach out around yourself. Take your attention down to the palms of your hands. Put your palms in front of you, facing your body, about one to two hands breadth away. Move your hands backwards and forwards using your palms to sense where the outer edge of your aura is. (It may feel slightly tingly or springy.)

Move your hands around the edges of your aura from your head to your feet. Begin in front of your body and go from above the head down to your feet. Then do the sides and finally the back of your body. (If you cannot reach with your hands use your mind to check out this area). Check how far out it extends and notice any places where the energy breaks up or feels different in any way.

If you find that your aura extends a long way out, try bringing it closer. Or if it is very close to your body, use your hand to pull or push it to a more appropriate distance just as though you would if it was made of tangible, physical substance. Bring it within arm's length and probably closer depending on the situation. (You can either grasp hold of the outer edge or use your hand like a magnet to which the field sticks to draw it in).

Go over your entire aura checking for breaks and 'holes', hooks or cold spots. Use your hands to pour extra energy into that place, pulling the edges of it together. You can picture healing light sealing it together. If you find a hook, take it out with the power of your mind and mentally send it back to whoever put it there. Fill where it has been with light. Ensure that your aura is not tangled up with anyone else's. If so, carefully separate the two (a Flint or Rainbow Mayanite crystal is helpful).

Experiment with the ability your mind has to control your biomagentic field. Close your eyes. Picture your aura expanding, and contracting. Really let yourself feel the process happening. Push it in, and draw it out until you feel competent, finally allowing it to settle at an appropriate distance from your body.

When you are ready, open your eyes. Take your attention down to your feet and feel your feet on the earth. Be aware that your feet are connected to the earth, grounding you. Take your attention to your forehead and picture a shield closing like that over an automatic camera lens. With your eyes wide open, take a deep breath and stand up with your feet firmly on the earth.

***If you find it difficult to visualise**, you can use a clear Quartz, Angel's Wing Calcite, Flint, Rainbow Mayanite or Selenite crystal to work over the aura, healing and sealing it.*

David Eastoe has anticipated the need for a shield that prevents energy leakage or undue influence passing through the aura but which still allows psychic sensitivity at the interface between two fields. If you pass his Petaltone Power Shield around your body before you begin the next part of this exercise, or before any psychic work, it will help you to be aware of the interface and work from that place.

When you have mastered the art of monitoring your own energy field, ask a friend to allow you to feel theirs. Impart to them any impressions you receive as you move your hands over their body about a hand's breath out from their clothes – some people find it easier to do this using a crystal such as Selenite, Charoite or Healer's Gold as an intermediary – it creates an interface between the your own energy field and the one you are scanning.

When monitoring someone else's aura, be sure to notice 'cold' or 'hot' spots, hooks from someone else, areas where the aura extends or is pulled outwards, places where the aura feels weak or has a hole, and whether your own body picks up any sensations particularly pain. If you hold your hand on a place where you feel a lack of energy, you can picture healing light or crystal energy (not your own energy) entering the spot and re–energising it – or you can apply Petaltone Plant Ally or Power Shield. Your hand will tell you when this has rebalanced – you may feel a tingling or a sense of quietude or a coming together to a place of stillness and balance of the energies, for instance.

This exercise can be enhanced if you move into your heart energy before seeing or sensing your friend's field. Try to sense whether this is happening at a physical, emotional or mental level – you can often pick up clues about this by noticing how far away from the body your hand is. Close tends to be in the physical level, next layer out is the emotional level, and then the mental level – although remember that the fields interweave and are not laid down in well–defined layers. You can also take note of what is happening in your own solar plexus at the time.

Exercise: Feeling the aura

Walk towards your friend with your hands out.
Stop when you feel a prickling in your hands or feel like you are pushing up against an invisible wall.
Feel the energy: is it hot, cold, happy, sad?
Once you are aware of how you sense this energy, put some ear plugs into your ears to shut off aural clues, close your eyes and ask your friend to walk lightly towards you from different directions. Try to sense from which direction the biomagnetic energy is approaching.

Energy sensing is an extremely useful skill for checking on the freshness of food and whether it still has energy. Some food has been over–processed or hangs around for so long that it loses its life force. Bioenergetic sensing warns you when this has happened.

You can also use your sensing ability to check out crystals to see if they have a clear energy or if they need cleaning and to check whether objects or substances will be good for you.

Cleansing the aura

It is essential that you keep your aura clean and free of negative energy, hooks or implants at all times. A simple visualisation carried out before you go to sleep is the easiest way to do this.

Exercise: Cleansing the aura

Picture a hand–held vacuum cleaner, the kind you clean out the car with. Picture yourself running this vacuum cleaner over the whole of your aura, hoovering up anything that is sticking to it. Make sure you do the back as well as the front.

When you have finished, picture taking the dust bag out of the hoover. See a shiny new dustbin ready to receive the dust and dirt. It will be emptied by the cosmic trash man and taken for recycling. When you have emptied the bag into the dustbin, replace it into the vacuum ready for use next time.

When you are ready, open your eyes. Take your attention down to your feet and feel your feet on the earth. Be aware that your feet are connected to the earth, grounding you. Take your attention to your forehead and picture a shield closing over your third eye. With your eyes wide open, take a deep breath and stand up with your feet firmly on the earth.

If you are kinaesthetic*, you may prefer to do your aura cleaning with a crystal. Smoky Quartz, Amethyst, Lemurian Seed, Selenite, Flint, Anandalite and Clear Quartz are excellent for this. Hold the crystal in your hand and slowly 'comb' all over your aura about a hand's breadth out from your body although you may need to go further out. Pay particular attention to the energy centres on your spine and front of your body. After you have finished, remember to cleanse your crystal.*

Aura sealing

Once your aura has been cleansed, it makes sense to seal the outer edges of your aura so that, whilst you remain sensitive and have clear sight through it, nothing can penetrate to contaminate or leach your energy. Wearing a crystal soaked in Petaltone Power Shield is the most effective way I have found to do this. Moss Agate, Labrodorite, Jade, Fluorite, Rainbow Obsidian and other protective stones work extremely well as carriers for this invaluable essence and to protect the aura.

Essences and crystals for auric close–down

Petaltone Power Shield, Heaven and Earth, or Plant Ally, Labradorite, Shungite, Actinolite, Nuumite, Hematite, Rutile, Rainbow Obsidian, Black Tourmaline, Flint, Healer's Gold.

The chakras

To understand the chakra system is to understand ourselves.
Swami Brahmananda

The chakras connect your aura with your physical body and act, amongst other things, as linkage points to higher consciousness and spiritual energies. They also subtly affect the functioning of the endocrine system and are a fundamental part of the body–mind relationship and are a component in the psychosomatic causes of disease. If a chakra is blocked or is stuck open it can affect your energy field, leaving you vulnerable. Your chakras need to be open and under your control if you are to use your psychic abilities wisely and with clarity and integrity.

Ancient drawings of the chakras show many more than the traditional seven that we tend to know today. In additional to those traditional seven chakras, several more chakras are opening in response to universal energy changes (see illustration p.92) and these 'higher' chakras facilitate psychic connection to high–vibrational realms and the beings who inhabit them. However these chakras should only be opened when you have the basic chakras under control, functioning fully and without blockages and when you have begun to take control of your psychic abilities. These 'higher' chakras vibrate at a different, faster rate and are more able to channel refined spiritual energies down through your body and up from the earth. By changing the core vibration of your bodies, 'lower' frequency energies simply cannot reach you. Many 'new' crystals have become available to activate these higher chakras, some of which are expensive and difficult to source. Angel's Wing Calcite is a reasonably priced Calcite that vibrates at a very high rate and is useful for opening the higher crown chakras. Anandalite and the more rare Rainbow Mayanite are excellent for this task. If you cannot obtain the exact crystals you need, when programming the crystals that are available ask that the energy will be lifted up to its highest level in order to receive the influx of new vibrations – or use the photographs in *101 Power Crystals* or *The Crystal Wisdom Oracle* as these encapsulate the energies perfectly.

The alta major chakra (see p.109) is becoming increasingly important in metaphysical work. Forming a merkeba–like shape within the skull, this chakra links all the important endocrine glands and chakras in the head with the throat chakra so that you can communicate metaphysical information with ease. The alta major includes the pineal gland, the 'inner eye' long believed to be the site of clairvoyance and 'second sight'. It has been postulated that

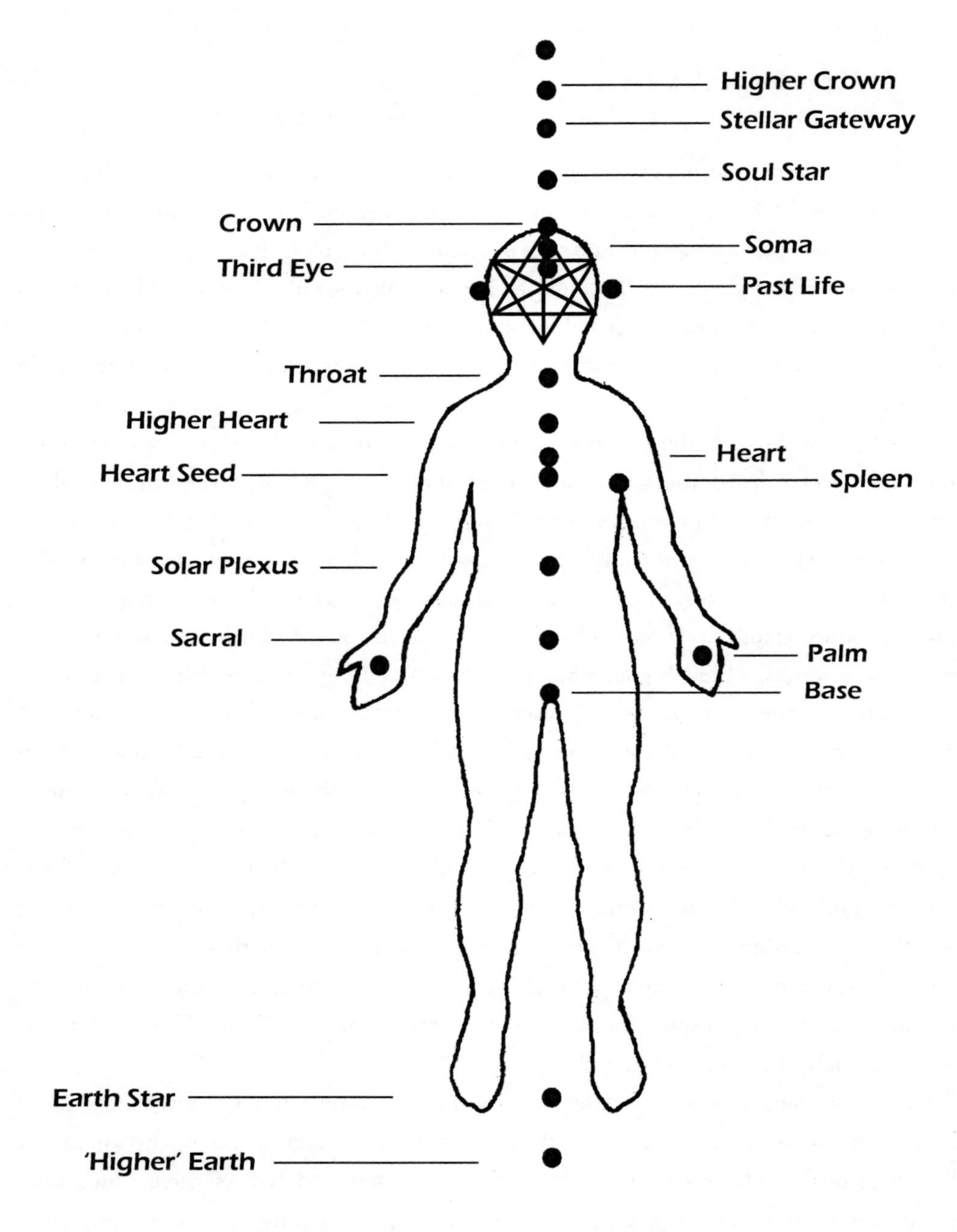

Chakra Points on the Body

the pineal secretes DMT, often called the 'spirit molecule', A natural psychedelic, DMT is involved in out–of–body, near–death and other exceptional human experiences that take the soul into multi–dimensions. So, when the alta major is activated in conjunction with the pineal, or third eye chakra, metaphysical abilities, especially telepathy and far sight, function with much greater clarity.

Earth Star (below the feet): This chakra grounds you in your body and connects you to the devas of the earth and the earth's energetic grid. It mediates the inflow of sacred earth energy that helps you to stabilise and assimilate refined spiritual energies reaching the earth whilst remaining grounded in your physical body. When this chakra is permanently closed, you will be spacey and find it difficult to operate in everyday reality. If it is permanently open, you can easily pick up negative energies from the ground, which may contaminate your psychic abilities and you will have no sense of personal power or inner stability, finding it difficult to operate in functional reality. You may also pick up 'spirits of place', either as attachments or as communication of events that have taken place. With the chakra functioning well you are held gently in incarnation and will be 'down to earth' in your psychic sensing.

Palm Chakra (in the palms of your hands): This chakra is highly receptive to energy and connects you to the external world. If you are kinaesthetic you receive much of your information through the palm by touching a person or handling an object. If the chakra is too open you will be overwhelmed by impressions from everyone who has touched an object. If it is closed you may experience difficulty in recognising tactile impressions. With the chakra functioning well, you have a strong intuitive connection to the sensate and material worlds.

Base Chakra (bottom of the spine): This is the chakra of survival instincts and basic security. It is where you have a sense of your own personal power and the ability for independent, spontaneous leadership. If it is stuck open then you may have a fear of annihilation or a death wish that colours your psychic perception. You may also harbour considerable anger and have a tendency to manipulate people particularly through your supposedly psychic sensing that is actually a projection of your own feelings or desires. If you keep the base chakra open when using your psychic abilities, it helps you to ground it into everyday functional reality.

Sacral Chakra (below the navel): The sexual and creative chakra that is a source of confident assertion. Stuck open, it can be the site of 'emotional hooks' that drain your energy and you are vulnerable to another person through sexual contact or powerful feelings such as lust or possessiveness that create attached thought forms. A blockage in this chakra can lead to feelings of inferiority that lead you not to trust your psychic connection.

Solar Plexus Chakra (between waist and heart): The solar plexus is a source of emotional empathy and emotional intelligence but it can also take on other people's thoughts. This chakra is an emotional linkage point and is where you store your emotional baggage. Psychic perception can easily be contaminated by your baggage, or that of someone else. Invasion and energy leeching also take place through this chakra. A 'stuck–open' solar plexus means you take on other people's feelings easily but if you can learn to open the chakra at will, you will be able to read other people's emotions and yet remain detached. You may receive psychic communications through your solar plexus as you unconsciously read other people's emotions.

Spleen Chakra (under left armpit): A source of psychic energy, if this chakra is stuck open then psychic vampires can leach your energy, as can past partners, children or parents. You may fall prey to psychic impressions that appear to show that you are indispensible and are the only person who can look after someone needy – indeed, you may feel that you have a duty or have made a promise to do so. Keeping the chakra protected and under your control restores your psychic energy and allows for clear psychic sensitivity as to when it is appropriate to assist someone and when it would be better to practise truly unconditional love and allow them to learn their own lessons and stand on their own two feet.

Heart Chakra: Another emotional and relationship linkage point, the heart chakra is the seat of love in all its manifestations. An open and fully functioning heart chakra is essential for metaphysical health. Most people find that their psychic ability functions best when their heart chakra is expanded. Sending love to someone from your heart naturally attunes you to their energies and helps you to communicate. A closed heart is disconnected from feelings and unable to show love or empathy. If the chakra is blocked then psychic awareness will be coloured by jealousy, possessiveness and insecurity, and may make you resistant to change so messages from your psychic connection will not get through.

Throat (over throat): The throat chakra links the emotional to the mental and is involved in communicating psychic awareness. If the throat chakra is open and functioning properly, you are able to speak your own truth and are highly receptive to psychic communications. A blocked throat chakra results in difficulty in communication – especially in not being able to speak your truth. Problems can arise from your own unvoiced intuitions and the dogmatic nature of a blocked throat chakra can leave you closed to psychic solutions.

Brow (third eye, slightly above and between the eyebrows): The site of the inner, 'mind's eye'. If this chakra is functioning efficiently you will be a perceptive visionary, functioning spontaneously in the moment. Strong beliefs can block this chakra, however, and may be caused by undue influence or thought form attachment. If the third eye or brow chakra is stuck open, you are vulnerable to the thoughts, feelings and influences not only of people around you on the earth level, but also on the etheric level. You will be spaced out and may feel constantly bombarded with thoughts and feelings that are not your own. You may also receive indiscriminate 'psychic messages' and not be able to filter these out. You may be prey to wild intuitions, premonitions of doom and the like – not all of which will come from outside yourself. If the chakra is blocked, then you cannot visualise or receive intuitions. You will be attached to the past, fearful and superstitious and prone to creating exactly what you fear most.

Past life (behind the ears): The past life chakras, as the name suggests, hold past life memories especially those of traumatic events such a violent death. If the chakras are stuck open, you will feel unsafe and overwhelmed by past life memories and fears – which may manifest as nightmares or premonitions of disaster. Any psychic sensitivity may be contaminated by residual fears. If they are stuck closed, you will not be able to access the lessons and skills your past lives have taught you. With the chakras functioning, you are connected to the wisdom your soul has garnered.

Crown Chakra (top of the head): The crown chakra maintains and filters a spiritual connection and a link to higher consciousness. It is the major line of defence and connection for the subtle bodies. When it is functioning efficiently it is mystical, creative and encourages you to be of service to others. If it is stuck open, then you will be overly imaginative, prey to illusions but arrogant in your assertions of true knowing. It also leaves you open to thought forms, spirit attachment or undue influence.

Controlling the chakras

The ideal situation is for all the chakras to be balanced, opening and closing at will, under your conscious control by the power of thought and intention. When you are starting out, however, it is the traditional seven chakras plus the Earth Star and the past life chakras behind your ears that are likely to be active, with possibly the palm chakra having opened spontaneously. The 'higher' chakras will come on line later and should not be activated too soon as otherwise you can be overwhelmed by an influx of energies and psychic communication that your subtle bodies and chakra system are not yet attuned to deal with.

Exercise: Chakra shields

Sitting comfortably in an upright chair, close your eyes and establish a gentle breathing rhythm.

Take your attention down to your feet and the point between and slightly below them. If this chakra is open, you will be aware of your connection with the earth and you may feel energy from the earth travelling up from this chakra through your feet. If this chakra is stuck, you may feel ungrounded and 'floaty'. Picture a pair of gates shutting off this chakra between it and the earth beneath it. Then let them open again. Picture the gates opening and closing until they come under your conscious control.

Now move your attention up to the base of your spine. Visualise a whirling vortex of energy and picture a pair of shields closing over the spot, shutting out the light (use your hands to cover and then open the site if this helps). Practise opening and closing these shields a few times until it becomes automatic. (You will be able to sense the difference within your body as the chakra opens and closes.)

Bring your attention to the sacral chakra below your navel. Picture this full of light, and close the shields across. Open and close this chakra until it is automatic.

Then bring your attention up to your solar plexus and once more visualise the chakra open, and close it off with shields. Take your attention out under your left armpit and find the spleen chakra and close it off with shields.

Probe the base of your breastbone and locate the heart seed chakra and open and close this a few times before putting the shield in place.

Move up to the heart chakra, opening and closing it a few times. (You may also be able to sense the higher heart chakra, in which case practise opening and closing this.)

Now take your attention to your throat chakra. Open and close it before moving up to open and close the third–eye brow chakra, the soma chakra above it and the past life chakras behind your ears, and finally move to the top of your head for the crown and higher crown, starseed and stellar gateway chakras.

Once you can open and close the chakras at will, practise running your mind up and down your spine to assess the state of your chakras.

Before you bring your attention back into the room, take your mind to your earth chakra. Check whether this is open or closed and sense if you are in an area of environmental or geopathic stress. Open or close your earth chakra as appropriate according to the energies of the place you are and check that your third eye is also closed.

Bring your attention fully back into the room. Stand up and feel your feet firmly on the floor. Have a good stretch and breathe deeply to ground yourself.

***If you are kinaesthetic**, you can use the energy of your hands and the palm chakras to 'read' your chakras and to open and close them. Once you have programmed in the opening and closing by moving your hands, it will become an automatic action carried out by your mind. If you find hooks or blockages during this exercise, take them out by doing the chakra cleanse below.*

Chakra Cleansing

Chakras hold on to negative energies or emotions. Cleansing the chakras is essential for healthy functioning and maximum protection, and to avoid contaminating psychic awareness. You can clean the chakras with visualisation or by a simple but powerful crystal layout.

Exercise: Chakra cleansing

Repeat the chakra shield exercise this time checking out the colour and spin of each chakra in turn. If the chakra looks murky or has dark patches, visualise light entering the chakra to cleanse it. If it is spinning too fast or too slow, use the power of your mind to set it to the right speed – you will know intuitively when it is right. If it feels like it is spinning in the wrong direction, pause it and start it spinning the right direction for you.

See the light whirling round until all the blackness is cleared. When you have finished, all the chakras should have an equal brightness and energy intensity (do not worry if some seem to spin in different directions so long as this feels right for you).

Complete the exercise by opening the earth chakra (as long as the environmental energies are clean) and closing the chakras along the spine and head. Bring your attention fully back into the room. Feel your feet on the floor and be aware of your connection with the earth. Breathe deeply and have a good stretch to remind yourself that you are fully present in your body.

You can also use a pendulum to dowse each chakra, checking for direction of spin and blockages so that your body tells you if all is well or whether some adjustment or clearing is needed.

Chakras cleansing can also be carried out with crystals. By selecting appropriate crystals, you can clean, re–energise and harmonize the energy centre.

Exercise: Cleansing with crystals

Lie down for twenty minutes with appropriate crystals placed on each chakra or work on each in turn spiralling a pointed crystal such as a Lemurian Seed out from and then back into the chakra (a crystal wand works well for this, use it point out for cleansing, point in to re–energise). It is usual to unwind the energy in an anti–clockwise direction and wind it back in clockwise, but check out how the chakra is spinning before you start and do what feels right for you. Some people have chakras that spin in an anti–clockwise direction which may be appropriate for you.

For a traditional chakra crystal cleanse, start at your feet with a brown crystal and work up your body using red and orange at the base and sacral, yellow for the solar plexus, green for the heart, blue–green for the higher heart, blue for the throat, indigo for the third eye, purple for the crown and clear or light amethyst for the higher crown chakras; or use the crystals indicated for aura cleansing or from the list below.

Useful chakra cleansing crystals

realignment: Aurora Quartz, Quantum Quattro, Graphic Smoky Quartz in Feldspar, Kyanite, Citrine, Quartz, Fire Agate.

align with physical body: Amber, Graphic Smoky Quartz, Que Sera.

balance: Graphic Smoky Quartz, Sunstone.

base chakra: Fire Agate, Garnet, Pink Tourmaline, Smoky Quartz, Red Calcite, Red Jasper, Bloodstone, Carnelian, Cuprite, Graphic Smoky Quartz.

blockages (dissolve): Clear Quartz, Lapis Lazuli, Bloodstone, Graphic Smoky Quartz, Rainbow Mayanite.

blown, repair: Fire Agate, Rainbow Mayanite, Graphic Smoky Quartz, Que Sera.

brow/third eye chakra: Apophyllite, Sodalite, Moldavite, Azurite, Herkimer Diamond, Lapis Lazuli, Purple Fluorite, Kunzite, Lepidolite, Malachite with Azurite, Royal Sapphire, Yellow Labradorite, Aquamarine, Iolite, Preseli Bluestone.

cleanse: Amethyst, Quartz, Bloodstone, Calcite, Citrine, Quartz, Tourmaline wand, Graphic Smoky Quartz, Que Sera, Gold and Silver Healer, Rainbow Mayanite.

crown chakra: Selenite, Angelite, Moldavite, Quartz, Purple Jasper, Clear Tourmaline, Golden Beryl, Lepidolite, Purple Sapphire, Petalite, Phenacite, Larimar.

earth chakra: Smoky Quartz, Graphic Smoky Quartz in Feldspar, Brown Jasper, Boji Stone, Fire Agate, Hematite, Mahogany Obsidian, Tourmaline, Rhodonite, Cuprite, Smoky Elestial Quartz, Flint.

energy leakage, prevent: Quartz, Labradorite, Ajoite with Shattuckite, Green Aventurine, Graphic Smoky Quartz, Que Sera.

heart chakra: Rhodonite, Rhodochrosite, Rose Quartz, Green Jasper, Green Quartz, Jadeite, Jade, Aventurine, Kunzite, Variscite, Muscovite, Watermelon Tourmaline, Pink Tourmaline, Green Tourmaline, Morganite, Danburite, Ruby, Chrysocolla.

heart seed: Tugtupeite, Mangano Calcite, Rosophia.

protect: Apache Tear, Jet, Quartz, Labradorite, Graphic Smoky Quartz.

sacral/navel chakra: Orange Calcite, Blue Jasper, Orange Carnelian, Topaz, Citrine, Que Sera.

spleen: Green Aventurine, Jade or Green Fluorite.

solar plexus chakra: Malachite, Jasper, Tiger's Eye, Citrine, Yellow Tourmaline, Golden Beryl, Rhodochrosite.

strengthen: Magnetite (Lodestone), Quartz, Graphic Smoky Quartz, Que Sera.

throat chakra: Turquoise, Amethyst, Aquamarine, Topaz, Tourmaline, Amber, Kunzite, Lepidolite, Blue Lace Agate.

Activating the higher chakras

Dormant chakras can be awakened that assist in connecting to the highest spiritual realms and which then channel and filter refined, multi–dimensional energy into your physical and subtle bodies and to the earth itself. By activating these chakras, you can ensure that the beings you communicate with are themselves of the highest level, thus avoiding spiritual illusion and gaining psychic enlightenment. These chakras are:

Heart seed (just beneath the breastbone): chakra of infinite compassion, the heart seed helps you to remember the reason you are in incarnation, your personal soul purpose, and connects you to the divine plan for your soul evolution and the tools available to manifest your potential. When it is open it allows you to psychically know the reason you are on earth. If it is blocked, you are rootless and purposeless, unable to connect to your spiritual self.

Higher heart (over the thymus above the heart): this chakra helps you to radiate forgiveness and acceptance out to the planet and to yourself from a place of unconditional love and compassion. A spiritual connector to all that is, it acts as a protector and filter for the heart and a powerful contact point for psychic guidance. If the higher heart chakra is tightly closed you will be spiritually disconnected, unable to express your feelings and shut off from your psychic connection or only open to those 'intuitions' that arise out of – and appear to fulfil – your own neediness. Inevitable disappointment accompanies such psychic communications.

Soma (on the hairline above the third eye): the linkage point for total spiritual connection and higher consciousness aligned with the purpose for which you are on earth. It links the subtle bodies to the physical. When the chakra is functioning efficiently, it automatically reels the soul back into the body following out of body journeys. If this chakra is stuck open, then you will be spaced out, ungrounded and prone to spontaneous out–of–body experiences or spirit attachment. You may fall prey to wild intuitions. If the chakra is blocked, then activities such as remote viewing and out–of–body journeying are impossible, or the soul never fully inhabits the physical body. It can also be the site of psychic overwhelm or spirit attachment. With this chakra functioning well you will always return to your physical body no matter how far you may travel in distance or time. It facilitates time travel and remote viewing.

Soul star (about a foot above your head): the linkage point for channeling the highest self–illumination and spiritual light into your physical body which raises its vibrations accordingly. The soul star connects to ancestral memory. It is the ultimate soul connection where the soul intertwines into the physical body with high frequency light. When it is functioning fully it communicates soul intention with an objective perspective on all lifetimes and takes you into the timelessness of all that is. Stuck open or blocked closed, it can lead to soul fragmentation, spirit attachment, ET invasion, or a messiah complex that attempts to rescue but does not empower. You may connect with beings in the etheric realms who do not have the best of intentions. Such beings can be misleading and malicious and psychic communications received via this source are extremely unreliable even though they may masquerade as the highest possible guidance. It can also mean that you are taken over by ancestral memories that may appear to be psychic but which hold you stuck in a place of fear. When working well it accesses higher consciousness and enlightenment. When functioning properly, intuitions are expressed with true humility.

Stellar Gateway (above the soul star): a cosmic doorway to other dimensions, the stellar gateway connects you to the highest energies in the cosmos, facilitating communication with enlightened beings. When it is stuck open, it can be a source of cosmic disinformation that leads to illusion, delusion, deception and disintegration that leaves you totally unable to function in the everyday world.

Alta Major Chakra (inside the skull): Opening the alta major creates a direct pathway to your subconscious and your intuitive mind. It is an anchor for the multi–dimensional energy structure known as the lightbody and for higher dimensional energies. A merkeba–like shape, the Alta Major links the endocrine glands in the skull with the upper chakras and controls metaphysical sight and intuitive insight. It holds your soul's plan and information about the ancestral past, karma and contractual agreements made with the Higher Self and others before incarnation. A blocked Alta Major causes feelings of confusion, 'dizziness' or 'floatiness', loss of sense of purpose and spiritual depression. A fully functioning Alta Major allows you to know your spiritual purpose and access the divine, drawing down information from higher dimensions.

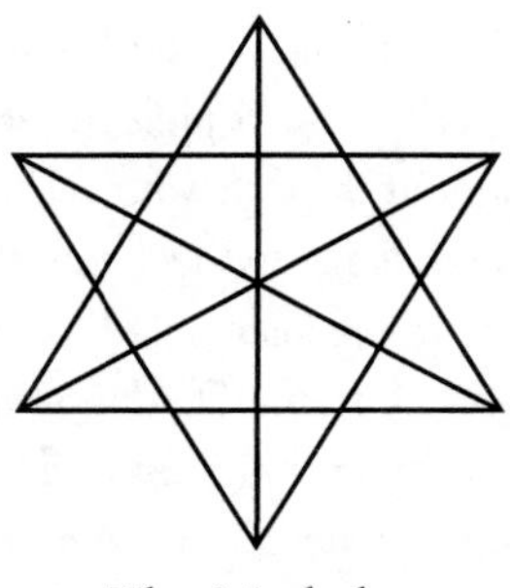

The Merkaba

Exercise: Opening the Alta Major

Lie down and place Anandalite or one of the other alta major openers (see below) in the hollow at the base of your skull. Place Preseli Bluestone, Flint or one of the other soma chakra crystals (see below) over the centre of your forehead so it touches the hairline and projects downwards. Lie still for ten to fifteen minutes and visualise a merkeba shape forming in your skull.

You may need to repeat this exercise several times before the alta major fully aligns.

Exercise: Activating your higher chakras

Hold all your crystals you will be using for a few moments, visualising them bathed in bright white light.

Lie down and position crystals as follows:

Smoky Quartz Elestial *about a foot below your feet.*

Smoky Quartz *between and slightly below your feet (point up if your crystal has a point).*

Tugtupite or Danburite *at the base of the breastbone.*

Rose Quartz or Mangano Calcite *three finger's width above the heart.*

Preseli Bluestone or Ammolite *on your hairline (soma chakra).*

AnandaliteTM, White Elestial Quartz, Nirvana Quartz or Angels Wing Calcite *on your crown.*

Phenacite, Satyamani Quartz or Angels Wing Calcite *about a foot above your crown (point down if your crystal has a point).*

Amphibole Quartz, Brandenberg or Satyaloka Quartz *above the Phenacite.*

Take your attention down to the crystal below your feet and be aware of the Higher Earth Chakra opening. Feel how it pulls in refined earth energies and radiates them up to the Smoky Quartz and through your whole body. Be aware of your connection to the earth's energy meridians and feel how the Elestial lifts them to a higher vibration. Feel yourself aligning to the faster, and purer, vibration that it carries.

Now take your attention up to the Danburite and Rose Quartz. Feel how the heart seed and higher heart chakra open and expand receiving and radiating unconditional love and awakening your innate compassion and connection with others. Feel how these chakras connect to the throat chakra so that you can communicate love out to the world.

Finally, take your attention up to the crystal above your head. Be aware of the connection to higher spiritual guidance. Feel how the energy flows down into the chakras, activating esoteric awareness and soul memory. Know that you are a spiritual being on a human journey.

When the activation is complete, slowly remove the crystals starting with the highest crown chakra and work down to the Earth Chakra. When you reach the Earth Chakra, be aware that there is a grounding cord which links your feet to this chakra. This cord keeps you grounded within your physical body and connected to the earth.

Finally, pick up the Smoky Elestial from the Higher Earth Chakra. Stand up and feel your feet firmly on the ground and your grounding cord in place.

Repeat the exercise daily until the activation is complete.

Crystals for the higher chakras

Alta Major: Brandenberg Amethyst, Apatite, Fluoroapatite, Anandalite, Rainbow Mayanite, Afghanite, Holly Agate, Red Amethyst, Crystal Cap Amethyst, Andara Glass, Aurichalcite, African Jade, Ethiopian Opal, Rainbow Covellite, Preseli Bluestone, Eye of the Storms (Judy's Jasper), Green Ridge Quartz, Petalite, Phenakite, Graphic Smoky Quartz, Fire and Ice, Azeztulite, Rosophia, Golden Herkimer, Golden Healer, Hungarian Quartz, Angel's Wing Calcite, Blue Moonstone.
Earth Star: Graphic Smoky Quartz, Elestial Smoky Quartz, Celestobarite, Flint, Golden Herkimer, Green Ridge Quartz.
Higher Heart: Mangano Calcite, Kunzite or Danburite, Tugtupite.
Heart Seed: Tugtupite, Danburite, Lemurian Blue Calcite, Mangano Calcite.
Stellar Gateway: Stellar Beam or Angels Wing Calcite, Amphibole, Nirvana Quartz, Trigonic Quartz, Fire and Ice, Phenacite, Azeztulite, Green Ridge Quartz.
Soul Star: Brandenberg Amethyst, Satyaloka Quartz, Anandalite, Selenite, Satyamani Quartz, Ajoite, Phenacite, Azeztulite, Green Ridge Quartz.
Soma: Flint. Preseli Bluestone, Faden Quartz, Green Ridge Quartz.

Note: If the crystals for the higher crown chakras are unavailable or too expensive, use Angels Wing Calcite or Selenite to cleanse and open all these chakras.

The psychic self

There is one spectacle grander than the sea, that is the sky: there is one spectacle grander than the sky, that is the interior of the soul.
Victor Hugo Les Miserables

Consciousness functions on many levels and there is far more to a human being than first meets the eye. You will be reasonably familiar with the part of yourself that is operating on the physical, emotional and mental levels. And will probably know that you have a subconscious mind that influences your behaviour without your being aware of it and that is home to fixed patterns and rigid expectations. You may also understand the concept of the collective unconscious: the point where we all join at the level of the psyche and a state of consciousness that houses archetypes and myths. You may think you know yourself as a spiritual being but what is often meant by that is someone who has religious or spiritual impulses or beliefs rather than someone connected to their soul and higher consciousness.

Few people are aware how much of them functions on a spiritual level. This is the 'higher self'. It is 'higher' because, like the subconscious mind, it functions on a different vibration to everyday awareness, although it pervades it. This vibration is finer, less dense and therefore it extends beyond the purely physical. This is why your psychic or metaphysical higher self can know so much more than your everyday self. The higher self is a vehicle for our soul consciousness. If you can raise your physical vibrations sufficiently to embody your higher self, to allow more of it down to manifest on the earth plane, you will automatically be more psychic.

The following exercise can be memorised but it could also be recorded, with appropriate pauses, or be read aloud by a friend giving you plenty of time to carry out each instruction.

Holding a Selenite crystal in your hand aids the process and you will have the crystal as a tangible reminder.

If you find raising your vibrations difficult, imagine yourself getting into a lift, pressing the button marked 'top' and stepping out to be met by your psychic self. Embody the higher self and return via the lift.

Exercise: Embodying the higher self

Settle yourself in a comfortable place. Breathe gently and easily. Lift your shoulders up to your ears and let go. Take a big breath and sigh out any tension you may be feeling.

Allow the sensation of release to flow through your body.

Take your awareness to your heart seed at the base of your breastbone, the heart and the higher heart chakras located above it (you can touch them to focus your attention there). Allow them to unfold, opening like the petals of a flower. Then take your attention up to the crown chakra at the top of your head. Allow this chakra to fully open. The chakras above your head will expand and you may feel a string pulling you up, allow yourself to go with this feeling. Consciously allow your vibrations to rise, to reach the highest possible level.

Invite your higher self to move down through these chakras until it fills your crown chakra. From the crown chakra, feel your higher self enfold your whole body. Experience the love that your higher self has for you. Bask in its warmth and draw that love deep into your being.

Spend time with your higher self, welcoming it, learning to trust and feeling safe. Ask your higher self to activate your psychic faculties and to ensure that you receive only the highest guidance and connection.

[Take as long as you need at this point]

Then, when you are ready, bring your higher self into your heart chakras. Embody your higher self at the centre of your being. Enfold your higher self within your heart chakras so that it is always accessible to you. Feel how different your body is when you embody your psychic self. How protected you feel, how much more aware you are at an inner level as your vibrations are raised by the embodiment of your higher self.

When you are ready to end the exercise, ask your higher self to remain with you, safely within your heart, and enfold your higher self within the heart chakras as you close them gently inwards.

Close the chakras above your head, letting them fold in on themselves like flowers closing for the night. Close the crown and third eye chakras and make sure that your earth chakra is holding you firmly in incarnation. Check that your grounding cord is in place. Slowly, bring your attention back to your physical body and the room around you. Move around, have a stretch.

***If you are kinaesthetic**, holding a Trigonic, Greenridge, Anandalite or other high vibration Quartz will help you to connect to your higher self.*

Receiving messages from your higher self

Once you have established a connection to your higher self you will always be able to receive messages. It will simply be a matter of establishing how that message communicates itself to you.

Exercise: Message from the higher self

Simply take your attention into your heart chakra, put your hand over it, and feel the connection open. Listen to what your higher self has to say.

7
Developing Your Psychic Awareness

When you let intuition have its way with you, you open up new levels of the world. Such opening–up is the most practical of all activities.

Evelyn Underhill

There now follow a series of carefully structured introductory exercises to expand and focus your psychic awareness and extra sensory perception. They will help you to expand your individual awareness and access wider consciousness. They should be worked through in order and built upon until you feel totally confident you are ready to move onto the next stage. Do not rush and do not skip anything because something else looks more exciting. You need to do the groundwork first so that you are in control of the process. This will make you all the more competent when it is time to explore other realms.

You can either read the exercises first and memorise them, or record them, with pauses when necessary, and play them to yourself. You can introduce appropriate music into the background if it helps.

Your psychic awareness

We need to be willing to let our intuition guide us, and be willing to follow that guidance directly and fearlessly.

Shakti Gawain

The best tools you can develop alongside your psychic awareness are common sense and discernment. Whilst some experiences may make you go "Whaaat?!" and yet still be valuable, others may be internal sabotage or external trickery from the subtle planes of being and it is essential to distinguish between illusion and a real psychic experience. Sensitively appraising your experiences, rather than blindly accepting everything, will make your psychic sensitivity that much more valuable – see the metaphysical journal.

Appraising your psychic function

It is important that you do the next exercise before you read any further in the book. It will help you to recognise exactly how your psychic faculties work, building on the work you did in Chapter 1. Ask a friend to assist you with this and to observe you carefully as you do it. It would be useful if your friend read the questions overleaf first and made notes for your metaphysical journal as you do the exercise.

(If you cannot ask anyone to assist, try to be aware of how your body and mind are behaving as you do the exercise, or make a movie of yourself giving the directions.)

Exercise: Assessing your psychic function

Give your friend directions from your house, or place of work, to the nearest supermarket.

You can give directions for either walking or taking some form of transport. (If you find it impossible to picture the route, a map is printed overleaf for you to use with alternative instructions.)

Be as specific as you can.

When you have finished, turn the page and answer the questions in consultation with your friend.

If you find it impossible to picture a route

If you find it impossible to see pictures in your mind don't be put off. It's not that unusual. You are probably kinaesthetic, that is you feel or sense rather than see. Forty percent of the popular are kinaesthetic and usually resort to gesture to point the way.

Exercise: Using sketch to give directions

Try the same exercise as above using the sketch map provided. You may find that you trace the route with your finger – confirming that you are kinaesthetic.

Tracing the route and the closing of your eyes and trying to picture the route can assist you to see images.

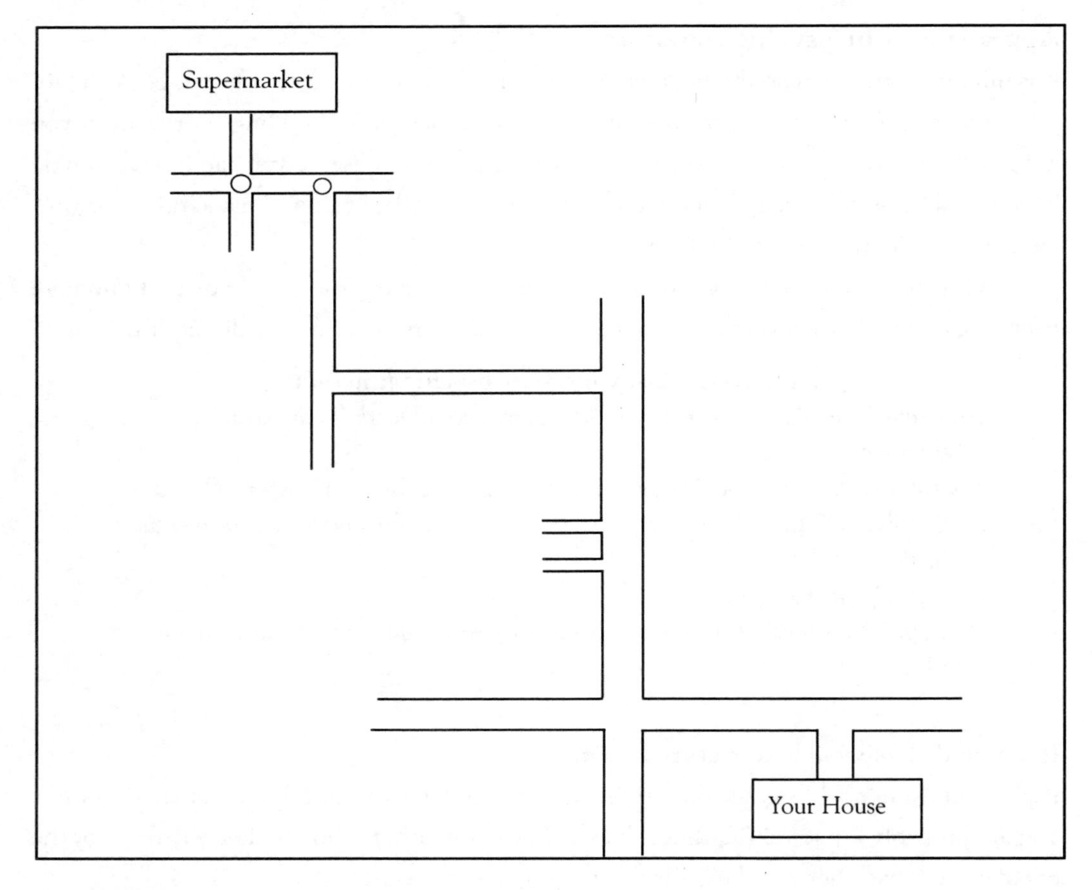

Questions to ask

- Did your eyelids flutter as you gave directions?
- Were your eyes closed or open?
- If they were open, in which direction did your eyes point?
- Did you see a mental picture of the route?
- Did you use your hands?
- Did you draw a map?
- Did your body move?
- Did you hear a voice giving directions?
- Did you 'just know' the way?
- Did you find it difficult to verbalise and needed to resort to gestures?
- Did you have difficulty distinguishing between left and right?

Assessing the result

When giving directions almost everyone visualises, although you may not be aware that you are doing this. Eyelids fluttering rapidly – as they do when you dream – are an indication that you are indeed visualising. If your eyes move around, you are accessing different parts of your brain.

If your eyes are up above the horizontal, you are using the visual cortex. If you close your eyes in order to see better, and especially if you saw a mental map, you are working at a visual level and your psychic sensitivity will function visually.

If you drew a map by using your hands to indicate direction or moving your body around, you are kinaesthetic. Your psychic awareness works through your body and through feeling. You will be prone to hunches and gut feelings.

If you heard an inner voice giving you directions that you passed on, your psychic sensitivity functions aurally. You may have supersensitive hearing, and are easily disturbed by noise. (In that case, you may find that playing music as you do the exercises in this book actually interferes with your psychic awareness.)

If you gave directions without moving, seeing or hearing anything because you 'just knew' them, you may find that you already function on a sensing or feeling level. If you found you confused left and right – and especially if you did not realise that you were doing so – you are most probably right brain dominant and will find imagery easy to access but verbalising more difficult.

You can also establish whether you are a visual person or an aural one by trying to remember a telephone number you don't know off by heart. Do you see it written down in front of you? Do you make writing motions as you try to remember or instinctively press an imaginary key pad and let muscle memory take over? Or do you hear the person saying the number? If it's the former, you are visual. If it's the latter, you are aural. If you make writing motions or press the key pad, you are kinaesthetic. Some people combine two or three different modes. If you are an aural person, orientated towards hearing rather than seeing, you may find it easier to drop your eyes slightly rather than raising them. If you focus on the area to the back of your ears, you may begin to hear your psychic awareness communicating with you. You may have to adapt the guided visualisations slightly. You could concentrate on sounds and smells, for instance, hearing birdsong or the sound and smell of the sea or a particular flower or tree.

Practise to perfect

Practising exercises as you go about your day to day business fills in those moments when you would otherwise be doing very little.

- *Waiting for the mail*: As you wait for your mail, close your eyes and try to anticipate who will be writing to you today and what they will say.

- *Answering the telephone*: Before you pick up the phone, take a moment to tune into who is on the other end and what they have to say to you.

- *Waiting for the train*: If you travel to work by train, intuit exactly what time it will arrive each day.

- *Colours*: Keep a pack of playing cards with you. Whenever you have a few moments, take them out, shuffle them face down. Before you turn each card up, foresee what colour it will be. Then you can progress to what suit, and finally to the number of the card.

- *Anticipating traffic lights*: As you watch traffics lights, try to anticipate the exact moment they will change colour. (Then try to influence the moment with your mind, saying 'change now'.)

- *Waiting for the elevator*: As you wait for the elevator to arrive, intuit which floor numbers it will stop at on its way.

- *Watching the cursor*: As you sit at your computer waiting for those boxes to pop up, position your cursor exactly where you expect it needs to be.

- *People watching*: Pick one person from a crowd around you. Try to anticipate what their next move will be.

- *What comes next?* Tune into conversations going on around you. Try to anticipate what someone will say next. (Asking what comes next in any situation is a useful way to flex psychic sensitivity.)

- *Who am I meeting?* If you have a friend to see or a business meeting, ask yourself exactly what they will be wearing today. Close your eyes and let a picture of them float into it.

- *What will I hear next?* Next time you have the radio on, try to forehear the next song to be played. Feel the words or the tune float into your mind.

Emotional intuition

The heart has its reasons which reason knows nothing of.
Blaise Pascale

Psychic awareness is not just a matter for the mind. It belongs to the emotions too. As psychotherapist and mythographer Jean Shinoda Bolen explains:

> *To know how to choose a path with heart is to learn how to follow psychic feeling. Logic can tell you superficially where a path might lead to, but it cannot judge whether your heart will be in it.*

Your emotions tell you how you intuitively feel about something. The site of your emotions is the solar plexus and the heart. You can recognise the part the emotional self plays in intuition and the intelligence with which your emotions can guide you *once they become conscious*. If they remain at the level of wishful thinking or subconscious traps they lead to suspect psychic sensitivity. Most people have emotional triggers and needs of which they are unaware. Knowing what is going on in your emotional centre is a powerful way of enhancing your psychic awareness. Automatically tuning into what is going on in your heart and solar plexus, and the feelings that you have about things and people, helps you to be more emotionally intelligent as well as psychic. Always remember that it is part of an on–going process, keep asking yourself 'how do I feel?' and let your psychic awareness lead you to the answer. It can also be useful to check 'is this me, is this you?'

Exercise: Enhancing Emotional Intuition

Stop whatever you are doing. Close your eyes and take your attention into your heart. How does it feel? Is it joyful, expectant? Or is it heavy and dull? Let your heart speak to you.

Now take your attention down to your solar plexus. How does this feel? Is it calm and peaceful or churning and uneasy? Are you harbouring destructive emotions such as guilt or anger? If so, let them dissolve or resolve to do something constructive with them.

If uneasy, check out which emotional buttons have been pressed. Look at the events that created those buttons, forgive anyone involved, and let them go. Switch that button to 'off,' permanently. If your frustrated hopes and wishes are involved, check out whether they are still appropriate. If not, let them go.

Now check out how you feel about things. Are you happy with the situation around you, the people with whom you are in contact? Is there anything you can do to improve things? Ask your emotional intuition to speak to you.

Then bring your attention back to the present moment and put your insights into practice.

Remember to record the insights in your metaphysical journal.

Signs and signals

When the secret corners of the forest are heavy with the scent of many men…
it will signal the end of living and the beginning of survival.
Chief Seattle

Once your psychic awareness begins to open, both the internal and external worlds will exhibit a host of signs and signals that point the way forward, answer your unspoken – or spoken – questions, or just let you know that you are on the right track. You might even get a signal, as my grandaughter did, without having formulated the question. I was planning to buy a flat in which my granddaughter was to live. She viewed one and was very enthusiastic so I went along to take a look. The otherwise empty flat was full of pictures of fish and books on fishing. On the same day, my granddaughter, who was doing a fill–in job and had been looking for work for several months, saw a vacancy advertised in the job centre. At 12.30 she picked up the application form. At 4.30 she had the interview. The next evening she had a trial and started work the following day. The job? Working in the aptly named 7 Fish Restaurant. So the universe had provided a very large hint as to where she would be employed before the vacancy had occurred. I didn't buy the flat but the message had been passed on. Only you will be able to interpret the unique message symbolism has for you.

Millennia ago, oracles listened as the trees at Dodoni in Greece whispered to them and those same trees still speak today – if you are listening. One of the most ancient of oracles is that of audible rumblings of the belly – it goes back over six thousand years to Mesopotamia although sadly that key is lost so we do not know how it was interpreted but such gurgles are often a signal that energy is moving or your gut is trying to tell you something. Nature oracles abound. Often such an oracle is a two–way process: bee–keepers have long whispered their deepest secrets or the latest gossip to their bees – who were usually the first to be told of a death in the family. And when there was trouble, the bees would be consulted for their wisdom and knowledge.

If you are lost, a crow sweeping in can show you the right way. If you are doing a card reading and one card jumps out from the pack, this will have special significance. If you are concerned about your security, a hawk might skim past your ear chasing a sparrow that finds safe shelter in a hawthorn bush right in front of you. You just have to be alert to the signals – and learn how to interpret them. You also need to be aware of the thoughts passing through your mind when these incidents occur, as they can have oracular significance too. We always know more than we think we know.

Catching your signals

The universe is a mirror that reflects back to you.
Christine Hartley

One of the ways in which you can teach yourself to catch the signals your psychic awareness is sending you is to meditate with a perceptive partner observing. One who is aware of your body response to psychic communication, or who is sensitive enough to detect a signal such as your eyelids fluttering, a finger twitching or an energetic surge through your body. Every time they see a signal, they should ask "What was your awareness just then?" This teaches you to catch the fleeting insights that pass through your awareness and associate them with the signal your body gives you as you receive them. Asking "How did you feel just then?" might elicit a different kind of answer, one from your emotional intuition. Take up the habit of monitoring yourself and be sure to note the signals in your metaphysical journal.

Another way to catch signals is to notice the outer world's response to your questions. I was once driving down a country road at dusk discussing a mutual friend who was missing. I was saying that whenever I tried to tune in to him, he was vague and confused, as though wandering somewhere he was unfamiliar with and most unclear as to what had happened to him. As my companion asked: 'Do you think he's dead then?' a barn owl flew straight at the windscreen of the car. It seemed to come, and go, out of nowhere. My reply to her question had to be 'yes, I do', as in many cultures the owl is the deathbird and in some an omen of evil. Some six months later his body was found dumped on a remote French hillside. It was no wonder he had been confused when I tried to communicate with him. An owl is also said to help you see behind the mask to what really is. Shortly after his body was found, his estranged wife, who had denied any knowledge of his death, was arrested and convicted of plotting his murder.

Everyday clues

Stones have been known to move and trees to speak
Augers and understood relations have
By maggot–pies and coughs and rooks brought forth
Shakespeare, Macbeth

Shakespeare chronicled how, for 'ordinary' people magical signs were inextricably linked to the world around them. The everyday world is still full of clues as to what you would – or would not – be doing if you are going with the flow of your psychic inner knowing. Learning to pay attention to these signals makes your life flow much more smoothly. If, for instance, you are trying to book a hotel for a weekend away and the system is down or the phone continuously engaged, stop and ask the question: 'Is this action what would be most beneficial – or appropriate – for me at this time? Is there a better/cheaper/more fulfilling or constructive alternative?' In one such case, where someone went ahead despite considerable difficulties without asking the question, illness prevented the planned trip at the last moment and the cost of the hotel was lost. Conversely, when the signal was noted and a trip postponed, a damaged tyre and an exhaust dropping off the car whilst close to home made it clear why a long journey would have been unwise. In another case, the answer was 'try somewhere else' and a much better deal was found.

Signs are everywhere. A woman I once knew had 44 as her signal from the universe that all was well. She saw it on emails, parking tickets, till receipts, number plates and so on. Each time it made her feel safe and secure, looked after by the universe and on the right path. When she sold her house, the buyers had 44 on their car number plate. I wonder what she made of Barack Obama being the 44th president of the United States? Such signals can become an obsession bordering on mental dis–ease so keep your common sense active when noting 'your number'.

You might also want to take note of the things that intrude into your awareness: in other words, notice what you notice. Say you keep seeing red, literally rather than figuratively. The car in front of you always seems to be red, the traffic lights flick to red as you approach. While you are waiting you see a red dress in a window or a pair of red shoes, red roses, and so on. You need to clear your mind and let the associations wash in. Red can be the colour of anger, danger – or of love and passion. Ask yourself who you associate with the colour red. Do you know anyone who is fond of this colour – if so it might be time to give them a call?

Is someone lusting after you and you haven't noticed? Or trying to capture your attention? Is someone or something trying to warn you of danger? Exploring and recording in your metaphysical journal will help you to make sense of such signals and develop your own set of intuitive meanings.

You will also find as you become more psychically aware that you learn a great deal about other people in the first few minutes. You instinctively look at their body language, the feelings they put out, and you also notice what they say to you. Many people tell you their whole story in the first sentence or two of a conversation, if you are aware of the story behind the words. Learning to pay attention helps you to hone in and know what to expect.

Signals from the body

Your body speaks your mind
Ken Dychtwald

Your body is often the first part of you to pick up on subtle clues or insights, beating your conscious mind by several seconds – and sometimes by weeks. Quite apart from those rumblings in the gut that the ancient Mesopotamians were so fond of, your body has a myriad ways of communicating with you: shivers, hair standing up, queasiness, buzzing in the ears, eyes going out of focus, the top of your head prickling and so on. Someone described the difference between a comforting 'it's ok' sensation and a warning 'go carefully' as: 'you know when you get tingles on your head – that tends to be good, positive, safe'. The same person said 'I feel as if something or someone is stroking my legs sometimes, a sort of beware, or be cautious.' He had clearly connected to his body signals. In my own case, the warning would be a hand on my shoulder gently holding me back.

Your 'ears burning' has long been associated with someone talking about you, itchy feet with travelling to new places and itchy palms with money coming your way. My hands itch and burn if someone needs healing or I feel discomfort in the part of my body that is troubled in theirs. Psychic healer Wilma Davidson says her upper arms itch when there's a need for spirit rescue. If you've been keeping your metaphysical journal you should by now have picked up some of the ways in which your body communicates with you.

Sometimes these signals can be hard to miss but not necessarily easy to interpret. I get cold sores when I'm not speaking what is on my mind, which is very clear when I have something accessible to my conscious mind to say but can be more difficult if it's something psychic that I'm missing. So I have learned to look beyond the obvious, asking 'is there more to this than I am consciously aware of? If so, please make it clear.' So often there will quickly be another clear signal from the universe, or my psychic awareness, to tell me what else I need to be saying.

For me one of the most powerful signals is through my eyes – I am a very visual person so this is my dominant mode for receiving information and I 'visualise' with my eyes open and 'see' subtle energies and beings who are invisible to others quite clearly and objectively 'out there' in the room. I have spoken in *Good Vibrations* about how, in the guise of giving me unasked for healing, someone who was trying to cloak things from me speeded up the growth of cataracts in my eyes: literally veiling them. When I realised what had happened I was able to reverse the process – for a time. The healing had been, on the surface, sent for iritis, an inflammation in the iris. The iritis began some years ago when an ex–partner was trying to conceal behaviour he knew would end the relationship if I found out. At that time I asked myself 'what am I seeing that is irritating me so?' But I received no answer. Not surprising since I was asking the wrong question. What I didn't ask is 'what is behind the iritis, what is being hidden from my eyes, what is it someone doesn't want me to see?' That would have been the better question. Since that time, whenever I get a flare up of iritis, I ask 'what is it people don't want me to see, or, what is it that I am not aware of?' A question that covers both the deliberate intention to conceal and the accidental or unintentional action. There is always something going on – which may sound paranoid, but paranoia has been defined as awareness at the edges of consciousness and there are times when apparent paranoia is actually a very clear signal from the universe or your own psychic awareness that something is indeed happening. If you keep looking over your shoulder, you are probably being watched at one level or another. Ask your intuition who is overlooking you and what you need to do about it.

Along with my iritis signal can go emotional irritation, a distinct but inexplicable feeling of angst and unrest that has no relationship to what is going on immediately around or within me, although it may apparently be linked to something else if I use my conscious mind to 'explain' it. This kind of sensation is not usually overwhelming, merely there in the background, nor is it neurotic, it is a sensitivity that falls most readily into kinaesthetic knowing but is also an emotional intuition. However, if I continue to ignore it, particularly when it links into a similar situation in the past, it can become overwhelming, almost hysterical and, when that is the case, I need an aware friend to ask me what is really going on as, even now, I find that the emotional charge I get from such situations can be so severe that it overwhelms my sensible non–metaphysical mind. When I was very much younger, and before I learned to ask what it was all about, I would sometimes come out in hives during such an episode, an outlet for the psychic feelings bottled inside me. Once I learned to ask 'is this mine and what is it about', the negative reactions ceased, but I still need to be quick to recognise what is going on as otherwise a powerful reaction can roll over me. So, if you experience inexplicable emotions and strong feelings, remember to ask what lies behind them and, most importantly, who they belong to and whether they are relevant to the present time. If they are 'yours', then you can get to the bottom of them. If they are not yours, then you need to recognise what they are signalling and who they relate to – and what they are telling you about that person or about a situation.

You will also need to learn to let go if you cannot get to the bottom of things at that particular moment. During the period when my iritis first flared up, my then partner had a car accident. He told me it had happened on ice close to home, while I was away teaching. The explanation didn't *feel right*, especially when he refused to do anything about the car which languished in a local garage. What surprised me most was that I wanted to kick the car savagely every time I saw it on the garage forecourt where it had been abandoned. But I couldn't get any answer as to why I felt like that and I had to let it go. Several years later, when we were breaking up, out of the blue he suddenly confessed where he had really been when the accident happened. Everything became clear: he had indeed been skating on thin ice. All I could do then was forgive myself for not having seen things clearly. It had not been the right time. However, this also illustrates a common problem: if someone else is deliberately blocking you because they don't want you to know what is going on, then you may have to work around that block or dissolve it (see 'What to do when things go wrong').

Ear 'problems' are common if you are an aural person who hasn't quite opened up psychic sensitivity or whose psychic ability wants to catch your attention. In psychosomatic medicine, earache tends to mean that you are hearing something you don't want to listen to and tinnitus can be something you are blocking out physically – or a remnant of a past life. The psychic Edgar Cayce once warned a woman suffering with tinnitus 'never again block your ears to the cries of those who need aid'. But it can also be a psychic condition. I always liken the whooshing and whistling sounds you hear in tinnitus to the voice of the universe speaking to you – you just need to tune it in properly to know what is being said (see opening the inner ear in Chapter 3).

My head has always prickled in the presence of unseen helpers and my nose wrinkles in the vicinity of lost souls who need rescue work – they tend to bring with them a miasma of sweaty socks and blocked drains – but I can also feel very heavy in my body, my head feels full of cotton wool, and I experience difficulty in breathing or a very fast or particularly slow heartbeat. I cough in the presence of suppressed emotion, yawn when someone around me feels powerless or when negative energy is being released. Fortunately I can channel this into the past life readings I do, but it is also useful when I work with people on workshops or one to one, as I have learned to listen to my body signals to reveal what is going on with someone else. Learning to listen to your body signals will help you to deal with the world better and grasp your psychic ability more clearly.

Signals from technology

The universe is an evolving integral system, staggeringly coherent and interconnected.
Ervin Laszlo

My computer now joins in sending psychic messages to me. Awhile ago I discovered that there was a Crystal Bible website in Canada purporting to be me which had cloned the material from my website. I was also encountering difficulties with a publisher who had hijacked the title of my best–selling book. I'd just commented in an email to a friend that I felt like a baby penguin adrift in a sea of walruses – I have no idea where that image came from as it isn't one I'd normally use – when on the bottom of the screen up popped 'Adopt a penguin today' with a picture of a penguin snuggly safe in a dog basket. Beneath it said, 'No you don't take it home, you leave it in the wild.' Then up flashed a sign saying 'Everything's bigger in Canada, even the deals!' So what did that tell me? Well, first of all I had to trust that everything was in hand, it was being taken care of. I had told my agent and the publisher of the situations so it was up to them to take action. Then I had to put it out of my mind. Within a week the site was taken down. In the States and Canada the book title was changed. A little while later several of my books were translated into French Canadian and are doing well.

Signals from the natural world

Is not the core of nature in the heart of man?
Johann Wolfgang von Goethe

As we have seen, animal medicine, natural oracles and omens have formed part of divination and psychic living since the beginning of time and a powerful tradition of meaning and cooperation with animal allies has been built up. Whilst it is preferable to develop your own psychic understanding of what these signs and signals mean for you, traditional meanings can trigger your own knowing.[22]

Signals from the natural world can come from the hare that suddenly crosses your path to signal watchfulness is needed, the birds that wheel in the sky to form a heart shape confirming you have just met your twinflame, or the stag that steps out into the moonlight in front of your car.

The latter happened to me at a turning point in my life. Everything had fallen away: my relationship, my home, my abundance, my health, my inspiration. It was clearly time for a change and I was musing on this as I crossed the New Forest late on a misty, moonlight night. What, I asked myself, was I to do next? Suddenly, from a grove of trees, stepped a white stag, huge antlers rearing against the sky. He stood in the middle of the road about two feet from my car – I'd hastily slammed on the brakes as he halted. Immobile, he stared into my eyes for about five minutes, a contact only broken by a car coming up behind me. He slowly moved aside, tossed his antlers and stood watching me as I reluctantly drove away. His majestic presence seemed to be telling me that it was time to regain my independence, to let go of the past, go through a purification and move on into my future. The next day I finally found a new home, two days later I found a publisher for my novel, and a week later a royalty cheque arrived that enabled me to live for the next year without worrying about money. I did a detox, found a homoeopath, my health improved and life moved on rapidly. I've seen that stag a few times since as I've crossed the Forest, he bows his antlers to signal a new book is on the way or that I've taken the right course of action. He once shook his head and I hastily reread a letter I was about to send, corrected a mistake that would have cost me dear and sent it on its way. He also appears in my dreams and this is another way that nature oracles can speak to you or power animals make themselves known.

Such animals may have a specific message for you, or they could be confirming the thought that you were having just as they appeared. Such thoughts can be elusive and you need to train yourself to catch hold of them before they disappear in the wonder of the encounter, but it can be very rewarding to do so.

Power animals, or allies, naturally belong to the shamanic landscape and may show up as guides or gatekeepers in all their myriad forms. Some can be somewhat unusual: I doubt if many people have Dumbo the baby elephant as a power animal, for instance, but I do. He arrived on my very first shamanic journey many years ago, happily running alongside me until I needed a lift over a chasm, then he invited me to hop on his back, spread his ears, flapped, and off we flew. He reminds me to stick with it, that it's possible to rise above anything and enjoy the most surprising situations – and to keep my sense of humour intact. Funnily enough he's dancing around on Aol today as I write this, above a line of rubber ducks so I take that as a sign that I should perhaps also recount another power animal incident from my recent past.

When I was studying the Crystal Medicine Wheel I was troubled by a cough I just could not shake off, it had already lasted several weeks. So, while journeying, I asked what I could do about it. An imposing tiger appeared, opened his mouth to roar, and out came a beautiful lily flower. Not quite the power animal I was journeying to meet but it was ok with me. The next day I went to see a Chinese Herbalist, told her of the imagery and she promptly gave me Tiger Lily as a remedy. It cured my cough immediately.

Exercise: Meeting your power animal

If you have a shamanic drumming CD, play it for this exercise.

Settle yourself comfortably and close your eyes. Take your attention down to your feet and check that your grounding cord is in place. In your mind's eye take yourself to your favourite place and spend a few moments enjoying this lovely place. When you are ready let your feet take you to the base of a big, old tree that stands to one side. Beneath its roots there is the entrance to the shamanic lower world. Wait quietly by this entrance and ask that your power animal will make itself known to you. You may hear or see your power animal.

When your power animal appears, spend some time together and ask your power animal how it will help you.

When you are ready to leave, ask your power animal to always be available to you when you call (arrange a signal if appropriate).

Make your way back to the centre of your favourite place.

Open your eyes, breathe deeply and become aware of your body once more.

Check that your grounding cord is in place.

Asking the universe for a sign

O God! That one might read the book of fate
Shakespeare, Henry IV, Part II

Sortes is latin for fate or chance lot. It is a form of divine guidance that uses a passage from a book, usually spiritual or philosophical, to answer a specific question. *Sortes* provides a rapid answer. It also operates when you have been mulling over a question and suddenly hear an answer from somewhere around you – from the radio, a line of a song or someone's conversation for example. This type of answer is known as a *Cledon*.

Sortes is useful where you need specific guidance quickly. Whilst it can be used for complex questions, it is particularly good for simple questions even when these are all–embracing: "What should I do?" for instance can be answered by a Sortes text. The secret of success is to choose a book that gives straightforward answers rather than obscure texts that have to be further interpreted or which could be understood in a number of different ways. The book that accompanies a divination pack can also be used without having to lay out a card spread. Switching the radio on when you have asked your question also works well.

Cledons operate even when you haven't asked for guidance. Studying for an M.A. in Cultural Astronomy and Astrology was an enormous shock to my reality. Used to operating psychically and, as an astrologer of thirty five years standing, convinced that astrology was a divine art in which I and the cosmos performed an intricate dance together, meeting academic pernickityness and skepticism was like running headlong into a temple wall. Especially as the practice of astrology per se was banned within the hallowed walls of academia. Thinking that exploring sacred landscape, one of the course options, might be a welcome change, I was horrified to find that, half way through the module, mandatory titles were suddenly imposed. I couldn't see how I could fit my ongoing experiential research into the sacred Dorset landscape in which I live into the compulsory title: 'Sacred space is a human construct. Discuss with reference to the work of at least three theorists'.

In deep despair I set off for the university. As I started my car the radio came on and I heard: 'In other words, the landscape wrote him'. It was a divinatory moment that I interpreted as indicating I could explore sacred space by drawing on my own self–reflexive experience and that of others within my local landscape and, whilst grounded in academic theory, I could reach beyond it. When I listened to the edited repeat of the program on the way home, those vital few words were missing. That essay not only got a distinction, it is being published in an academic journal and its experiential content helped to change the way that particular module was taught. It also became the foundation for *Crystals and Sacred Sites* which took me far from the world of academia into intuitive and sacred landscape.

Sortes tends to give an answer which is straight and to the point. In M.R. James *Ghost Stories of an Antiquary*, there is an account of a man found dead after he received the answer: 'Seek ye me in the morning and I shall not be there.' The Roman Emperor, Gordianus reigned but a few days after receiving the oracular warning from the *Aeneid*: 'Fate only showed him this earth, and suffered him not to tarry'. In a modern example the journalist John McCarthy, who was held captive in Lebanon in the 1980s, heard a commotion and feared he might be executed. He opened the only book he had been allowed, the Bible, and read: 'Open thy doors, oh Lebanon'. Later that day he learned that one of his fellow captives had been released. The Bible is often used for Sortes and the early Christian bishop St. Augustine recommended its use in cases of spiritual difficulty but philosophical books can be substituted. Traditionally, from classical times onwards, the works of Virgil, especially the *Aeneid* were also consulted.

Exercise: Using Sortes

Before opening the chosen text, focus on the question for a few moments, holding the book between your hands, and to send up a request for divine guidance. This 'prayer' can be addressed to a specific deity, or simply to universal guidance.
Allow the book to fall open where it will.
Without looking at the text, simply place your index finger anywhere on the page.
The passage indicated is your answer.

8
The Downside of Being Psychic

If you are in a field of anger, you will sense and experience that anger.
If you are in a field of fear, you will sense and experience fear.
William Bloom [23]

It would be irresponsible to pretend that using your psychic abilities is purely sweetness and light. Unfortunately, as everyone who is psychic knows, it is easy to pick up negative energies from places or people and the nastier side of life sometimes makes itself known in advance and when it does, the effect can be distinctly unpleasant. There are times when your own expectations and fears – or your ego – get in the way or when they attract to you exactly what you wish to avoid or when the voice that is apparently telling you something unpleasant is actually your own. The voices of the subconscious mind take on many guises and may believe that attack is the best form of defensive action. You will, however, experience it as external attack.

Sometimes you can specifically be targeted by those who would prefer that you did not use your psychic abilities (if so see What to do when things go wrong.) The good news is that the more honed and skilful your psychic abilities, the less impact the negative stuff has – and the more accurate and precise the information about such events becomes. You will no longer be prey to overwhelming premonitions of doom and gloom. It is also sensible to learn how to protect yourself and close down after working psychically and this chapter contains further psychic–protection information that you need to practise before opening your psychic awareness further. You will find more assistance in dealing with the unexpected consequences of psychic working, such as spirit attachment, in the chapter on 'what to do if something goes wrong.'

Heights and depths of consciousness

The human mind must always be aware that there are two very separate airwave frequencies. Either of these frequencies can tune into the mind, but they are completely the opposite of each other.

Wilma Davidson

When you open your psychic abilities, especially when you begin to meditate, you often find that you go into 'peak experiences', what the Buddhists call bliss or enlightenment and other disciplines call cosmic consciousness or wholeness. Such experiences are expansive, light floods in, the inner world becomes the outer world, the outer world the inner. When the painter Vincent Van Gogh had such a vision, the starry night he was observing metamorphosed. The stars turned into enormous whirlpools of light and energy and the trees flamed towards the heavens.

But, as so often happens, Van Gogh crashed into the deepest despair. He was experiencing two opposite polarities, bliss and despair, bouncing between the extremes of higher and lower consciousness. The peak and the despair are merely experiences, but many people confuse them with emotions or absolute truth. Physiologically, endorphins are characteristic of bliss states, adrenalin of the pits. Healthwise, physiologically and psychologically, too much adrenalin has a detrimental effect so you need to switch it off in order to keep a metaphysical balance.

In the 'pit' state of lower consciousness fear rushes in. The lower levels of consciousness tend to take over at night. You wake up, heart pounding. You find yourself hot, dizzy, unable to breathe. Adrenalin is pumping round your system. This is when you have intimations of doom. You will doubtless hope when you go to bed: "It won't happen again" but of course it does because you have given it attention and the brain does not understand 'not'. 'I am free from...' is a much better way to phrase it. When you learn to switch this response off, life stabilizes. You have the bliss moments, but the fear recedes.

Exercise: The adrenalin controller

In your brain there is a switch marked 'Adrenalin On/Adrenalin Off'. In charge of this switch is a controller. The controller switches the adrenalin on whenever you get worked up, stressed or fearful whether or not the situation warrants it.

In your mind, picture this switch. Set it to Off and mentally tape it into position. Inform the controller that it is now in charge of making sure no one interferes with the switch. It is the controller's job to keep it in the Off position and to shout 'Stop' before you go into fear mode. The controller is responsible for keeping you happy and healthy.

To fully control fear, you also need to be aware of your negative thoughts. Everyone has about 55,000 thoughts a day. Many of them are negative and you need to switch them to positive. Negative thoughts create what you most fear because you come to expect it and can also create thought forms. And, as the brain does not understand the word 'no', telling yourself it will not happen is counter–productive. What you have to do is learn to catch the thought before it happens and stop it in its tracks or the adrenalin reaction before it is switched on. Similarly self–doubt needs switching off.

An actor friend of mine always shouted 'retake' when he'd said something he didn't mean to say. Someone else I knew kept saying 'erase, erase', but it is much more productive to learnt to listen to your thoughts *before you speak* and change the negative to positive before it comes out of your mouth. Stop the toxic thought before it hits your brain. The old, but tried and tested, remedy of counting to ten before you speak allows you time to monitor what it is you are going to say, to catch a negative thought and transform it before it is spoken.

Worm's eye view, eagle's eye view

Fearfulness and lower states of consciousness can be likened to a worm that has popped its head above the earth. It cannot see much, a few blades of grass, a worm cast or two it left behind last time it was here. It has no idea of the bigger picture and it cannot see what is coming. At any moment a blackbird might pull it from the ground.

Higher consciousness and psychic states are like an eagle's eye view. The overview is there, the bigger picture, and yet the eye can focus in on the smallest detail. If you get into the habit of seeing the world from the eagle's eye view rather than the worm's, life takes on a very different look.

Exercise: A different view

In your mind's eye become a worm, feel yourself wriggling your head out above the grass. Smell the earthy smell, see the green grass in front of you, try to see beyond it.

Now become an eagle soaring high overhead. Feel the cool air slide past your wings. Let your eyes see the bigger picture. Then focus your eyes on the worm and recognise how restricted that viewpoint is, how narrow and un–insightful. Now pull back and see the bigger picture with all the benefits that insight brings. Promise yourself that you will see life with an eagle's eye from now on.

Projection and wishful thinking

Look clearly at your psychological history so that it does not haunt you.
William Bloom

Projection occurs when your own fears and expectations subtly influence what you psychically see or sense. It also occurs when what you refuse to face in yourself is 'seen' in the people around you. So, for instance, everyone has an inner terrorist who could wreak havoc. This can contaminate what you sense in the world around you, so that many of the doom–full scenarios that untrained psychics apparently perceive can actually be coming from their own subconscious mind.

Wishful thinking can likewise colour perception. If you intensely wish for something to happen, you may believe that your psychic awareness is telling you it will occur when it is actually your own overpowering desire, your vanity or your ego at work. Facing up to your fears, accepting and integrating the qualities of your shadow self and learning to recognise and control intense desires help to 'clean up' your psychic sensitivity. If you need further assistance, seek out an Emotional Freedom Technique practitioner. This is the fastest and most effective way I have found to neutralise and transform fears and negative programming, or you could check out Crystal EFT in *Good Vibrations*.

Psychic attack from within

If you are lost in your own emotions and ambitions and drama, and always reacting to the events and activities around you, you will find it impossible to feel safe.
William Bloom

Psychic attack is created by ill wishing from another person and is dealt with at length in *Good Vibrations* but an apparently external psychic attack can come from within yourself and what you unconsciously wish for, and much of the confusion around your psychic sensitivity is generated by inner figures such as the inner saboteur. Remember that, as astrologer Margaret Koolman puts it:

> *It's not the world that makes you feel small.*
> *It is your own inner voices.*

Saboteurs subtly obstruct your purpose or trip you up. They have been created at some time in your past, often during childhood, and have had a protective function. Unfortunately, when you outgrew the need for that particular help, you did not necessarily outgrow the figure that became lodged in your subconscious mind and still tries to 'keep you safe'.

If you find it difficult to develop your psychic abilities, it could be a saboteur that lies at the root of the problem. Children are extremely psychic – until adults tell them it is all nonsense. They then have to make the difficult decision between being psychic and being rational. If your saboteur was formed during this process, it could be 'keeping you safe' by blocking your psychic awareness. Meeting this figure and explaining that you have matured and now have different needs will usually release the sabotage, and the figure may be persuaded to take a more constructive part in your inner life.

If you accept reincarnation and past lives, you may find that the prohibition against being psychic goes back to a time when you were persecuted for your gifts. Reminding yourself that you are now in a new incarnation and talking accordingly to the saboteur figure can release this prohibition.

Exercise: Meeting the Saboteur

Sit quietly and let yourself relax. Take yourself to your favourite place. Spend a few moments enjoying being in this space. Walk around and enjoy its unique feel.

When you are ready to seek the inner saboteur, look at what is beneath your feet in your favourite place. You will see that there is a trap door in front of you. Open this trap door and descend the ladder below – remember to take a light with you or look for a light switch as you go down the ladder.

This is where your inner saboteur lives. This figure may be reluctant to come out into the light and may prefer to stay in a dark corner. It this is the case, try to reassure it and coax it into the light so that you can communicate more easily.

Ask the figure what purpose it serves. [Wait quietly and patiently for the answer, do not push].

You will probably find that the figure once had a positive purpose but that this has changed over the years. If so, thank it for its care and concern and explain how things are different now.

Ask the saboteur if it will help you by taking a more positive role in your inner life.

If the answer is yes, discuss this and ask for a new name to go with its new role. If the answer is no, ask the saboteur if it is willing to leave you and take up residence somewhere where it will not frustrate your purpose. [You may need to do some negotiating here. Most saboteurs eventually agree to become more positive or to leave. If yours absolutely refuses, it may need a different approach under the guidance of someone qualified in de–possession techniques.]

When you have completed your discussions or negotiations, leave by the ladder and close the trap door. The figure may come with you and can be encouraged to find an appropriate place to settle. [If the saboteur has been particularly obstreperous, sending it to outer space for the duration could be a solution.]

When you are ready, open your eyes. Take your attention down to your feet and feel your feet on the earth. Be aware that your feet are connected to the earth, grounding you. Picture a shield closing over your third eye. With your eyes wide open, take a deep breath and stand up with your feet firmly on the earth.

***If you are non–visual**, take your mind around your body and allow yourself to feel psychically where your inner saboteur lurks. Communicate through sensing, asking the same questions as above. A Scapolite crystal facilitates this process.*

You can adapt the exercise to meet other inner figures such as the critic or persecutor, the victim or the martyr and the scapegoat or to meet your self–doubt.

Inner voices

Then, there is the plague of self–doubt that descends on us all from time to time and causes us to misread all the signs and signals that surround us.

Jonathan Cainer (www.cainer.com)

I've already mentioned the inner voices that can plague us and subtly alter our perceptions without our realising it. But it has become even more apparent to me lately, from a variety of sources, just how much these inner voices can distort our reality whether psychic or consensual and how they can lead to misinterpretation or distortion of our intuitive faculties. A little self–doubt can be a useful check to the over–confident ego but it can go overboard.

Most people are familiar with the 'plague of self–doubt' that Jonathan Cainer mentions which leads us to question 'is it me?', 'is it my fault?', 'is what I think I'm picking up true or am I distorting it?' 'am I imagining it?'. When we doubt our inner knowing, it goes awry and the voice of the self cannot direct us. So it becomes a self–fulfilling prophecy of doubt and doom. Of course we'll 'get it wrong' if we don't believe we're getting it right. But, being too certain has its pitfalls too.

The other inner voice that is so subtle and soooo seductive is that of the ego: 'of course I'm right', 'I'm here to save the world', 'I know what's best for you', 'because I can see what you need I have the right to intrude on your private space without permission', and so on. This is where a healthy dose of scepticism comes in, 'is it really an Ascended Master telling me this or has my ego taken on a new guise?', 'do I really have a monopoly on truth?', 'am I the only one with the answers?' If you always work in truth and love, so it is said, you cannot go far wrong. Well............. that depends on whose truth it is and whether the love is unconditionally applied to everyone. As I've already said, ego is perhaps the biggest trap in the metaphysical world. I've seen too many good psychics ruined because they came to believe that they, and only they, had all the answers. Equally I've seen very promising psychics not make the grade because they couldn't believe that they deserved to be a vessel for high level information.

So how do you distinguish between the inner voice of the heart, soul and intuition and those that arise out of the ego and the subconscious mind?

Learning to listen is the first step. Most of these voices pass through our mind so rapidly that we can't always 'hear' them but we automatically react. So:

- Every time you have one of those thoughts no matter how fleeting, write it in your metaphysical diary.
- Question the question or statement. Write freely, whatever flows into your mind around that thought. Look for patterns and preconceptions, lack of self–confidence and the doubts that creep in – or the egotistical certainties.
- Ask yourself who is speaking. Then go up to your higher self and assess things from that perspective. Your higher self can rein your ego in and blow away the self–doubt to reveal what really is.
- Mentally step into someone else's shoes and view the situation from their perspective.

Then you can learn to respond in an appropriate way. Simply by catching the thought or the doubt before the automatic reaction kicks in you can change it.

- ➢ Find the positive statement that negates a doubt. Find the humility that mitigates the ego. Affirm these.

Work with humility, light and love and always aim for the highest. Then you'll know that your inner voices are those of heart, soul and higher self.

Thought forms

Thoughts are things.

Source unknown.

You have only to look at the photographic work of Masaru Emoto regarding the influence of thought and emotion on water and that of Dr Bruce Lipton on how beliefs affect genetic activity to realise the power of thought could be very potent indeed. [24] Although this work has still to be scientifically validated, it appears to demonstrate that different kinds of thoughts or emotions affect the structure of the water, which is then frozen and the resulting patterns photographed and that thoughts encourage or discourage genetic patterns or predispositions to kick in.

To say that thoughts are tangible things is not an exaggeration. Thought is what creates, the thought is there before the action or the product of the thought comes into being. Thought forms are another source of unwanted influence and, as the name suggests, are created by the power of thought – your own or someone else's. One type of thought form is created by negative thoughts, or emotions, that take on a life of their own. You can literally be haunted by your own mind. Strong beliefs, emotions or fears, may create a thought form as can someone else's or your own desires. Thought forms feed off desire, jealousy, envy, hatred but also love. People who want 'only the best for you' are creating a strong thought form that may not actually be in your own best interests or for your higher good because it is that person's idea (or thought) of what you need to be or do that is trying to control you. Such forms are very controlling and often appear to be human – or demonic depending on your belief system – and may communicate in the guise of a 'real person'.

You can be haunted by your own obsessive thoughts, although it may not be obvious that that is the source as the thought can externalise. However, if a thought goes around and around in your head and you can't let it go, then you are obsessed by a thought form.

Such thought forms stop you moving forwards in your life, as do thought forms from other sources that are trying to operate 'for your own good' (a Banded Agate placed on the third eye is an excellent removal tool).

There are a great many old thought forms that are simply hanging around. Some get strongly attached to a person, or a family – and many are actually passed down the family. Others are what the Tibetans call 'hungry ghosts' created from all the unsatisfied desires of humankind that hang around close to earth. They are easy to contact and all too happy to communicate – usually garbage but sometimes frightening. The problem is that a thought form's knowledge is extremely limited. So any 'intuition' that comes from such a source is rarely useful.

It is possible to create a thought form. Some years ago, parapsychology researchers in Canada conducted an experiment. A group sat together in meditation and thought a 'communicator from the other side' into being. They gave him a detailed history and a name: Peter. Despite the fact that this was fictitious, a communicator called Peter was contacted through several mediums and gave the same history. The more he communicated, the more certain he was that he was a real person. Eventually, the researchers had to think him out of existence.

Thought forms can also arise from emails etc. that threaten you with dire consequences if they aren't sent on – or rewards if they are. (Simply burn a printed copy or just delete and send it out to the great cosmic recycling bin for dispersal, then forget about it. Let it go totally.)

When you have some experience of working psychically, it is easy to recognise a thought form. Although it can appear powerful, it somehow lacks vitality and is inflexible. A most effective way to deal with a thought form is saying firmly: "I don't believe in you." Laughter also dissolves them. You can always visualise a Light Wand (see 'What to do when things go wrong') or use a crystal wand.

Exercise: To disperse a thought form

Zap it with an Aegirine crystal wand or Laser Quartz or imagine a laser beam breaking it up.

Place a Banded Agate over your third eye.

Put a drop of Petaltone Plant Ally, Special 8 or Power Shield on your hands and pass these all around your aura a couple of hand's breadths away from your body.

Psychic vampires

> *One of the most common forms of subtle invasion is energy leeching or psychic vampirism. Someone, knowingly or unknowingly, sucks out your energy to feed their own.*
>
> *Judy Hall*

Psychic vampires are energy pirates who home in on power–full (or even not so power–full) people and leach their energy. As you become more psychic, your power builds and these sad and needy people can latch on. Keeping your spleen chakra – just under your left armpit – properly protected helps. You'll know if anyone is hooking in here as there'll be a sore spot or a pain in your ribs (as an emergency measure place a Green Aventurine over it or draw a green triangle in felt tip pen from just under your left arm down to your waist above your belly button, round to the spine at the back and then back up to your armpit). But, if you become aware that this is happening and know who is doing it, you can perform a powerful invocation and banishing ritual that will keep your energy free for your own use. Keep a picture of the person in your mind as you direct these words straight to his or her heart. You might like to place yourself in a protective pentangle (a five pointed star) or a protective layout of Black Tourmaline stones to do this.

Exercise: Keeping the vampires at bay

I call on my guardian angel and the power of Archangel Michael and his warriors, I call on my guardian and my gatekeeper. I call on all my power allies known and unknown, seen and unseen. I call on the protective powers of universal love. By all those powers, I demand that I be freed from this psychic vampirisation, that it will cease and desist immediately for all time. I take control of my energy. I am free and clear of this parasite whom I forgive for being so needy. I am free, I am whole. I am protected forthwith. My power is my own, my energy is my own, my psychic awareness is my own. I am that I am.

See the person getting smaller and smaller, shrinking away to nothing, banished back to his or her own space. Remove your attention and let them go with love and forgiveness. Then forgive yourself for having let it happen.

Stamp your foot firmly on the floor.

Know that your power and your energy are now in your own guardianship. Feel forgiveness and compassion for the poor needy soul, *but don't allow the parasite back into your energy field.* Don't think about him or her, don't speak about it, don't have any contact if at all possible. Only you can now give away your power and allow a parasite back in, no one can take your energy unless you allow it. Be sure that you do not succumb again. Be strong. Be power–full. Trust your psychic knowing. (See also my book *Good Vibrations* for further protective and strengthening measures for your energy field.)

Visions of impending disaster

> *And there came flashes of lightning, rumblings, peals of thunder, and a violent earthquake, such as had not occurred since people were upon the earth… The great city was split into three parts, and the cities of the nations fell… And every island fled away. And no mountains were to be found, and huge hailstones, each weighing about a hundred pounds, dropped from heaven on people, until they cursed God for the plague of the hail, so fearful was that plague.*
>
> Revelation of St John the Divine 16:17–21

As anyone who has sat in St John's cave on the island of Patmos and who is the least psychic will know, some places seem to be preprogrammed to create the most vivid visions of heaven and hell. It's no wonder St John wrote his Revelations there. But it is also possible to, as it were, pluck premonitions out of the Akashic Record or to come up with them out of the blue in an instant. It can be an overwhelming experience. Without trained psychic awareness, and even with it, you may become disturbingly aware of an impending disaster; with honed psychic abilities you will recognise what is about to happen and will know what can be done to meet it in the most constructive way possible. With foresight, it may be possible to circumvent the event altogether but this is not always so. Sometimes we need the challenging events in our life to put us on another path. But, with foresight, you can face the challenge with a psychic plan of action and on–going guidance.

Some of the biblical prophecies were so vivid and ubiquitous that they are still being interpreted as pertaining to the present day two, three or four thousand years after they were written. What needs to be borne in mind here, though, is that the prophets were speaking to the people of their time. 'The Great Whore of Babylon' was Rome in the first century C.E. It was not America or Britain in the twenty first century. I've grown very tired of being told that crystals belong to the devil. A huge misinterpretation and misconception of a biblical telling off that occurred over two and a half thousand years ago but which is today being attributed to something entirely other than its original source. A chapter in Ezekiel proclaims:

> *Moreover, the word of the Lord came to me:* Mortal, *raise a lamentation over the king of Tyre, and say to him. Thus says the Lord God:*

You were the signet of perfection, full of wisdom and perfect in beauty.
You were in Eden, the garden of God,
Every precious stone was your covering,
Carnelian, Chrysolite, and moonstone, beryl, onyx, and jasper, sapphire [or lapis lazuli], turquoise, and emerald;
And worked in gold were your settings and your engravings.
On the day that you were created they were prepared.
With an anointed cherub as guardian, I placed you
you were on the holy mountain of God;
you walked among the stones of fire.

Ezekiel 28:13–14 (NRSV)

I just loved the idea that when walking in the Garden of God a king was covered in crystals from the moment he was created. But when I looked at web commentaries on this particular chapter of Ezekiel, I was surprised to find it linked to Satan and his fall from grace and yet it forms part of Ezekiel's tirades against neighbouring kings – it is addressed to the King of Tyre and Satan isn't even mentioned (he rarely is in the Bible). By verse 20 Ezekiel is admonishing the king of Sidon and then in Chapter 29 he turns his attention to the Egyptian Pharaoh and threatens dire punishments that are today being applied to contemporary events. Why? Ezekiel wasn't making predictions for a few thousand years ahead, he was prophesying for his own time. However, a quick trawl through the internet revealed a host of sites under titles such as Delving into Demons. Utterly ridiculous, especially as crystals were elsewhere in the Bible instruments of God's will – there's even a description of prophecy by crystals in the Breastplate of the High Priest and the Urim and Thurim. But, of course, people apply these dire warnings as they see fit, not as the prophet intended and the same thing can happen with modern prophecies. Knowing what is applicable and when it is applicable to is one of the great psychic conundrums, and the greatest downside of being psychic is, perhaps, being quoted or misquoted out of context. But this is only one of the dilemmas facing someone who, apparently, foresees the future.

As all professional psychics know, seeing death is one of the most difficult dilemmas. Death may signify an ending or a change. It can be an extremely upsetting thing to hear, especially if it turns out not to be literally true. It does not necessarily mean a physical death. If it does, however, being prepared brings equanimity to the situation. Much depends on how the knowledge is communicated and how aware you are of *knowing*.

Many people who foresee death feel guilty about it: as though they were somehow to blame for having caused it. Many years ago, before I had trained my psychic abilities, I subconsciously tuned into the imminent death of a friend's father with whom he had had a major row. I urged Anthony to ring his father, who was about to travel to another country, saying that it was important he phoned before his father left. Anthony insisted that he would ring the following month when he had the results of an examination he was taking.

The next day he rang me from an airport, saying that his father had had a stroke as he stepped off the plane and was now in hospital. Anthony was on standby. "Don't worry", I said, "You will get there in time. It will be alright." I could not have stopped those words from coming out of my mouth, but I had no prior knowledge of what I would say beforehand. When Anthony arrived at the hospital his father briefly regained consciousness and they were able to resolve their differences before he died.

When Anthony phoned to tell me the news, he said: "You knew, didn't you. You must have known because you kept telling me to phone." Trying to explain that whilst I had known he needed to phone, I had no idea of why, was useless and it took sometime to get over the feeling of guilt that arose from his accusation of prior knowledge.

Nowadays I would still urge someone to phone in similar circumstances but I would have a much clearer *knowing* of why I felt it was so important. I would explain that, whilst I felt an ending was coming, it need not necessarily be a death but that it was an opportunity for forgiveness and reconciliation. But, because of all that I have learned about the process of death, I would also offer, if the person was receptive, some guidance about the best way to help someone make the transition and how to keep psychic contact with them as they passed into another dimension. And I would certainly not feel guilty. Foreknowledge can be a wonderful thing as it can turn the most negative event into a positive happening. In the Old Testament, for example, we see what happens when Jacob interprets Pharoah's dream of seven years of plenitude followed by seven of famine. By putting aside sufficient grain, the disaster was adverted.

Nevertheless, there are times when the events that premonitions foretell cannot be turned around and there will be times when the predicted events, personal or public, do not materialise. Many more predictions turn out to be untrue than true, it's not an exact science even for the most skilful psychic and there are alternative realities. Even when the details are clear, the timing or precise location may be difficult to ascertain. There are times when you can do nothing except register and record what you see and let it go. It is important to learn how to handle the capricious wildness of uninvited precognition.

Dealing with premonitions of doom

- Stop, sit down, and let your eyes go out of focus. Slow your breathing down and relax. If you have just awakened from a dream, sit up.
- Take your attention into your solar plexus. Clarify what you are sensing or have dreamt, finger dowsing if necessary to check the answers.
- Ask: "Is this premonition valid and real?"
- If the answer is no, picture white light surrounding your aura dissolving the experience. Open your eyes and proceed no further. (Although you may like to work on releasing your own fears, or send white light and positive thoughts to the collective to counteract any fear.)
- If the answer is yes, ask for precise details. Who is involved? What will happen? Why is this occurring? When?
- Ask if there is anything you can do. Do you need to say anything to anyone? Is it preventable?
- If the answer is no, write up the premonition in your metaphysical journal. Ask that universal light and love will be sent to the situation. Get up and walk away from it. Your psychic awareness has told you there is nothing more you can do. Remind yourself that you are not responsible for what you see – you are however responsible for how you deal with it.
- If the answer is yes, ask for precise guidance. What do you need to do? Who do you talk to? What do you say? When do you need to say or do it?
- Be sure to take any action necessary, or pass on exactly what you are told, do not inflate it or agonise about it. When that's done, put it aside, let it go.

Precognition and disaster

> *Abraham Lincoln dreamed of his own death six weeks before his assassination. However, his dream was not of being shot and dying, but of being an observer after the fact. He saw a long procession of mourners entering the White House. When he entered himself and passed the coffin, he was shocked to find himself looking at his own body. American presidents John Garfield and William McKinley [also] experienced foreknowledge of their deaths.*[25]

There are many recorded cases of premonitions and precognitions of disaster and these can be disturbing both to hear and to experience. It helps if you remember that this is only one possibility amongst many. As might be surmised, there were many psychics who claimed to have foreseen the events of September 11. A British man, Chris Robinson, dreamed the event intensely on several occasions in August 2001 whilst being tested by Professor Gary E. Schwartz of the University of Arizona. On September 9, two days before the attack occurred, Robinson apparently wrote to the US Embassy in London to warn them an aircraft was to be used by terrorists as a weapon of destruction against a tall building in New York.

Another Briton, Dave Mandel, drew a graphic representation of the destruction of the twin towers by an aircraft – which he dreamed five years to the day before it occurred. Mandell took his drawing to the local bank and was photographed in front of a calendar and witnesses. Six months later he had to repeat the process when he again dreamed of the twin towers splitting apart, with great chunks falling off them before one of the towers started to topple. This was by no means the first precognitive dream Mandell had received. He predicted Concorde crashing, a river boat sinking and numerous earthquakes, floods, assassinations, and the like.

An English psychic, Valerie Clark, appeared on BBC TV's *Kilroy* programme three months before September 11. She described a disturbing vision she had had several years previously in which she was wandering around during bombing of the World Trade Centre and saw a plane going past. She was, however, unclear whether it went into the building or not. After September 11 she was convinced that this was what her dream had foretold. After–sight is infallible. Foresight is not always so.

Real life often emulates fiction. Stephen King, writing as Richard Bachman, ended his story *The Running Man* by the hero crashing an empty plane into the plate glass window of a tall tower out of which a media boss, who had double crossed him, was staring. The media man's last sight was the hero giving him the finger. It could be deemed to be prophetic, although the details are far from exact, but it could also be the writer reaching into the *zeitgeist* to pluck out a suitable revenge. Then again, it could be skilful use of a vivid imagination.

Illusions, delusions and wishful thinking

> *It will, I imagine, be an uncomfortable passage as we work through the profoundly negative effects of celebrity culture and mindless global capitalism but, in my opinion, in my heart and my gut, I feel that all will be well.*
>
> *www.williambloom.com* [26]

Do you subscribe to an end of the world theory? Sadly a great many people did in the period leading up to the end of 2012. I wonder if the doom and gloom merchants ever gave a thought to the fact that their thoughts might create the very destruction they were predicting or that, as William Bloom has suggested – their fears come out of a past life experience which they are projecting on to the present day. As we've seen thoughts are very powerful things and can manifest what is so feared or, that they can create what we most wish for but it might not be what is best for our higher good. If we are working psychically it is always as well to bear in mind just how our thoughts – and those of the people wanting readings – create a 'reality' or a possibility that may not be the true one. 'Consensual reality' is created from the thoughts of the many. 'Psychic reality' stems from the intentions of the few. Personally I believe that the end of 2012 signalled a huge shift in consciousness, a spiritual and psychic opening up. But whenever you work psychically you need to ask yourself 'is this true for me, is this something I (or someone else) am creating, is this part of my (or my querant's) soul path, is ego or wishful thinking at work here?' Don't let yourself get caught up in what I call the pitfalls of the psychic path. I've seen so many promising psychics who, because of ego, failed to fulfil that promise as they succumbed to the seductive lure of the cult of celebrity. No matter how sincere they were in the beginning, subtle pressures and expectations amended their ability into people–pleasing or doom and gloom mongering.

Pitfalls of the psychic path

> *The main feedback was that I was tending to lecture the reader rather than guiding them along with me. Luckily my bruised ego did not stop me from seeing the constructiveness of this feedback.*
>
> *Ian Lawton* [27]

So, finally, we come to what is perhaps the greatest pitfall of all. That of ego and celebrity and thinking that you know it all when really you've only just started out on the path and, as you will soon discover, have a lifetime's learning in front of you. After seventy years of being psychic and over forty five years as a professional psychic, I know just how seductive it is to feel you have all the answers. 'Spirit has told you' or an ascended master has communicated through you and your ego has gone overboard. You are the chosen one. The only one who has this special ability. You can fix someone or make them better, help them get their life on track, provide evidence and convince them, and so on – even when they haven't asked you. You have the evangelical zeal of a prophet, you can't wait to share this new understanding of the world. How wonderful it feels when people fall at your feet, giving all their power away to you because, they believe or you have caused them to believe, you have all the answers.

Money and greed is another pitfall as is the present day cult of celebrity. This can attract egotistical, flamboyant, showy people who are skilled in marketing and self–promotion. They soon become 'experts' beloved by the media. But just because they are on television doesn't necessarily mean they know what they're doing or have the best of intentions.

Remember! No psychic can possibly be all things to all people. Nor can any one person have all the answers. Sadly I have so often seen extremely promising psychics and healers propelled from obscurity to the bright light of fame, only to come crashing down *because they believed their own spin*. They began to believe that they, and they alone, have caused the miracle, given perfect guidance or found the complete – and only – explanation. And the effect on their psychic or healing abilities is devastating. It opens them up to so many undesirable influences on so many different levels:

One of the most essential tools of the psychic path is humility

So, how do you avoid the pitfalls of the psychic path?

- Let your higher self take the credit, not your ego.
- Practise, practise, practise and never stop learning.
- Never assume you know it all.
- Don't interpret, offer what you see with humility.
- Always work at the highest spiritual vibration you can attain and from a place of rightness.
- Check your sources, use psychic protection and be aware.
- Wait to be asked or at the very least volunteer your services gently.
- Never assume that, just because it worked before or was right in the past, it will be the same in the present.
- Offer your suggestions as to what might be rather than ramming them down people's throats.
- Open up a dialogue rather than assuming you have all the answers.
- Never think even for one moment that you know best or that your guide – or you – is infallible.
- Listen to feedback, it's the best way to learn.
- Never say 'I think you'll find I'm right'.
- Never be afraid to say 'I don't know'.

- Learn when it's appropriate to keep your mouth shut.
- Be content to work quietly in the service of others.
- Monitor your body's responses and signals, check in with your solar plexus and see how you feel, if it doesn't feel good you can be sure it isn't so don't pass it on to anyone else.

    - And – and I know this one comes from my own prejudice but it is based on long experience – avoid like the plague anyone who claims to be a guru or to be able to instantly fix you. Psychic plagues and virtual infections based on ego are as bad for your spiritual health as physical ones are for your bodily well being.

    - Remember, the greatest teachers are the ones who are often content to work in anonymity and always with humility.

9
In Two Minds

There is an immense ocean over which the mind can sail, upon which the vessel of thought has not yet been launched.
Richard Jefferies

Psychic awareness is a function of consciousness but the more scientists and psychologists try to pin down the source and location of consciousness, the more elusive it becomes. Yes, areas of the brain can now be mapped that function during specific processes but in the opinion of Professor Stanislav Grof:

Ideas about the nature of consciousness and the relationship between consciousness and matter (particularly the brain) have to be radically revised. [28]

Brain activity is not necessarily an indication of consciousness or awareness. An apparently brain–dead person can have – and later report – experiences while there is no measurable brain activity and the ancients always claimed that mind was an independent and ongoing entity. Something that science is at last beginning to recognise. As Dr. Melvin Morse points out:

Although our modern brain began evolving more than two hundred thousand years ago, it didn't come with a manual. We are just starting to learn to use it fully. [29]

From the psychic standpoint, it might perhaps have been better if he'd used the word mind or consciousness rather than brain, although the three are often confused, as that is where the excitement and the potential lies.

Mind, brainwaves and consciousness

If brain function won't support [an] experience you have to argue that mind and brain are separate.
Dr Peter Fenwick

Have you ever said: 'I've just had a brainwave'? You probably did! Everything of which you are aware, including intuitive ideas, has to pass through your brain and its electro–neurological activity – which includes the frequency measurement that is a brainwave. But, while it is clear that psychic awareness is mediated through the mind, it is far from clear whether, as many scientists would like to believe, mind and consciousness as a whole is generated purely by the brain and ceases when the brain ceases to function. Metaphysicians would agree with Willis W. Harman, Professor of Engineering–Economic Systems, Stanford University when he says:

Mind is not brain

and some scientists are in accord with Dr Peter Fenwick when he states:

> *we are left with a real scientific problem... it looks as if mind and brain – if the data is correct – are separate.* [30]

However, it is apparent that the brain mediates what happens to psychic awareness as in order to be communicated experiences have to go through the brain to be turned into speech, sight and body awareness.

With the sophisticated imaging equipment now available, neuroscientists are able to pinpoint the parts of the brain involved in psychic activities. But that does not mean they are able to explain them fully. For instance, when brainwave research was carried out during past life regression, it was found that not only did the regression therapist's brainwaves synchronise (a process called entrainment) with the patient's, but that simultaneous beta and delta waves were present – a situation that, according to orthodox science, cannot occur and yet researchers have monitored similar combined states during meditation and dreams.[31]

Each level of brainwave has its own frequency, each one slower, more focused and one–pointed than the last. It is this focusing of the attention, or awareness, that produces an altered state of consciousness. As Dethlefsen puts it:

> *There is a narrowing of consciousness to one point, as if, when a wide angle lens is replaced with converging lenses, the light becomes more and more concentrated, and a strongly focused light beam picks out a tiny point, plunging the surrounding areas into increasing darkness. The intensity of light at this point is far greater than when the light was diffused.*

Five types of brainwave frequency have, so far, been identified: beta, alpha, theta, gamma and delta each having their own frequency. Although all the waves are present at any one time, one or more will be the dominant frequency. Beta is present in the waking state during everyday awareness and when processing information. It is also present, in combination, during lucid dreaming and precognition. High frequency gamma has been described as the optimal frequency for brain functioning, being connected with enhanced levels of empathy, compassion, mental abilities and increased awareness. Having a tiny amplitude that is barely detectable it nevertheless binds the brain together regulating memory and perception and assisting focus and integration of information. Gamma waves are stimulated by meditation, yoga and hypnosis. They are dominant during the REM period of sleep alongside Theta waves and on waking which may be why so much psychic and creative information is available at this time and during dreams. Alpha, a slower frequency, occurs during meditation and altered states of awareness such as dreams and imaging. Theta, a slower frequency still, also occurs during deep meditation and 'bliss' states and can bring about profound healing and psychic awareness. Theta connects to the subconscious mind and the Akashic Record. Delta, the slowest of all, is produced in 'dormant' states and can occur during past life regression. It is a form of universal awareness and taps into what Rupert Sheldrake has called the morphogenic field and mystics the universal mind. It is not detectable during 'ordinary' dreams but is active in lucid dreams and extra–sensory experiences such as pre–cognition and out–of–body states and seems to act as bridge to higher knowledge. If you are purely in theta, however, you will tend not remember anything when you return to everyday awareness so some degree of beta is also required or a combination of entrained delta and beta.

When psychic dreamer Chris Robinson was tested by Professor Gary E. Schwartz of the University of Tucson, he spent ten nights wired up in a sleep laboratory to test his brain wave patterns. During his precognitive dreams, his patterns were different to anyone else who had been tested there. Robinson had the kind of paroxysms or discharges that would normally be seen in epilepsy. The anomaly is being closely monitored but may point the way forward for researchers to understand exactly what does go on in the brain during precognition.

It is apparent from bio–feedback techniques that it is possible to train the brain to maintain or attain certain brainwave combinations and this is a fruitful area for research and the development of psychic abilities.[32] When leading–edge imaging equipment is applied to the brain during psi–states and so called paranormal activities, it is locating the exact sites in the brain where precognition and the like are processed just as other areas of the brain are now being mapped. It is likely that, like a muscle, this site is present in everyone but, as with someone who exercises a muscle daily, it will be more strongly developed and visible in psychics or meditators. Researchers are already aware that people who use their memory a great deal have a much more extensive 'memory' area in the brain – to the extent that adjacent sites are often taken over. It may be that by meditating and stimulating your gamma brain waves, you can increase both memory and psychic awareness.

The mind link

Research has shown that when minds are in rapport, they do not have to be in the vicinity to synchronise – the brains 'entrain' that is, they come into resonant harmony sharing the same brainwave pattern. One research subject was isolated in a remote location and wired up to an EEG machine to measure brain wave patterns. A research 'partner' was subjected to intermittent strobe lighting and a careful note of time kept. The person at the remote location showed brain wave changes that accorded exactly with those strobe lights despite the fact that there were no visual or auditory clues. It was impossible for the subject to have known when the strobe light was flashing and yet the brain waves had synchronized.

For the last fifteen years or so scientists have been investigating mirror neurons in the brain or, as V.S. Ramachandran has dubbed them, "Dalai Lama neurons". In 2000 he predicted that these neurons will 'provide a unifying framework and help explain a host of mental abilities that have hitherto remained mysterious and inaccessible to experiments'.[33] As with all such discoveries, however, neuroscientists are sharply divided as to their significance. I personally find the idea extremely exciting and am sure that it has profound significance for intuition, although I'm not yet sure quite how and what.

What is known is that people with autism don't have functioning mirror neurons, which could go a long way towards explaining how difficult they find it to put themselves in someone else's shoes, in other words to have emotional empathy. Well functioning mirror neurons, on the other hand, have been shown by brain scans to 'fire up' when a person sees someone else doing an action or feeling an emotion, or *imagines those things* (that is, the action or emotion or indeed the other person does not need to be present). This mirroring or modelling is seen as enhancing not only empathy but also evolution.

It may be that mirror neurons, like brainwaves, can fire up in sync even when two brains are separated by a vast distance but connected by consciousness. Now isn't that an exciting thought? After all, if we are reflections in a hall of mirrors of a single cosmic reality, then it makes sense that all the parts can communicate. Indeed, it may lie at the bottom of why when we think of someone, they often find themselves thinking of us or they telephone at virtually the same time. The difficulty lies in persuading science to do the experiments that would 'prove it'. But fortunately we metaphysicians don't need 'proof' in order to utilise the idea in our intuitive, interior lives and in our conscious connection with all that is.

The enhanced empathy that results from mirror neurons might also explain why practitioners of regression and many psychics find that breathing in harmony with their client, mirroring their gestures and their language can greatly increase the success and the depth of a session, and why bringing someone to mind at the start of distance seeing or healing facilitates connection.

The bicameral mind: right and left brains

The main theme to emerge… is that there appear to be two modes of thinking, verbal and nonverbal, represented rather separately in left and right hemispheres respectively….

Roger Sperry

Even though views of the brain are changing due to scanning and imaging research to map the brain, all metaphysicians would assert that consciousness is not confined to the brain and many neuroscientists would probably disagree. In metaphysics, one part of the brain is specifically orientated towards psychic connection. The human brain has four parts to it: the left and right hemispheres and the front and rear brains. The rear brain is the oldest, holding both personal and collective memories, and is concerned with autonomous bodily functions such as breathing but may have connections to the intuitive body–mind that registers physical sensations as a part of knowing and which also holds ancestral and past life memories.

The left and right hemispheres appear to be concerned with different ways of thinking and perceiving the world and utilising them in this way assists psychic development.[34] The left brain thinks in straight lines, the right in starbursts. The left brain 'gets a grip' while the right, is imaginative, psychic and, like a muscle, can be strengthened with use, which is what this book is all about. How you communicate psychically is closely related to which hemisphere of your brain is the most active. Left brained people are precise and organised and value intellect and reason over intuition, whereas right brained people tend to be more visual and creative and value intuitive responses. The hands often do the talking when words fail the right brained person – and they frequently confuse left and right. The left hemisphere is logical and rational. Where the right brain will make a huge intuitive leap and rarely knows how it got its result, the left brain reasons things through a step at a time. The left side of the brain dislikes complexity and ambiguity, the right side thrives on it.

If you are left handed, you are more likely to use your right brain (the right hemisphere controls the left side of the body) and this in turn may affect your career. Many musicians, artists and actors are right brain dominant and 40% of architects are left handed. This is not surprising as it is the right brain that handles geometry and spatial awareness and the left hand links to the right side of the brain.

Left brain	**Right brain**
Rational	Emotional
Logical	Illogical
Linear	Random
Sequential	Simultaneous
Fact focused	Imagination focused
Intellectual	Creative
Analytic	Synthetic
Verbal	Non–verbal
Safe	Takes risks
Practical	Impetuous
Time orientated	No conception of time
Relies on sensory input	Does not need sensory input
Mathematical/digital	Spatial
Detail orientated	'Big picture' orientated
Pattern perception	Meaning

Relates to:

Left brain	**Right brain**
Reality	Fantasy
Strategies	Possibilities
Linguistics	Music and the arts
Intellectual processes	Feelings and emotion
Syntactical Language	Symbols and imagery
Categories	Integral wholes
Boundaries	Unity
Math and science	Philosophy, religion
Past and present	Present and future

Left or right brain dominance

Although the theory of right and left brain dominance has fallen out of favour somewhat lately following on from sophisticated brain scanning, it still works efficiently for stimulating psychic abilities. The idea is that people use one side of their brain rather more than the other, although some people have balanced hemispheres. If you use your right brain, you will be artistic, perceptive and feeling orientated. Visualisation will be easy. You will resonate to metaphors and myths. That gives you a head start when it comes to communicating with your psychic awareness.

To assess which brain hemisphere you use, stop reading now and tick the appropriate boxes below.

Are you left or right brained?

Tick the boxes that best describe your thinking processes (you can tick boxes according to what you are doing at any one time):

List 1		List 2	
Safe	[ ]	Innovative	[ ]
Linear	[ ]	Holistic	[ ]
Word–orientated	[ ]	Visual, non–verbal	[ ]
Logical	[ ]	Non–rational	[ ]
Analytical	[ ]	Looking for synthesis	[ ]
Pedantic	[ ]	Open minded	[ ]
Intellectual	[ ]	Imaginative	[ ]
Practical	[ ]	Idealistic	[ ]
Symbolic	[ ]	Metaphoric	[ ]
Judgemental	[ ]	Feeling–orientated	[ ]
Time–orientated	[ ]	Outside time	[ ]
Sequential	[ ]	Boundless	[ ]
Abstract	[ ]	Spatially perceptive	[ ]
Categorical	[ ]	Insightful	[ ]
Theoretical	[ ]	Experiential	[ ]
Goal–orientated	[ ]	Process–orientated	[ ]
'Masculine'	[ ]	'Feminine'	[ ]
List orientated	[ ]	Confuse left and right	[ ]
Hands stay still	[ ]	Hands do the talking	[ ]
Practical	[ ]	Daydreamer	[ ]

If you tick mostly boxes in the first list, you are left hemisphere orientated and may need to develop your psychic side more by painting your feelings, writing stories and other right–brain activities. If you tick more boxes in the second list, you are right hemisphere orientated. You may be psychic already, but find it hard to function in the practical world. Making lists is an excellent way to bring more balance into your brain.

Equal numbers of boxes indicate that your hemispheres are balanced. This means that you can easily access your psychic ability and put it to work in a practical way. (In some people, particularly those who are left handed, the hemispheres may be reversed – the brain is wired up differently. A following exercise will reveal this.)

Touring your brain

Two simple exercises assist in identifying whether you are left or right brained. There is no right answer to the questions. They are simply there to assist you.

One side of your brain may feel more active than the other. If the left side is dominant, you will have found it much easier to write the mental shopping list than to trace the spiral – unless your hemispheres are crossed. (In this case, the right hand side will have felt more active.) If the right side is stronger, you will have struggled to write the list and, most probably, promptly forgotten it.

Exercise: Touring your brain

Close your eyes and relax. Take your attention into your brain. Move around it, left to right. Does it feel bigger or more active on one side than the other? Is one side lighter than the other or emptier? Does energy radiate from one side only? Are they both equal?

Make a mental shopping list of the things you need to buy next time you are at the store. Notice which side of your brain is active.

Now think of a point that is moving inwards, tracing a spiral pattern. Visualise it in your mind's eye. The point moves from just inside your skull to deep within your brain. Which side feels active?

A simple exercise will also reveal whether your left or right hemisphere is dominant, or whether you are equally balanced. It is as useful to have a friend read the exercise to you, or record it yourself with pauses to give you time for the images to form.

Exercise: Where's the donkey?

Settle yourself comfortably. Close your eyes and look up to the point above and between your eyebrows. Onto your inner screen a picture of a field is being projected. It is a lush green field with plenty of grass. There are wild flowers in the grass. Across the centre of the field, from one side to the other, there is a worn earth path. Walking on this path there is a man with his donkey. Notice which side they enter from, and which way they walk. Now bring your attention back into the room.

If the man and his donkey entered from the right hand side, you are left hemisphere dominant. If they came from the left, you are right hemisphere dominant. If they appeared in the middle, your hemispheres are trying to unite and are almost balanced. If you could see the field but not the donkey this means that your hemispheres are equally balanced.

Modern physics and the right and left brains

I have been discussing the difference that getting into your right brain can make with Dr Andrea Kary, a classically trained scientist who has turned to energy medicine and uses a method of deconstructing fixed beliefs that involves visualisation and body awareness. She has some useful insights into how the right and left brains relate to quantum and classical physics and affect how your psychic awareness can operate:

> *I have struggled with the whole issue of "non–duality" for the past several years. It seems impossible to even begin to achieve because of the way our brains are wired. Everything we think is about comparing, judging, measuring. But, from a physics viewpoint, classical physics versus quantum physics may be represented by our left and right brains. Our left brain is a linear processor and can process 9 bits of information per second. Our right brain is a serial processor and can process 40 BILLION bits of info per second. And of course our left brain is what compares, judges, measures... operating primarily in "duality". The suggestion has been made that when we are operating out of our left brain, we are subject to the laws of classical physics, particularly the Law of Entropy. The Law of Entropy says that all energy being sent out will dissipate, getting weaker and weaker as it goes. (This is probably why left brain affirmations are often a lot of work with little tangible change.) The right brain and the heart field may be a direct link to the world of Quantum Physics and the Zero Point Field (Field of all Potential/Possibility).*
>
> *The zero point field is the energy present in the emptiest state of space at the lowest possible energy, the closest that motion of subatomic matter ever gets to zero. It represents huge amounts of potential that does not have a fixed polarity or charge. It's a boiling sea of energy in a continual state of transformation.*

She has drawn extensively on the work of the Heartmath organization in her understanding of how intuition works:

> *The heart and brain are in continuous 2–way dialogue with the heart sending far more information to the brain than the brain sends to the heart.The signals the heart sends to the brain (the heart energy field) can influence perception, emotional processing and higher cognitive functions. Neurocardiology researchers call this system the "heart brain". The heart produces the body's most powerful electromagnetic field. The heart field is a carrier of emotional information and a mediator of bioelectromagnetic communication, inside and outside the body. There is an intimate relationship between the heart and the intuitive process. Researchers concluded from their study: "our data suggests that the heart and brain, together, are involved in receiving, processing, and decoding intuitive information.... There is compelling evidence that the heart appears to receive intuitive information before the brain." (Heartmath.org).*

She goes on to say:

> *So, maybe to really see change, particularly in belief systems, we have to get out of classical physics and our dualistic left brain. Or our left brain has to get to the point where it is OK with the way things are, or is OK with things changing. Maybe the paradox is that to see powerful change, we actually shouldn't care whether it happens or not. I've been watching this in myself as I facilitate the energy sessions. The sessions where I am actually feeling a little tired, just going with the flow or being more concerned with following my guided imagery format, than being invested in results, seems to produce the most response in people. When I get too concerned with my own ego/goals, or focusing on a specific thing I want to change, it is not so powerful. Or maybe that's where the trust comes in.*

It may, however, be that when she does a session when she is 'a little tired' she is working during an ultradian rest period that allows her intuition to function at a much greater level and she is able to let go of controlling the process. This is very similar to my own view that once you have set an intention or a process in motion, you need to let it go. To invest no more emotional energy in the outcome otherwise you interfere in the process.[35]

Confusing the left brain

Putting your left brain into a state of disorientation where it gives up trying to think linearly assists your right brain to become more dominant and do easily what the left brain cannot. So, if you want to stimulate your psychic awareness, confusing your left brain can kick–start the process. This can be done by using your non–dominant hand (that is, the hand that you do not normally write or draw with) to draw an everyday object such as a chair that is upside down and therefore not familiar. Concentrate on drawing the spaces rather than the chair itself. The intent is not to draw a perfect picture but rather to trigger a right brain response so don't be critical, just draw. The exercise works even better if you can ask a friend to present the upside–down object to you to draw.

Exercise: Right brain problem solving

Think about a problem or question to which you would like a solution. Set it out logically, step by step and try to think of an answer.

Now take an everyday object such as a chair and turn it upside down. Look at it carefully. Take your mind round the hard edges and look at the shadows and angles. Keep thinking about your problem. Then, using your non–dominant hand, draw the object in front of you in as continuous a line as possible drawing the spaces you see rather than the hard edges.

You will find that you stop thinking about the problem and, as you relax and let your right brain take over, the solution will rise to the surface of your mind.

Brain synthesis

Ideally both brains work together in people with optimum mental ability. This coordinating ability may be the key to superior intellectual abilities.

Dan Eden [36]

Balancing the brain hemispheres is achieved by activities that stimulate the under–used side. If you are a dreamy right brained person, make lists, do your accounts or Suduko, read a map or write a business letter. This will stimulate your left brain. If you are a pragmatic left brained person, you can deliberately choose a right brained way of expressing yourself. Listen to music, daydream, write an imaginative story, draw with your eyes shut. Left brained people tend to find it hard to express emotions. If you draw, using colours and patterns, you will be able to access your feelings more easily. You can visualise your hemispheres into balance. If you find visualisation challenging, use Lemurian Quartz or a Tourmaline wand to 'stitch' the two sides together. Or you can simply place Eudialyte in the crown chakra and let it balance the hemispheres for you.

Exercise: Balancing the hemispheres

Take your attention to the middle of your head, going from your forehead to the back of your head and back again. Immediately below this line is where the two hemispheres unite. Imagine that there is a zigzag line of light moving from the front of your head to the back. This light stitches together the two halves of your brain and stimulates the neural pathways that cross between the hemispheres. Picture the light flashing backwards and forwards across the pathways, uniting the different parts of your brain. Let the light continue its work until the two sides feel balanced and in harmony.

Repeat this exercise twice a day for a week and you will see an enormous difference.

This exercise brought up a question from my editor who is always very intuitive but who also has to be extremely focused and anal most of the time due to her work. She said 'I find there is always constant oscillation, a zigzag motion going on in my head and I've never heard it described until this bit. How do I stop it so there is a sense of calm? I find it almost impossible to switch off.' This made me stop and think, so I gave her some options to work with – there is no substitute for personal experience. Auralite 23 crystal had not been discovered at the time, if it had I'd have suggested that as it's brilliant. It switches off the brain in mid sentence even in the most hyperactive and talkative person. I've also found that Rhomboid Calcite, Blue Selenite or Bytwonite placed over the third eye has the same effect. The effect is heightened if you place a drop of two of Petaltone Greenway essence on it. Place it over your third eye for instant stillness and mental balance.The options were:

- Take your mind to the front end of the zigzag and gently bring it round in a horizontal circle so that the zigzag smoothes out and quietly encircles your brain at about the level of the third eye. Allow the 'thread' to slowly disappear into your third eye and coil into the calm still centre point of your brain. This allows your mind to switch off and achieve a peaceful sense of calm and non–doing.
- When you need to start thinking again, ask your bi–cameral mind to work in harmony with itself without the need for the constant zig–zagging.
- Take your mind to the front end of the zigzag and gently pull the energy thread out of your third eye and down the front of your body until you read the dan–tien just below your navel. Curl the energy thread into your dan–tien where it can be stored until you need the mental energy.

- Imagine that at the centre of your mind a lotus flower is opening petal by petal. As the flower opens, it draws the zigzag of energy down into its depths so that it reaches a still, calm place.

The feedback was that number one worked brilliantly so the other two hadn't been needed. If you have a problem settling your mind you can always combine the zigzag stitching the two halves of the brain followed by one of the 'zigzag swallowing' exercises to achieve total peace and harmonious balance. (See also entering a meditative state with ease).

I have also found that deliberately opening the base chakra and putting your grounding cord in place before starting any kind of meditation, visualisation or brain synthesis can be very helpful as it anchors you into everyday awareness and yet allows you to reach expanded consciousness at the same time.

10
Body Awareness

My beliefs I test on my body, on my intuitional consciousness, and when I get a response there, then I accept.
attributed to D. H. Lawrence

One of the most ancient of oracles, mentioned in early Mesopotamian texts over four thousand years ago, is that of interpreting 'audible oracles of the belly'. Diviners from that time valued the strange gurglings and rumblings that, for the most part, more 'civilised' communities today find embarrassing and try to excuse. A Mesopotamian would simply have assumed that his body was speaking. It is now time to let your body speak.

Body talk

The language the bodymind uses is surprisingly simple to understand.
Debbie Shapiro

Your body will have been trying to communicate with you psychically all your life. Most people are familiar with the notion of body language: the unconscious stance that says so much about how a person feels. If you observe someone hunched up, covering their solar plexus with one hand and an ear with the other, not only are they not liking what they are hearing, they are none too happy about the vibes that someone is giving off. But you can also get those shudders down the spine and queasy feelings when you meet someone new who turns out to be not so nice. However, body talk goes deeper than this and it's not only the signals from your own body you need to watch out for.

Many people unconsciously grimace or twitch when they hear or speak a lie or something that does not ring true for them. A pain in the neck can indicate someone around who is exactly that. If you can bring these unconscious reactions to your attention, you can tune into your body's intuitions and learn to recognise its signals. To do so, you will need the help of an observant and perceptive friend.

Once you have your friend's observations, repeat the exercise trying to be aware yourself of your body's responses.

Exercise: Body reaction appraisal

Prepare in advance a list of statements, some of which you strongly agree with, others with which you strongly disagree; some of which are lies, some truth. Include several 'yes' or 'no' questions to which you will not give a verbal answer but will think the replyin your mind.

First you, and then your friend, will read out your list.

Ask your friend to closely monitor your body's reactions. Paying attention to such things as jerks, rumblings, grimaces and twitches.

Small signals will be important. For instance, the left index finger could twitch for yes and the right for no.

Expanding body awareness

Research has shown that the heart communicates to the brain in four major ways: neurologically (through the transmission of nerve impulses), biochemically (via hormones and neurotransmitters), biophysically (through pressure waves) and energetically (through electromagnetic field interactions).

Heartmath Org.

Develop the habit of paying attention to what your body is telling you at all times. The major areas of psychic response, beyond finger twitches and the like, are in your gut and solar plexus or through headaches or yawning when you're not tired.

- Next time you are in the middle of a conversation, stop paying attention to what is being said. Half close your eyes and let them go out of focus. Bring your attention into your body and pay attention to what it senses is going on, taking your mind down to your solar plexus and gut.

After a while, this becomes automatic and you will act on psychic information received in this way without thinking about it.

The body scan

One of the easiest ways of getting to know your body and learning to listen to it is to make a regular, daily scan. Not only will it help your body communicate any dis–ease it may be feeling, but you will also become much more aware of your body when it speaks to you at other times too.

Exercise: Body scan

Before you get out of bed in the morning, lie quietly for a few moments. Feel your body resting quietly, the weight and pressure where it touches the mattress, the areas where it is hot or cool, relaxed or tense. Be with your body.

Now slowly scan from the top of your head down to the tip of your toes, letting your attention move down without judging or assessing, simply be with what is and noticing how each part feels. Notice any noises or gurglings, twitches or lack of sensation. Allow your body to speak as it will.

This scan can be repeated during the day or at night just before you sleep, at first you will need to give it your attention but it will become easier as the communication is established and you automatically monitor the feelings your body has. You can also biomanipulate your brainwaves by instructing your body to enhance your gamma waves to optimum functioning for you during the day – gently tapping over your third eye or at the base of your skull whilst repeating 'gamma waves to optimum' helps you to do this.

Bodily psychic awareness

> *Get out of your head and into your body so that your body can respond spontaneously from the body–mind not the intellect.*
>
> *Judy Hall*

Body responses can be highly psychic and very intense, as we have seen from St Teresa's description of her encounter with an angel. If you have ever had a gut feeling or felt like something has smacked right into the centre of your being, you have had a psychic intuition via body awareness. If you have ever entered a room and the hairs on the back of your neck stood up, your body was psychically reacting to an unseen presence or to danger. If you have ever held an object belonging to another person and had a shudder run through you or felt a frisson of excitement, you have had an instinctive body response.

Psychic body responses

- gut feeling
- hairs standing up or skin prickling
- body 'clicks' as though two things have come together
- heat beat changes – races or slows down
- breathing changes – deepens, slows, speeds up

- dizziness
- queasiness
- breathlessness
- anxiety/agitation (ceases on tuning in)
- sudden calm, a feeling of being enclosed in a silent bubble
- sinking sensation or heaviness in belly or legs
- hearing becomes acute
- eyes go slightly out of focus
- deep yawning when not tired

These physiological responses occur through the psychobiological systems of the body. Quantum research has shown that cells communicate with each other – not only in the body but across vast distances – *and that they transcend space and time*. Past, present and future have no place in the quantum field (see chapter 16). Research has also shown that the cells in our body, our skin and especially our heart, respond to a stimulus *several seconds before it occurs*. That is, they access information *before* the event not after it.[37] It appears that the heart receives a stimulus several seconds before it reaches the brain but that even the brain and the autonomous nervous system can anticipate an event. In what has been called 'anomalous anticipatory skin response', research 'participants generated significant galvanic skin conductance responses before engaging in higher risks even though they were not consciously aware of the higher risk.' [38] They showed what was called 'body knowledge' or 'body cues'. So it should be no surprise that our bodies are innately psychic and the physiological response will most probably be bound up with the dominant perception mode (kinaesthetic, aural, visual etc.). This is a carry over from the earliest times, before speech had been invented, when it was essential to be totally tuned in to the natural world and to respond before an event occurred. This survival mechanism was the basis of all intuition.

The Bodymind

The body does more than read vibrations or react in an instinctive way. The body has what Ken Dychtwald christened 'the bodymind'. This is an awareness of its own that can communicate its psychic sensitivities directly through the body. To Dychtwald, the body is a highly intelligent, all–knowing system with far more potential than it is usually given credit for, as he puts it, 'I view the bodymind as the evolutionary storehouse for all of life's potentials'.

It is possible that this bodymind has its seat in the heart – valued by the ancient Egyptians as the seat of the soul and the spiritual self. As we have seen, researchers have found that the heart has its own electromagnetic field that can communicate its perceptions – picked up before an event occurs – to the brain and it is possible that this same field may also be implicated in the minute muscle changes that occur during dowsing and kinesiology.

Posture

There is another way in which the body can be involved in your psychic ability. Your posture may affect how clearly you receive psychic impressions and how efficiently your psychic sensitivity and energies can operate. When I was first sitting in circle to learn clairvoyance, we had to sit on hard, very upright chairs 'so that the energy could flow straight up the spine'. However, I noticed that when I was doing psychic readings or regressions, I instinctively chose a chair that allowed me to lean back and expand my belly rather than scrunching it up. This helped me to work much more efficiently. During clairvoyant demonstrations I noticed that some people liked to march up and down 'getting the energies up'. Such activity merely exhausted me! I needed to drop into a deep quiet space within myself for any psychic work, which meant my body had to be totally relaxed and I channelled energy through my belly to assist the healing, the regression or the seeing that was taking place. I find the same thing happens when I'm running a workshop or giving a talk. I simply have to sit down comfortably so that the energies flow freely.

An occupational therapist who was advising a friend of mine who has Parkinson's Disease said 'if you get muddled or forgetful, sit down. The brain and the feet can't work together with this condition'. It worked brilliantly for her and I feel that it is wisdom that applies to my own body when doing psychic work. I connect through my feet and the base chakra to the earth and then up through the higher chakras to spiritual realms and that connection is broken if my brain has to think about balancing on two feet at the same time. So, if you are having difficulty in getting clear impressions or in tuning in to your body try altering your posture. If you've been sitting in a very upright position, slouch. If you've been slouching, try sitting up. And if you're one of the marching brigade, trying slowing down and perhaps even sitting down. Or get up and walk. It allows your body to receive information in a different form. You'll soon learn to recognise when your body has dropped into that still silent space in which your intuition can speak.

Harnessing bodily reactions

When you learn to dowse, a whole new world of possibilities is opened up.
Wilma Davidson

Dowsing is one of the fastest ways of tapping into your body's psychic awareness. You can use rods, pendulums or the like. But it is possible to dowse without any equipment at all, just by using your fingers or your body. As with most metaphysical activities, no one quite knows how dowsing works. It has been suggested that the subconscious mind, which can move beyond space and time to access information not available to the conscious mind, 'twitches' muscles that suddenly jerk dowsing rods upwards or sideways, or cause a pendulum to rotate. It may be difficult to believe that a twitching muscle can create the complex star patterns that some pendulums trace but it is possible to accept that the subconscious mind can control your fingers, holding them firm if the answer is yes but releasing them if the reply is negative. You can take advantage of this simple method of accessing guidance to all kinds of questions, including testing your food, vitamin supplements and such like to see if they will be beneficial for you or not. Remember to regularly cleanse your dowsing tools as you would a crystal.

Finger dowsing

There is nothing magical about finger dowsing – although it often looks like magic. The power of psychic awareness to hold your thumb and finger together for a 'yes' answer and to let them part for a 'no' has no logical explanation. But you can replicate the action time and time again and finger dowsing is a reliable method of contacting your psychic awareness. It is an excellent way to check a course of action and to guide your day to day life.

Exercise: Finger dowse

Hold the thumb and finger of your right hand together to form a loop. Now interlock the thumb and finger of your left hand through the loop to make a chain.

Ask your question clearly, precisely and unambiguously. It must be phrased in such a way that it will have a straight 'yes' or 'no' answer It does not have to be spoken aloud, although it can be, but your mind must be focused as you ask the question.

Try to pull your hands apart. If they hold, the answer is yes. If they part, the answer is no.

Pendulum dowsing

> *Dowsing is an amazing gift from our Creator, it's 'Free', and is available to all of us to answer questions about our food, health and everyday problems in our life.*
>
> *Wilma Davidson* [39]

Using a pendulum is an excellent way to locate lost objects, to ask advice from your inner guidance, to check out information and to answer virtually any yes/no or timing question. If you want to identify food allergies, or choose remedies, or oils you can list the possibilities, run your finger down, and stop at the one that says yes. You can use this method to make other choices.

You need to be strongly focused and to phrase your question correctly. If not, the pendulum will return to neutral or the energy will go out of the swing. Before starting a dowsing session it is usual to check if it is alright to dowse and ask that the dowsing be for the highest good of all concerned.

Clarity of intention, focus and trust are essential for good dowsing. The answer may not yet be settled, in which case the pendulum will reflect the uncertainty. An unclear response often indicates that you are not asking quite the right question. You need to be precise and avoid ambiguity. Having asked your question, do not keep checking. Trust!

You can use a purpose made pendulum of wood, metal or stone but if you do not have a pendulum, any suitable object on a chain or cord can be used – wedding rings on cotton were traditionally used to determine the sex of an unborn child. If you get incorrect answers, check that your pendulum is energetically clean and that wishful thinking is not clouding your ability to dowse.

Exercise: Mastering the pendulum

Hold the pendulum between your thumb and forefinger with about a hand's breadth of chain hanging down. Wrap the spare chain around your fingers so that it does not get in the way. Begin by programming in 'Yes' and 'No'. Set the pendulum moving backwards and forwards in a straight line. Tell yourself this is 'No.' Then set the pendulum swinging in a circle. Tell yourself this is 'Yes'. (If the pendulum hesitates or does not swing well, ask whether this is because your yes and no signals are different, then ask your pendulum to show you' yes' and then 'no'.)

If the pendulum stops or wobbles, the answer will be maybe or it could indicate that it is an inappropriate question to ask or not the time to be asking. You may also find that your yes and no signals are different, in which case note which is which.

Check out your yes and no by holding the pendulum over your knee. Ask out loud: "Is it correct that my name is '....'?" And give your correct name. The pendulum should respond with a circle if this is your yes. Then give a false name and the pendulum should respond with a backwards and forwards swing if this is your no. If your signals are different, adjust your expectation accordingly.

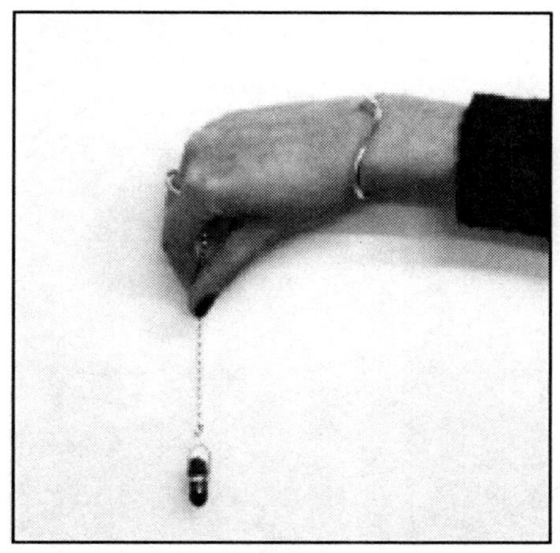

How to hold a pendulum

Map dowsing

Hold the pendulum over a map or plan and move it around slowly in a grid. This can be used to locate lost objects, to find a good place for a holiday or to chose a new area to live. You must hold a clear intent and strong picture of what you want to know to be successful. The stronger the yes swing, the more emphatic the answer.

Use your pendulum or finger dowse to:

Find:

Lost objects
Missing people or pets
Unknown information
Underground water
Buried treasure
Minerals
Oil
Electric cables

Choose the right:

- Mineral and Vitamin supplements
- Remedy/Medicine
- Food or diet
- Place to live
- Holiday destination
- School
- Career
- Car
- Crystal
- Therapist or teacher

Check:

- Potential for success
- Allergies
- Course of action
- Doubtful situations
- Someone's integrity
- Whether it's safe to go ahead
- Compatibility with partners, friends, employers
- Food suitability
- Water purity
- Chakra functioning
- Timing

Make:

- Good business and personal decisions
- Consumer choices
- Career Moves
- Health diagnoses

Answer:

- Yes/no or timing questions

Embodying psychic awareness

To believe that the body is a separately operating, purely mechanical organism is to miss the point entirely. It is to deny ourselves this source of great wisdom that is available at all times.
Debbie Shapiro

Your body knows much more than you know you know. It can be demonstrated that your body has answers to questions on which your mind has no knowledge on which to base a decision or prediction, and that your body can distinguish between true and false information even when this information is totally new to you. By dowsing or muscle testing, you can ascertain whether substances and foods are beneficial for you, and assess the outcome of a course of action or the timing of events.

Muscle testing

Muscle testing is a useful way to access your body's psychic awareness. If you are alone, finger dowsing is appropriate (see below). However, if you have a friend who can help you, you can considerably extend your access to your body's awareness. Muscle testing is particularly appropriate for health questions, but it can be used for psychological and emotional matters. It centres around the body having strength when the answer is 'yes' and the matter is good for you, and its lack of strength when the answer is 'no'.

This method can be used to test food allergies or to choose complementary remedies or supplements. You can also test how strong the organs of your body are by putting your hand on them and trying to resist a downwards push on the outstretched arm. When you become adept at muscle testing it can answer all kinds of psychic, physiological and psychological questions. If you want to know which parent had the strongest influence over you as a child, for instance, put your hand on your heart. Say 'mother' out loud and have your friend push down on the wrist of your outstretched arm. Then say 'father' and do the same. The parent associated with the weakest push down was the more dominant one – that is, the arm will stay strong for the non–dominant parent and go down easily when pushed for the dominant parent. You can test for chronic destructive emotions in the same way. Place your hand over your heart, name the emotion, have someone push down on your outstretched arm, and check the body's response.

Exercise: Muscle testing

Stand upright with your feet slightly part. Put one arm straight out sideways from the shoulder (if you are right handed you will probably find it best to put out your right arm and if you are left handed, your left arm.)

Ask your friend to stand behind of you, with a hand on top of the wrist of your outstretched arm. When your friend says: "Resist" and pushes down on your arm (without undue pressure), try to keep it as firm as possible. You should be able to resist quite easily.

Now put something in your other hand that you suspect is bad for you (such as cigarettes, sugar, chocolate, a food to which you are allergic). Place that hand over and slightly above your heart. Your friend should once again say: "Resist" and push down on your wrist. Your arm will probably feel extremely weak as it drops to your side. If it is good for you, your arm will remain firm.

Try this:

Exercise: Body knowing

Ask a friend to select two pieces of information, one true and one not (preferably something cut from a newspaper, magazine or printed from the internet so that they have minimum contact with the information) and place them in two separate plain envelopes. The friend should do this at a distance from you and send the two envelopes to you in an outer envelope.

Now ask another friend who knows nothing about the experiment to muscle test you holding first one envelope and then the other. See which one you test strong for and which one weak.

When you check with the first friend, you will find that the one you tested strong for was correct information and the one you tested weak for was false information.

Research has shown that your body will know if a statement is true or false even if you have no prior knowledge of it and even when you have not read it. You can easily demonstrate this *body knowing* to yourself.[40]

That same *body–knowing*, separating truth from fiction operates when you listen to someone speak, so learning to listen to the hidden clues your body is giving you is vital.

What do my hands tell me?

> *The past is entombed in the present, the world is its own enduring monument.... The discoveries of Psychometry will enable us to explore the history of man.*
>
> *Joseph Rhodes Buchanan*

Your fingers and palms have great sensitivity and there are chakras in your palms. This sensitivity can be used for intuitive massage, where your hands will know exactly where to go without your conscious mind intervening. Such massage is excellent for taking the aches and pains out of your partner's back, or for soothing children. However, the hand's sensitivity can be used to learn more about other people. Psychometry picks up impressions from objects that belong to someone else.

As with so much else in the psychic world, the first step is to recognise how you receive the impressions. They may come at a feeling level. You may feel exceedingly sad or highly joyful. You may shake with fear or apprehension or bubble with anticipation. You may find you see pictures or hear a voice telling you about the owner. You may have to trust yourself and start talking, you will probably be as surprised as the owner of the object at what comes out of your mouth. Most people are adept at hiding their deepest feelings, so even if the object belongs to someone you know, you can still be surprised at how they feel or what secrets they hide behind the facade. The first time I tried this I was holding the car keys of someone who was, outwardly, calm and stalwart. I immediately began shaking so hard I absolutely had to say, 'I feel incredibly anxious'. 'So do I' came the reply.

Feedback is extremely useful when you are practising, so be sure that you choose someone who will wholeheartedly share with you how accurate your impressions have been. Continue to hold the object as they talk as you may get more impressions along the way.

Exercise: Psychometry

Open your palm chakras by bringing your hands together several times and then parting them again until you can feel a ball of energy between your palms which will grow hot and tingle.

Sit quietly holding the object in your hand, hands comfortably in your lap. Breathe deeply and exhale slowly. Do this three times. Drop your shoulders. Do not strain to make things happen. Take your time, gently opening yourself up to the impressions that you receive. Notice how you are feeling. Has this changed since you picked up the object? What thoughts go through your mind?

Share what you perceive with the owner of the object. Do not try to interpret, tell them exactly the impressions you received, no matter how silly they may seem.

11
Psychic Dreaming

One certainly ought not to underestimate the gigantic importance of dreams.
H.P. Lovecraft, Beyond the Walls of Sleep

Oniromancy, the study of dreams, goes way back into pre–history. Dreams were valued as messages from the gods and many ancient temples had rooms set aside for healing or prophetic dreams. To those skilled in interpretation, the future was revealed. Today, anyone can understand dreams.

Dreams are usually thought to be messages from the subconscious mind but they can come from your intuition too. The subconscious mind is not limited in the way the rational mind is. It is psychic, reaching beyond time to embrace past, present and future. Dreams can show the root cause of illness or events, stimulate latent creativity, and highlight unconscious desires. They reveal a great deal about state of mind, drawing attention to what is ignored or rejected in the waking state. Dreams can also be a 'dress rehearsal' to try out different scenarios. It is possible to ask for a dream to answer a specific query.

The dream state

The dream is the small hidden door in the deepest and most intimate sanctum of the soul, which opens into that primeval cosmic night that was soul long before there was a conscious ego and will be soul far beyond what a conscious ego could ever reach.
C. G. *Jung* [41]

According to myth, dreams are the time when the soul leaves the body to go wandering in other realms. The Tibetans, who have been studying such matters for millennia, state that the realms the soul enters are those that it also encounters after death. For the Tibetans, mastery of dream states means that, after death, the soul can traverse these realms and be freed from the pull of reincarnation.

As a dream is an altered state of consciousness, a dream may take only a moment or two of so–called real time, and yet last for hours, days even weeks in dream–time. It can move forwards and backwards in time or outside it altogether. If you understand the stages and processes of sleeping and dreaming, you can use your dreams as a vehicle for your psychic awareness, although you don't need to be asleep to have a dream, daydreaming is a time honoured way of allowing full rein to your psychic abilities and it harnesses the ultradian resting mode discussed earlier.

Altered states

A dream is an altered state of consciousness, as is a 'bliss' experience or hypnosis. Characteristics of altered states are:

- Distorted sense of time
- Perceptual distortions
- Alterations in cognitive thinking
- Change in emotional expression
- Different meaning or significance

The physiology of dreams

> *We do not have the dream, the dream has us.*
>
> C.G. *Jung*

As the 20th century progressed a great deal was learned about the physiology of dreams and dream sleep. By measuring the brain's electrical activity during sleep, four stages were identified which cycle throughout the night. Three of them are non–REM sleep and one is the REM state. REM means rapid eye movement. It occupies twenty to twenty five percent of sleep, although the need for REM sleep apparently decreases with age. Hypnagogic images and dreams occur in this lighter level of sleep, characterised by specific physiological signs and brainwave activity.

REM sleep starts soon after you fall asleep. At this stage, it is fleeting and you quickly move through into the deeper stages. REM sleep occurs at approximately ninety minute intervals during the night but the period of REM sleep lengthens as the night progresses and is longest between 5 and 8 a.m. when the body's physiological processes of food digestion and absorption are complete. This is the most likely time for precognitive and lucid dreaming as 'processing' or 'recycling' dreams occur early in the dream cycle.

Sleep Stages

Stage 1: (sleep onset and active sleep phase). Low amplitude, fast EEG pattern, frequency 8–12 cycles per second, alpha, beta or delta waves may be present. Hypnagogic images: fast, fleeting, flowing. Myclonic movements: jerking, feeling of falling. Moves into REM sleep and dreaming

Stages 2 and 3: higher amplitude, lower frequency delta and theta waves. May contain random thoughts and slight movement.

Stage 4: Inert sleep, slow brain waves, 4–8 hz, characterised by 'spindles' in the brain's electrical pattern, approximately 50% theta waves.

These stages cycle throughout the night with REM sleep increasing in length.

Research has shown that during a dream brain cells fire as they would during a conscious experience, with two crucial differences. Movement during sleep is inhibited and external sensory input to the cortex of the brain is restricted – although feelings of cold, heat and so on can be transferred into or out of a dream. Memory and emotion continue. The subtle subliminal perceptions of esp – and the ability to move around in time – are incorporated into a dream as imagery or memory but rarely into physical movement.

REM Sleep

Rem sleep is characterised by:

- Rapid Eye Movements
- Shallow, rapid breathing
- Slow pulse
- Alteration in muscle tone
- Changes in facial muscles
- Decreased spinal reflexes
- Nasal dilation
- Emotional arousal
- Genital arousal in men and women

Researchers observing sleepers wake them whenever rapid eye movements are discerned. Dreams accessed during the early part of the night are unlikely to be psychic or lucid. A partner who wakes early and who waits until your rapid eye movements cease and wakes you gently, asking "What were you dreaming" is the best aid to stimulating psychic, lucid, dreaming you can have.

My publisher, Margaret Cahill, strongly recommends *Dreaming Reality: How Dreaming Keeps Us Sane, or Can Drive Us Mad* by Joe Griffin and Ivan Tyrrell as an excellent way to understand the way daily life can influence your dreams. By separating outside influences from dreams it becomes easier to recognise any genuine psychic messages.

Dream Chemicals

The German biochemist and pharmacologist Otto Loewi, a Nobel Prize Winner, experimented with the vagus nerve. Stimulated electrically, the nerve slowed the heart but Loewi theorised that a chemical was responsible. Unsure how to prove this, however, in 1920 a dream showed him the way. He reported that:

> *The night before Easter Sunday of that year I awoke, turned on the light, and jotted down a few notes on a tiny slip of paper. Then I fell asleep again. It occurred to me at 6 o'clock in the morning that during the night I had written down something most important, but I was unable to decipher the scrawl. The next night, at 3 o'clock, the idea returned. It was the design of an experiment to determine whether or not the hypothesis of chemical transmission that I had uttered 17 years ago was correct. I got up immediately, went to the laboratory, and performed a single experiment on a frog's heart according to the nocturnal design.*
>
> *O. Loewi (1921) "Über humorale Übertragbarkeit der Herznervenwirkung. I.**

The day following the first forgotten version of the crucial dream was, according to Loewi, 'the longest day of my life'. Waking after the second dream, he went into his laboratory at 3a.m. and followed the experimental design from his dream. He stimulated the vagus nerve of a frog, then took its blood and injected it into another frog, whose heart slowed. Isolated and analysed, it proved that the chemical, neurotransmitter acetylocholine, induced dream sleep and improved cognitive functioning. The chemical occurs naturally in lecithin but needs vitamins B1 and 5 for assimilation.

Vitamin B6 (found in meat, salmon, herring, brewer's yeast, cabbage, soya, broad beans, pears, bananas, green vegetables, wheat germ, molasses, whole grains and egg) and nutmeg have also been shown to induce dreams and promote recall as do various crystals. Sleeping with clear Quartz under the pillow is an excellent way to induce lucid dreams.

---

* *Pflügers Archiv, 189, pp. 239–242 doi:10.1007/BF01731235, "An Autobiographical Sketch" by Otto Loewi, in Perspectives in Biology and Medicine, Autumn 1960.*

The psychology of dreams

The skilful interpreter of dreams is he who has the faculty of observing resemblances.
Aristotle

Throughout the last century, psychoanalysts were fascinated by dreams, believing that these were a pathway into their patient's unconscious mind. Analysing dreams threw light on inner processes and unfulfilled wishes. According to Freud, deep–seated desires and primal images from a dark layer of the psyche slid into dreams suitably sanitised and disguised. Many of these were black impulses that could not be voiced in the light. For Jung, dreams were full of symbolism and imagery, much of which came from a collective rather than a personal level but which nevertheless could be psychic intuition talking. The opposite view said that dreams merely processed what had happened during the day: a kind of mental recycling bin. Those who thought in this way saw little of value in exploring dreams further.

'Premature Closure'

Dream work practitioners believe that dreams have, amongst other things, the function of drawing attention to where our thinking has prematurely solidified. As Jeremy Taylor put it:

> *It's comfortable to think we know it all and that we have everything sussed. But dreams challenge our assumptions, point out where we've sold ourselves short or made a mistake.*

When premature closure occurs, dreams convey messages from the psychic mind. A woman dreamt, for example, that she was on a snowmobile, travelling over ice alongside her ex–partner. He zoomed on ahead and disappeared down a crevasse. For a while she remained detached, watching to see if he would re–appear. She became very agitated and went to see if she could help. Eventually he appeared from a totally different direction, completely frozen. She immediately found herself thinking: "If only I'd gone down sooner, I might have saved him. I didn't do enough."

When she woke she realised that she had slipped back into an old pattern. Her relationship had broken up after she became seriously ill with a heart condition and realised that her partner's frozen emotional attitude towards her was breaking her heart. It had taken her months of work to detach herself. Feeling as though she had 'done it', she had relaxed. The dream graphically showed her that she was being pulled in again. Her ex–partner was working on her new house and was unloading all his emotional angst on to her once more. She was trying to help him get in touch with his feelings – frozen feelings he had no intention of facing. She rapidly detached herself once again.

The Metaphysics of Dreams

What is life, without a dream?
Edmond Rostand

When Edmond Rostand asked his question, he may not have had psychic awareness in mind but he was making a profound statement. Mystics believe that life is a dream and that dreams can give you a glimpse of a greater reality. C.G. Jung had a dream that reflected this. He was a butterfly dreaming that he was a man on earth who was dreaming that he was a butterfly. Jung asked which was the true reality? Psychic dreams offer guidance and show what is to come. Inducing dreams was a standard healing practice in ancient Egypt and Greece and they have been used down through the ages to gain insight. Many famous inventors and scientists solved their difficulties through dreams.

Dreaming Solutions

Dmitri Mendeleev spent many months working out the Periodic Table of Elements, the basis for modern chemistry. But its ultimate form was revealed to him in a dream.

Elias Howe, inventor of the sewing machine, was having problems with designing the needle. He dreamed he was chased by cannibals carrying spears with holes in the end. He repositioned the hole to the tip of the needle, and the sewing machine was born.

When the chemist Kekule could not understand how the formula he had found for benzine could possibly be correct, he daydreamed the answer. Seeing a snake swallowing its tail showed him that it was a ring. It was not the only time his answer arrived in a dream. Asleep on a bus, he dreamed of pairs of atoms attracting others 'in a frenzied dance'. He had found the basis of atomic structure.

Creative dreams

All our dreams come true, if we have the courage to pursue them
Walt Disney

Dreams can be an important part of the creative process. Milton, the 17th century poet, 'put reason aside and wrote in his sleep'. When he awoke 'his muse' would have given him thirty lines or so that he used his reason to refine. Milton recorded that his inspiration was 'not to be obtained by the invocation of Dame Memory and her Siren daughters, but by devout prayer to that eternal Spirit who can enrich with all utterance and knowledge, and sends out his seraphim, with the hallowed fire of his altar, to touch and purify the lips of whom he pleases.' In other words, he invoked what the Greeks would have called his *daimon*. Devout prayer, as with REM sleep, produces an altered state of consciousness in which psychic perception can be accessed.

An ancient Egyptian ritual can help you to know whether a dream, a psychic communication, or a situation is truth. Questions were traditionally judged by Maat, the goddess of truth weighing them against her symbol, a feather:

Exercise: Testing truth

Before you go to sleep, sit with a straight spine. Picture an old–fashioned pair of scales. On the left hand pan, place the situation you wish to know the truth about. On the right hand pan, place the feather of Maat. The pans may quickly move into balance, which indicates that the situation is in accord with cosmic harmony. They may continue to swing, which indicates that the situation is still being weighed up. If the pan with the situation on immediately sinks to the bottom, it is not in accord with truth.

(If you are kinaesthetic use your hands as the scales with an actual feather in one hand and something to represent the situation in the other. Allow your hands to 'float' and to intuitively move up or down.)

Petition Maat that, by tomorrow, the truth of the situation will be revealed. Tell yourself that if the answer comes in a dream you will remember it but that you are open to the truth revealing itself in the most appropriate way including a cledon.

The life saving dream

A dream may be precognitive. This does not necessarily mean that what you see will come to pass, it can be symbolic. Notwithstanding, it may be a timely warning that allows you to change the future.

Many years ago, I had a vivid dream. I was working for a sceptical scientist and, as he featured in it, I felt compelled to tell him. In my dream he and his wife were driving along a quiet country road when suddenly a car hurtled towards them on the wrong side of the road, into a head–on collision. No one could get out alive from a crash like that.

After the weekend, a very shaken man stood at my desk. "Yesterday my wife was driving. I looked at the road and thought 'this is the road Judy described'. At that moment a car came hurtling down the road towards us, on the wrong side. I grabbed the wheel and steered us onto the grass verge, shouting at my wife to brake. Thanks to you, we managed to avoid a head–on collision." Knowing what was coming allowed him to avoid what could otherwise have been inevitable.

Remembering your dreams

We keep dreaming the dream long after we awake
Diane Skafte

Everyone dreams. But not everyone remembers. However, you can program yourself to remember. Each night, before you go to sleep, repeat three times:

"I remember my dream when I awake."

Tell yourself that, whenever you have had a significant dream, you will naturally awake so that you can record it in your metaphysical journal. Train yourself to wake up fifteen minutes before the alarm clock goes off so that you will have time to recollect and record your dreams in tranquillity. If you can hear a chiming clock, program yourself to awake when the clock strikes five, six or seven, and to remember.

Aids to remembering

- Vitamin B6
- Nutmeg
- Clary Sage essential oil in carrier lightly rubbed on the third eye, temples and base of neck.
- Diaspore, Green Jade, Selenite or Red Jasper taped on your forehead or under your pillow.
- Abstain from alcohol or drugs
- Set the alarm clock for a half hour earlier than you normally wake

The throat chakra connection

Research has confirmed what Tibetan Dream Yoga has known for hundreds of years. Stimulating the rear throat chakra and its connection with the brain stem activates the dream state.

Exercise: Stimulate the throat chakra

Focus your attention on the back of your throat. Picture a bright white light activating this point and passing through to the stem of your brain. As you do this, drink a glass of water or hot chocolate with added nutmeg.

***If you are non–visual**, massage the hollow in the back of your neck where your spine enters your skull.*

Recording your dreams

Although some dreams involve the brain, those that take place away from the body or are psychic do not directly involve the brain but have to pass through the brain to be recalled. Record your dream as soon as you awake in your metaphysical journal, kept beside your bed, or record them. If you use a voice activated machine, you can keep your eyes closed and make the minimum of movement (research shows that movement destroys dream memory). Keep the light level low. Record everything without embroidering, judging or censoring; even fragments or odd words. The smallest details could be significant.

Some people like to record the main events of their day briefly before going to sleep so that they can immediately recognise any connection with dreams that night.

When you awake

Do not move

Pay attention to the thoughts and dream memories that go through your head.

Record your dream with the minimum of movement possible

Recording tools

- Voice–activated recorder
- Easy flowing pen
- Metaphysical journal
- Torch or small light
- Clock

Ritual dreaming

Earth is the mother of all dreams.
Euripides

Using ritual can stimulate dreams. In ancient times, temples were dedicated to dreaming and the ritual involved a long process of preparation, purification and incubation. Today, it is possible to undertake a dream ritual in the comfort of your own home. The more involved your body is in the ritual, the better chance it has of succeeding. Make all your movements slow and deliberate. Rituals work better at certain times than others so time your rituals accordingly. If you menstruate, experiment to see which part of your cycle is most fertile for dreaming – it is often the middle or just prior to your period. The dark of the moon was a traditional time for going within and dreaming, but placing a Diaspore, Moonstone or Selenite crystal under your pillow at the full moon can stimulate a powerful dream. It was traditional to undertake a fast before incubating a dream and you can follow this process if your body can accommodate it, in which case choose a weekend when you can go quietly through the day without food. Make your dream ritual a special occasion. Note the dates on your calendar in advance so that your psychic awareness can get to work out of time.

Exercise: Ritual dreaming

You will need:

Rose oil or clary sage

Candles

Crystals, Diaspore, Amethyst

Herb pillow containing Artemisia Vulgaris (mugwort) – do not use if pregnant – and Lavender

Hot chocolate with added nutmeg.

Take a long leisurely bath to which you have added rose or clary sage oil (do not use if pregnant). Burn candles and gaze into an appropriate crystal such as Diaspore. Program it so that when you place it under your pillow, it will help you to dream true and wisely. Use the throat chakra activation, drinking your spiced hot chocolate. Dress in clean night attire. Place the herb pillow on top of your usual pillows so that you are sleeping higher than normal on your right side. Place your crystal under the herb pillow. As you go to sleep picture yourself entering a dream temple, laying down on one of the specially prepared beds and moving into your dream.

Remember to offer thanks afterwards for your dream.

Dreaming an insight

I was once asked to help a friend cut the cords with her ex–partner who had left but it proved to be a very difficult exercise and she felt it was incomplete. I asked for a dream to show me the way forward. These are the notes I made at the time:

Marie had been kidnapped by Marcus. Was at a squat – old stately home but in the back servants' quarters. A woman came to dump some stuff from a room she had been clearing out. There was a beautiful cushion although it had got very dirty – sun symbol on it. Also some old gardening tools including a very complex, intricately geared cutting tool for getting into difficult places. I found Marie in a room and in the wardrobe was her bag, which had the keys to the back door in it. Large, old fashioned bag rather like a doctor's bag or briefcase but bigger. I put my arms in to get the keys out, got my arms stuck, ended up on the floor with my feet trying to push it off. Asked Marie to help but she was zombified/sleeping/hypnotised/enthralled.

Realised the tie is in a very difficult to reach place, subtle, and complex. Marie has her sun in Libra, she is still caught in the romance and hopes she had for the partnership – the 'great love of her life' – but these are no longer fresh and new. She has the key and the tool but wont/cant/hasn't used it. The cutting is intricate, many layered. She has to do the work, no–one else can.

I communicated the dream to her and we did a higher chakra tie–cutting together involving her and her ex–partner's higher selves, which successfully freed her from the strands of the old relationship and allowed her to move forward.

Incubating a dream

If you need guidance on a particular subject, incubate a dream.

Exercise: Incubating a dream

Choose a night when you can take time in the morning to process the dream. Abstain from alcohol or drugs (including caffeine and nicotine) and, if you wish, perform the dream ritual. Contemplate the issue on which you need dream guidance. Look at the solutions you have already tried, action you have taken. Ask yourself whether you are ready to resolve it. If there are emotional issues, are you prepared to let go? Tell yourself that when you awake, you will remember the answering dream. Place a Diaspore under your pillow. Then sleep. As soon as you wake, record your dream.

Expanding a dream

A powerful way to expand an intuitive dream is through dream dialogue especially if the dream seems to be incomplete or foreshortened by premature awakening.

Exercise: Dream dialogue

Close your eyes and go back into your dream at the point where it left off. Look at the dream from the standpoint of one of the characters – yourself if you featured in the dream. Ask questions: "What is the meaning of this?", "Why am I doing this?", "What insight does it give me?", "What am I hiding from myself?", "Where will this take me?"

Question other characters: "Why are you doing that?", "What does it signify?", "Do you have any guidance for me?" Then step into the shoes of another character (it does not have to be a human being). Ask the same questions. Let the dream run on and see how it ends.

Interpreting your psychic dreams

There is some ill a–brewing towards my rest
For I did dream of money–bags tonight
Shakespeare: The Merchant of Venice

The meaning of some psychic dreams will be immediately apparent whilst others are shrouded in mystery. On waking, quietly contemplate your dream and ask your psychic mind to clarify it. Say: "If I were to know what this means, it would be..." Allow answers and images to arise spontaneously. If the answer does not come within five minutes or so, put it aside. Often the answer makes itself known as soon as you stop focusing on it.

A guide to dream meanings can easily be purchased, but the most useful interpretation is the one that arises spontaneously from your own psychic mind (Ulexite crystal can aid understanding). Dreams contain puns, metaphors, colloquialisms, body language and symbolism that are personal to you and many of the characters symbolise parts of yourself – dreaming that you have a pain in the neck may indicate that someone is a pain to you but it can mean that one part of you thinks another part is a pain. Places can indicate your state of mind, weather your emotions. So, when you record your dream, add anything else it brings to mind: connections, word plays, similarities and so on. Look for themes that link to previous dreams and to situations you are involved in. Notice images from the recent past and people you know or characters who remind you of people you have known, and what the dream behaviour tells you.

Dreaming with awareness

Dreams offer themselves to all.
They are oracles, always ready to serve
As our quiet and unerring counsellors
Synesius of Cyrene

A lucid dream is a dream in which you are aware that you are dreaming and, as you become adept, can influence the course of the dream. Lucid dreams belong to the category of psychic experiences now known as EHEs (exceptional human experiences). Many lucid dreams start, or end, as flying dreams and may be linked with out–of–body experiences. Dreaming with awareness is extremely powerful and can have great healing properties. It expands personal reality and transcends limitations. You become aware of the nature of your true self. Skilful lucid dreaming means that waking consciousness can be maintained during dreams, and dream awareness can be carried into waking consciousness. Sometimes, when you become expert at lucid dreaming, it can be difficult to know which is which as you will move fluidly between dream awareness and waking consciousness and may, at times, seem to be living parallel lives through the lucid dreaming process – this can be used to try out different solutions and choices or to change patterns and outcomes but remember to anchor yourself back into everyday reality at the end of a session.

Facilitating a lucid dream

Researchers into lucid dreaming use a red strobe light to remind a dreamer that he or she is dreaming. But there are ancient techniques for inducing lucid dreaming.

- **Hand signals**: Whilst intuitive and lucid dreams usually take place away from the physical body, nonetheless in the dream you will usually have a dream–body. The classic way of inducing a lucid dream taught across all traditions for thousands of years uses a body signal. Before you go to sleep, tell yourself that when you see your hand (or your feet) in a dream, you will know that you are dreaming and will continue the dream in a lucid way.
- **Program a lucid dream**: As you fall asleep tell yourself: 'I am aware I am dreaming, I am conscious of my dream. I know I am dreaming. I step into my dream.'
- **Tibetan dream yoga**: Tibetan Dream Yoga is an ancient way of facilitating and gaining control of a lucid dream. Practitioners are not allowed to lie down. They are put in boxes too small to stretch out in. Propping yourself high on pillows, on your right side, and placing a brick wrapped in a towel at your feet so that you cannot stretch out simulates this method.
- **Crystal lucidity**: Use Danburite or Moonstone, especially at full moon. A gem essence made from the stone is particularly effective if sipped before you go to bed.
- **Awaken yourself**: Researchers found that waking up two hours earlier than you would normally rise, getting up and being active for an hour or two, and then going back to

bed was effective in instigating lucid dreaming. Once you become adept, shorten the period you are awake until lucid dreaming arises naturally during sleep.

- **Fall asleep again:** When you awaken from an early morning dream, go over the dream telling yourself that next time you dream, you will be aware of it. Let yourself fall back to sleep.
- **Visualise as you fall sleep**: You can find yourself stepping effortlessly from visualisation into a lucid dream. Go into your favourite place and proceed from there.
- **Put yourself into alpha**: Visualise your name printed in dots and then the words LUCID DREAM also in dots to induce alpha brainwaves.

Controlling a lucid dream

Once you become aware that you are dreaming, remind yourself that you are. At regular intervals say to yourself: 'This is a dream' You can go along with the dream whilst you get used to the situation. As with out–of–body experiences, you can direct yourself to different places. Some people find that closing their dream–body eyes and opening them again transports them to where they want to go – although it may take you back to your bed. (If so, remind yourself it is not time to wake up yet and move away again.) It is easier, certainly in the initial stages, to make small, gradual changes and to use the people you meet in your dreams to assist you.

The people you meet may surprise you. It can be helpful to remind yourself that you are indeed dreaming and that this is your experience. These people have no independent life within your dream, you are dreaming them. However, you can use their wisdom and expertise to solve problems, find creative possibilities, obtain healing, guidance and so on. An extremely powerful technique, once you are an adept, is to call into your dream anyone with whom you have a problem. Working it out in your dreams will transpose into your outer life. You can also use a lucid dream as a rehearsal for an event still to come.

Dream paralysis

Sometimes you will encounter the distressing condition known as dream paralysis. You awake, or want to wake, but your body will not move. It is as though you are set in concrete. The easiest way to move out of this state is to twitch your little finger just the tiniest bit. That will release your muscles. Or, pay attention to the breath passing through your nostrils or the beating of your heart. Allow that flowing movement to increase until you are released.

Meeting the dream healer

If you have a problem with your health, you can invite into your dream a Dream Healer to give you exactly the treatment you need for maximum well being. Some of the treatments can be unusual to say the least but remind yourself that you are dreaming. The benefit when you wake is worth whatever it takes in the dream. (This technique can be adapted for any situation where you require assistance or knowledge from the Dream Teacher.)

Exercise: Meeting the dream healer

Holding an Amethyst in your hands to enhance your visualisation abilities, close your eyes. Breathe gently and evenly, establishing a natural rhythm.

Without opening your eyes, raise them so that you are looking at your third eye in the centre of your forehead. Picture this eye opening and revealing a beautiful place into which you can step. (If you find this difficult initially, place your Amethyst on your third eye to stimulate its opening.) Spend a few moments exploring and enjoying this beautiful place. As you explore, you will become aware that there is a figure joining you. This figure is the dream healer (it is not necessarily human).

Explain to the dream healer exactly what kind of healing you need, whether it is physical, emotional, mental or spiritual. If you don't know the source of your dis–ease, then ask the dream healer to tune in and give you the right kind of healing. Request that tonight you will receive healing and that on waking you will recall your dream clearly and will know exactly what it means.

Place your Amethyst under your pillow. Tell yourself firmly that you will be meeting the dream healer and that you will remember your dream.

When you wake up, write the dream down and any insights you have about it.

12
Reading the Akashic Record

In the days before I knew of pre–birth planning, I felt sympathy for others who appeared to be less fortunate than I, pitying a homeless person on the street, for example. Now aware that this seemingly 'bad' experience may have been planned, I feel only deep respect.
Robert Schwartz , Courageous Souls

The Akashic Record is a cosmic memory bank containing all that has been and all possibilities that are to come. The concept of an Akashic Record has existed for at least five thousand years. In ancient Mesopotamia, it was called The Tablets of the Destinies and in India the Akasha or cosmic sky. The Akashic Record is a not a record of a fixed fate but rather an outline map of a soul's journey with all the potentialities that opens up. We can view the Akashic Record as a hologram of all that is and might be – it is not in any one place as it permeates our whole universe but we can nevertheless access it as though it were indeed a Hall of Records. Our souls are connected to this hologram, each carrying a small piece of the hologram within that contains the whole. Souls play out the destinies we planned for ourselves in the space between lives – the interlife – although this plan may be powerfully affected by the karma we have accrued and by soulplans from others lives that, although outdated, still overlay our soul's intention. So, through accessing the Akashic Record we can see both what we have been (our previous lives) and what we might be (our potential futures depending on what choices we make). Many seers connect to the Akashic Record when doing readings of various kinds, although they may call it Spirit, Source and so on. I access the Akashic Record via my client's higher self and soul memory when using far memory to explore my client's past lives.

Science is finally catching up with the idea of the Akashic Record through the connectivity hypothesis which says that there is a subquantum energy field in which everything that happens has been holographically – and permanently – recorded. Quantum physics can also be used to 'explain' how future possibilities are also encoded in this field. The term 'Akashic Experience' is being adopted to cover many experiences previously termed anomalous, peak, psi or 'paranormal'. Rather than simply being a record that can be accessed, the term Akashic Field now covers much of what I would term psychic: telepathy, intuitions, creative insights, healings, near death experiences, clairvoyance and other non–sensory and spontaneous experiences. As Ervin Laszlo puts it, 'in a popular, though overused and misused formation, the Akashic experience is a lived experience in the extra– or non–sensory mode.'

Fortunately, however, we don't have to understand how the field can exist nor how it works in order to be able to utilise it for psychic work. The first method is one I've taught for over forty years – having been myself taught it by my mentor Christine Hartley, who stated it was ancient but had been revived by her magical mentor Dion Fortune. While everyone 'sees' the Record in their own way, the underlying experience is always the same. It is a connection in to what we can call the wisdom of the cosmic mind or the cosmic memory field. Successful reading of the Akashic Record needs practice and becomes much easier as time goes by. As Christine always emphasised, it is important to distinguish between what you really see and what you'd like to see. As a writer herself Christine was all too aware of wanting to bring the threads together into a coherent whole, which is when the conscious mind starts to intervene and clarity is lost. It is important to record your impressions immediately, as I do, by speaking or writing them at the time.

As you become more competent at reading the Record you can use it to answer many psychic questions and to develop your connections with guides and your higher self, perhaps attending the interlife planning meeting where you set out the outlines for your present life and exploring the lessons you were intending to learn. You can also read the record for someone else if you have their permission.

True or not true?

Knowing your past lives can be extremely useful as it pinpoints patterns, root causes, unfinished business, blockages, soul purpose and so on. People always ask 'but is it true' and I reply 'does it matter?' What a past life seeing, accessing far memory or reading the Akashic Record does is to give you an overview, a picture of your soul history and that to me is more important than whether it is actually, factually true or not. I think the higher self presents the information in a way which is easily understood by the small self that is in incarnation. What you need to do is ask 'is this true for me?'

Accessing the record

One of the best things about reincarnational teachings is that gives us a long sense of our spiritual journeys, so that we can be more patient and understanding. It also supports a powerful tolerance.

William Bloom

Christine Hartley worked in such a deep state of inner withdrawal that she rarely remembered her perceptions afterwards – having to play the tape back or read the notes to recall her 'seeings'. Her concentration was so intense and so inwardly focused that, in a session in London during the war, she once failed to hear an air raid siren to which, as a part time air raid warden, she would usually respond automatically. I've known people not hear a fire alarm test going off at full blast in a building in which they were in regression and I rarely hear anything around me. I found it easy to train myself to either write or speak, without going so deep that I lost awareness, so it becomes, in my terminology, 'a straight through job'. I rarely retain the memory afterwards, which is beneficial as I could not possibly hold onto all the impressions I receive in the course of a year let alone a lifetime. Nowadays too I rarely actually 'see' anything and I simply have to trust that the impressions are there and start speaking, whereupon it all spills out. At other times I clearly see a figure and have to describe how it is dressed before I can continue.

When you first begin, you'll find that you have what Christine called 'practice runs'. That is, you'll get glimpses but they may not relate to the time period or the person you are interested in. I explain this as rather like tuning one of those old–fashioned television sets in. You get a lot of static and snow, and a few glimpses of images that move on quickly before you can fix them in place, and then gradually you can tune into an image, hold it and have the scene move on slowly enough to describe it. Because moments of great emotional trauma and soul dramas seem to make the biggest impression on the record, these are what tend to be seen first and it is possible to tune into a specific historical event without actually having been there and certainly without being a major player *although it may seem as though you were*. If you find a scene distressing, remember that you are seeing it objectively at a distance, not reliving or embodying it. As with all past life work, the scene can be reframed into a different outcome if it needs healing, and the same goes for if you are seeking to see the future rather than the past. You can then attune to the various potential futures that exist in each moment – every one the outcome of a different choice. This also works well if you want to see the potential outcomes of choices you or someone else has to make in the present life.

I have adapted Christine's basic method – concentrated withdrawal onto the inner planes and focusing the third eye – to incorporate an 'assistant' who would guide me to the right chapter of the Record as it were. I use a connection to my higher self, who then contacts the higher self of the other person – and I would never read the Record for someone for whom I don't have permission whether from the person themselves or their higher self in an emergency. These days I don't actually have to go to visit the Record in order to tune into the information – and anyway, as I believe we hold a hologram of the Record in our soul, it's more a case of withdrawing from the outside world and there it is – but I did when I started and so that's how I teach this method. Once you become practised you can adapt the method to suit yourself and the information you are seeking.

Christine advocated sitting relaxed in an upright easy chair with the spine fully supported, without shoes and wrapped in a cloak to shut out the outside world. I often semi–lie down as I find my belly is very much connected into this work and sitting upright compresses the energy point and I don't need the contact with the earth through my feet that Christine used (I remain connected through my base chakra and grounding cord). You will need to experiment for yourself as to which works best for you. She, as I, also found it useful to have a companion with you when you first try this and it can be very productive to have a small group who meet regularly. Obviously it is helpful if companions are psychically aware, but it is more important that they possess common sense – and a few instructions such as 'don't try to yank me out suddenly if you think I'm contacting a traumatic scene', 'treat me gently and only intervene if I ask you' (you can arrange a signal such as lifting your hand to indicate you need help). What is essential is that this companion is appraised of the script which is the way to bring you back safely should you wander too far.

Exercise: Calling back

Withdraw your attention from that scene and disconnect your energies and awareness. Make your way back to the lift, asking your guide or higher self to accompany you. Step into the lift and press the button for 'everyday reality'. The lift will bring you down through the vibrations until you reach the place you started from. Step out of the lift and be aware of leaving the past (or the future) behind. Cross the meadow until you reach your starting place.*

Slowly return your awareness to the room, come into the present moment [If appropriate state the date and time]. Take a few deep breaths and then slowly open your eyes. Wiggle your fingers and toes. Put your feet firmly on the ground and make sure your feet make a strong connection to the earth and that your grounding cord is in place.

**If there is any hesitancy about returning, your companion should ask if there is any unfinished business that needs attention and then find a creative way to deal with it if there is – guides and higher selves are usually all too willing to offer assistance with this.*

Putting your shoes on, and having a cup of tea and a biscuit usually completes the process of return to everyday awareness.

As with all things psychic, sensible precautions make the whole experience much smoother. Always work in a safe space with people you trust implicitly. Christine talked of the 'borderlands' through which she travelled that contained entities that may do harm so she 'stood by to repel boarders'. She also spoke of the 'Lands of Illusion' where you may happily lose yourself in what might be or have been – what I called a fantasy in fancy dress. If you are properly protected psychically and have followed the suggestions throughout this book, you will not encounter these (if you do meet unpleasant entities use a laser wand light zapper to dissolve them or call on your gatekeeper to protect you). This method is specifically designed to bypass those realms and go straight to a safe space in which to read the Record and then to return safely. Try to train yourself to speak what you see as you see it, or if that is not possible write it down immediately afterwards.

Reading the Akashic Record

Settle yourself comfortably in a quiet place where you will not be disturbed. Turn off the phone. Close your eyes and place yourself in a pyramid of protection. Open your base chakra and let it hold you safely and gently so that you can bring the information down to earth.

Breathing rhythmically and easily, withdraw your attention from the outside world. If any thoughts pass through your mind that do not relate to this work, let them pass on by. Focus your attention on your third eye and open your inner screen (which may actually be some feet in front of you rather than inside your head).

Now see yourself in your favourite place. Feel the ground beneath your feet, smell the air and enjoy being in this beautiful place. Let your feet take you over to a small building that is away to one side.

When you reach the building, open the door and go in. In front of you you will see a lift with its doors standing open waiting for you. Inside the lift are several buttons. One is marked 'Akashic Records'. Press the button and let the lift take you up through the dimensions to where the Record is housed.

As the lift doors open, your higher self and your guide step forward to meet you. They will conduct you through the multi–media experience that is the Akashic Record. They may take out the Book of your Life for you to read, or hand you a DVD to play. They may show you the many rooms and dimensions of the Record. Simply let the experience unfold before you with your higher self guiding the process for your highest good. If you have any specific questions, put them before your guide and higher self and ask to be shown the answers as and when appropriate.

...

When you have completed your Akashic session, disconnect your energies from the scene, thank your guides and your higher self and ask them to accompany you back to the lift. Step into the lift and press the button for 'everyday reality'. The lift will bring you down through the vibrations until you reach the place you started from. Step out of the lift and be aware of leaving the past (or the future) behind. Cross the meadow until you reach your starting place.*

Slowly return your awareness to the room. Take a few deep breaths and then slowly open your eyes. Move your fingers and toes and make sure your feet make a strong connection to the earth and that your grounding cord is in place.

**If there is any hesitancy about returning, ask your higher self if there is unfinished business that needs attention and then find a creative way to deal with it if there is – guides and higher selves are usually all too willing to offer assistance with this or consult a qualified past life therapist.*

A cup of tea and a biscuit completes the process of return to everyday awareness. Don't forget to record your session in your metaphysical journal.

Some people will never 'see' the Record as vivid pictures but they will get bodily sensations and intuitions. Recording everything that you feel and sense in addition to seeing assists you in ascertaining how you will read. If you feel a sensation in any part of body or an emotion, let is grow and become stronger. Let the feeling tell you what the story is that lies behind it. Say to yourself 'if I knew what the story was it would be….' You'll be surprised how often the answer just pops into your awareness. Then let the feeling or sensation go or reframe it into something positive and joyful if it has been traumatic.

Crystals for accessing the record: Brandenberg Amethyst, Trigonic Quartz, Amphibole.

To read the record for someone else

Before you read the record for someone else there are several things to do:

- Ask their permission
- Ask their higher self to assist
- Examine your motives in offering to read, ensure that you are not simply trying to confirm something you have suspected or that they believe. Don't get caught up in hidden agendas, your own or another person's
- Always protect your spleen chakra when reading for someone else (see Psychic vampirism p.140)
- Open your higher chakras (see p.99) so that energy can flow down through them

And after you've read for them there is a further essential stage:

> **Let it go. Don't try to hold onto what you saw for them. This applies to all psychic work for other people. You are not the keeper of their information so don't try to hold on to it. Let it go or you'll get psychic indigestion.**

It is my opinion that, when regressing people, as in healing, my energy is used to facilitate the process. I was, almost always, simultaneously seeing the life they were experiencing as they regressed. There was an interaction between my consciousness and that of the other person, my soul and their soul, my higher self and their higher self. I could feel, but more objectively, the same feelings. This meant that I could assist with reframing and healing the events that occurred – this is something that needs proper past life therapy training and is not covered here. But the same thing pertains to conducting a past life reading for someone. I am engaged at a very deep level. However, I came to recognise that I needed to protect my spleen chakra and not allow my energy to be taken from there as otherwise I would be exhausted. I deliberately channelled energy through my highest chakras to facilitate the process. When the reading is complete, there is a need to disconnect.

Before you begin to read for someone else, ensure that you have the other person's permission and are connected to their higher self. Then follow the steps you took to read your own record, asking that you be shown the appropriate record for the other person and that you will be able to access only what is for their highest good and guidance. Speak or write your perceptions while you are connected as it is unlikely that you will remember them once you have disconnected and forcing yourself to do so would be detrimental to your own future well–being.

Particularly when first reading for another person, offer your findings with humility and gentleness. Say 'this is what I see, how do you feel about it?' rather than 'this is what was'. Be prepared for them to choose not to accept what you see. If this is the case examine your motives, your preconceptions and the possibility of self–deception or illusion, but do not get into self–blame, and do not allow your feelings to be hurt in any way or become argumentative or belligerent. This is not a rejection of you. It is simply that the other person cannot connect to what you say *at this time*. It may be different later. Or perhaps you are saying it in a way that they cannot hear, denial is a strong force especially if you are offering a view that is far from what they'd hoped to hear. What's true for you may not be true for them as we each live in our own reality so do not force it on them. Always show compassion for that person and what they have been through in their other lives, as you would to yourself. And, where possible, look at the potential for reframing and healing any trauma or completing unfinished business from that life.

If the other person accepts all too readily, saying something along the lines of 'Oh yes, I've always known I was Cleopatra' check out that you were actually reading the record and not tuning to their wishful thinking – and that you haven't inadvertently linked into a 'fantasy in fancy dress' which is all too easy to do if you don't keep your perceptions and critical faculties sharply focused and your common sense to the fore.

Once you've had practice at reading for other people , the preliminary stages – other than connecting to their higher self –, and the need to visualise yourself going to the records office, fall away as the higher selves will pass the information directly to you for onwards transmission.

Psychically reading a body

The ability to sense through the body can be extended to 'read' people and what has happened to them in the past, near or far. Body language tells us so much about a person but it can go further than that. Sometimes it is the small clues, the body stance or the way someone walks or wears his hair that tells you what was going on before. You pick up the clue and your psychic awareness does the rest.

The following is part of an email from one of the regular attendees on my past life astrology retreats regarding spontaneous past life seeings triggered by physical characteristics.

It was sent from an Arab country in which he works. It beautifully illustrates the combination of reading a body, aural sensing and psychic sensitivity, I've used it elsewhere but I have no hesitation in repeating it here to remind you:

> *I am struck by the number of bods here (me included!) who have had significant past lives as Jews. Two guys on the bus – both wear glasses and one studies all the time – he even walks across the road reading a book – he has a special torch in his pen. His shoulders are very rigid – I was trying to recall what you said in Principles of Past Life Therapy – then it occurred to me that the rigidity in his case comes from the Jewish thing of rocking back and forwards.....*
>
> *The other guy only needs sidelocks and he'd be perfect. His glasses are so thick – he's very short–sighted and can't even drive – wow! I can see him with his black velvet cap on – so both have PHYSICAL characteristics that stem from past life causes. The first guy I can also see as a smarmy vicar going round to people's houses for free grub. He is so ingratiating – he has a fixed smile that he must have honed [elsewhere] ....*

While I don't recommend taking yourself deep into your own past lives – or other people's – without proper training as it is all too easy to get stuck there and reactivate problems into the present life, as we've seen it is possible to allow yourself to see past personas, both for yourself and for others. This exercise is not designed to take you deeply into a past life but rather to have a glimpse of what might have been.

Each time you practise, you will be aware of more detail coming in. Remember to pass it on if appropriate, and then to disconnect and let it go. If it becomes obvious that either you or the person you are reading for has an injury or an experience that is carrying forward into the present life, then it would be sensible to consult a properly trained past life regression therapist to heal the effects of that other life. If you need a 'first aid' measure in the meantime, ask the person to picture healing, forgiveness or insight being sent to that past life persona from the higher self so that it will not carry forward. The person might also need to 'reframe' the ending, either seeing it end differently or understanding more fully why it occurred. Be sure that both of you have both fully disconnected from the experience by closing down the chakras – especially the past life chakras at the back of the ears.

Exercise: Seeing a past life persona for yourself

Stand in front of a mirror in a dimly lit room. Allow your eyes to go out of focus and look from the corner of your eye rather than straight on. Ask that you will be shown your own past lives without having to enter them, that you will see the faces superimposed over your present face in the mirror. Wait quietly until you can see and allow whatever information that wants to make itself known to rise into your awareness.

Tell yourself that when you switch the light on and can see clearly again, the past life connection and any problems that life carried with it will be dissolved and healed.

Exercise: Seeing a past life persona for someone else

Always seek permission before reading for someone else.

First of all make a note of any physical characteristics, mannerisms, figures of speech or actions you have noticed that could be clues to the other person's past lives.

Either use a photograph of the person or ask them to sit against a plain background in subdued light. Study them quietly for a few minutes, noticing their body stance and physical characteristics.

Allow your eyes to go out of focus and look from the corner of your eye rather than straight on. Ask that you will be shown their past lives without having to enter into them, that you will see the faces superimposed over their present face. Wait quietly until you can see and allow whatever information that wants to make itself known to rise into your awareness.

Tell yourself that when you switch the light on and can see clearly again, the past life connection will be dissolved and you will disconnect yourself from that person and let the memory go after passing it on if appropriate.

Connecting the higher selves

When I read the Akashic Record for someone else, I work higher self to higher self. I deliberately connect to and request the cooperation of the other person's higher self – and I never deliberately try to read the record for another person unless a reading has been requested and permission has been given, or the information arrives spontaneously without my seeking it (in which case I then have to check out whether to pass it on or not and the best way in which to do this). In this way I can be sure that I only access information that will be for the highest good of all concerned. Amphibole or Brandenberg Amethyst helps you to make a higher self contact. The following 'triangle' exercise connects the higher selves whether or not the person is actually present and is best done before reading the Akashic Record.

Connecting the higher selves

Picture a connecting cord of light that goes from the top of your head up to meet your higher self.
Then picture a cord of light connecting your higher self to the other person's higher self who is standing close to your higher self.
Finally, picture a cord of light connecting your heart to that of the other person.
When the reading is complete picture the cords of light dissolving and falling away so that you disconnect from the other person.
Thank your higher self for the assistance you received.

Disconnecting the higher selves

Whenever you have completed a reading for someone else, remember to disconnect your energies and the higher selves and to close your higher chakras. I find clapping my hands down through my chakras from above my head to my feet is a fast and effective way to release. If the sound is hollow I consciously see my connection at that level falling away.

Accessing far memory

As we've seen, reading the Akashic Record is just one way in which far memory can be accessed. Sometimes you will be able to see past lives graphically unfolding before your eyes like a film. At other times you receive impressions and glimpses. When I first began to read past lives it happened spontaneously (although I'd always had glimpses of my own). I would see a person's head disappear as I looked at them. A kind of mist would replace it and then another face would be superimposed over the top – you can use this method with photographs, see below. Opening your third eye and asking to be shown someone's lives is efficient – at first it's rather like tuning in a picture as it will be spotty and fuzzy but it will clear. Gazing into a crystal is a time–honoured way of seeing other realities. The Christos Method used forehead and feet massage to put the subject into an altered state of consciousness which sometimes took several hours, but you can do this much more quickly by stimulating the past life chakras which lie just behind your ears on the bony ridge that continues down to meet your spinal cord at the base of your skull. These chakras hold a reservoir of memory – personal, ancestral and collective. Stimulating these chakras helps you to access memories especially if you are kinaesthetic rather than visual.

Exercise: Accessing far memory

Massage along the bony ridge from the back of the ear to the hollow where your spine exits your skull and then repeat on the other side. As you do this, memories will rise up into your awareness. You may see them as though on a screen in front of you, feel as though it is going on all around you, or experience bodily sensations and impressions.

Researchers in the United States found that by stimulating the past life chakras (they didn't call them that) 'memories' of traumatic events, especially deaths, were triggered. They took this to mean that the brain was producing bizarre hallucinations. No one on the television programme which reported this – so long ago that I've forgotten what it was called – seemed to consider that it might actually be stimulating real memories. In my experience, it is the traumatic events, particularly deaths, which imprint themselves most strongly in these chakras so it is wise to have someone on hand to assist you if this occurs. Once you are in control of accessing far memory, you will move beyond this stage and begin to see life patterns and relationships.

Far memory through photographs

An excellent way of practising reading past lives is through the use of photographs. These can be of people living or dead (but remember to ask permission if it is someone you know).

Exercise: Accessing far memory through photographs

Holding the photograph in your hands spend a few moments gazing at it.
Ask your higher self to connect to the other person's higher self.
Ask your guide to assist the reading.
Let your eyes go out of focus and continue to gaze at the photo.
The face will go fuzzy and you may see another face or figure superimpose itself. Note how the new person is dressed and how they look. Ask what century they are from and listen for the answer.
Ask to be shown the appropriate past lives. These may appear on the photograph. If not, close your eyes and picture a screen inside your head or just in front of your third eye on which they will be projected. You may also need to speak, without worrying what will come out of your mouth, or to write spontaneously…
When the reading is complete, turn the photograph face down to disconnect and ask the higher selves to disconnect themselves.
Close your third eye and ensure that your grounding cord is in place. Get up and move around.

13
Expanding your Psychic Ability

Our minds have the most remarkable ability to provide those resources that we most need at any given time.

David Michie

By now your psychic ability will be working efficiently. The more you use it, the better it will function. It is then a question of building on your strengths, putting the knowledge you have about how your psychic awareness functions into practice, paying even more attention to signs and signals, and trying out new ways of stimulating your innate ability. It can be helpful to join up with one or more friends at an agreed time each week so that your psychic knowing is ready and waiting – you can do this at a distance as it makes no difference whether you are physically together or not. The following are some suggestions to expand your inner awareness, but it is more fun to make up your own – if you listen your psychic perception is sure to suggest something.

Telepathy

Telepathy is not "reading a person's mind" as most people's minds are full of a lot of junk. Telepathy is communicating with another person by thought.

Stephanie Relfe

Telepathy games can be played at an agreed time each day or in a spare moment. For this you need a partner, present or at a distance, and a pack of coloured or Zener cards.

Exercise: Telepathy

Decide in advance who will be sender and who will receive (you can change over after an agreed time). The sender should shuffle the cards and turn them face up one at a time (without the receiver seeing them). Concentrate on sending the colour or the symbol to your partner. Fill your mind with it to the exclusion of all else. The receiver sits with a quiet, receptive mind and writes down whatever floats into his or her mind. The sender will need to make a note of the card. Then change around. At the end of the time, compare notes and check the scores.

As your telepathic ability strengthens, try sending your partner messages at pre-arranged times, and intermittently at any odd moment. Remember to be receptive to any message your partner might send you.

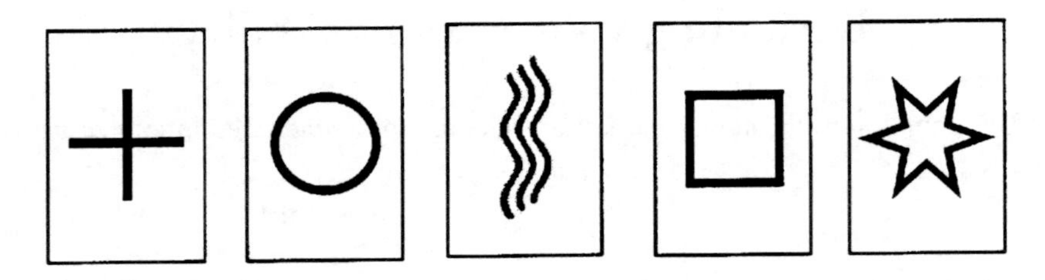

Zener Cards

Similarly, you can have a set of coloured cards or playing cards and concentrate on those, or use numbers or dots like dice.

Once you've developed your telepathic ability with your group or a specific friend, have fun sending 'psychic emails' at odd moments that have not been pre-arranged. Initially these can be simple things like 'phone' or 'text me' but as you get better at it you can expand and send information such as 'meet me at .... (remember to give a time and place)' and then turn up to see if the psychic email was picked it (it will be!). Then, move on to connecting with people with whom you haven't been practising (but be sure to do this ethically and with complete integrity, you will not benefit from prank psychic emails as they will rebound onto you). If you haven't seen an old friend in awhile, send him or her a psychic email that you'd like to be in touch again and then expand further in more creative ways.

Inner wisdom

Accessing your own inner wisdom becomes easier the more you meditate. Sit quietly and ask specific questions, or allow a stream of wisdom to rise up in your awareness. As this can easily be forgotten, record it at the time in your metaphysical journal.

Reading a sealed envelope

You can develop your ability to see beyond the norm by practising reading the contents of sealed envelopes or unopened books. This can be a useful technique with unexpected consequences. In the thesis for my first university degree I quoted from a book with extremely relevant research that confirmed a theory I was proposing but I did not reference its date.

I could not lay my hands on the book again and when I consulted the library catalogue, I could find no trace. Two years later, browsing in a bookshop I came across it. It had recently been published for the first time. When I met the author, I found that she completed the manuscript at the time I wrote my thesis. I had plucked it out of the ether. The page number and publisher I gave were correct although these had not been decided at that time. Initially, practise on actual books or unopened correspondence and then, if you have a friend to assist, move onto more complicated reading.

Exercise: Reading a sealed envelope

Sit down quietly, relax, breathe gently and bring your attention to the envelope in your hands. If you don't know who it is from, allow a picture of the person or knowledge of who it is to arise in your mind.

Picture yourself opening the envelope, unfolding the letter, spreading it out and reading it. If you cannot get it word for word, try to absorb the sense of it.

Then open the actual letter and see how you did.

Finally, disconnect.

You can adapt the above to 'read' a book. Decide in advance which page you are going to 'open' it to, picture yourself doing this and reading it. Then open the book and check it out. Remember to record the results in your journal.

Automatic writing

There are two forms of automatic writing. One is totally automatic. You hold a pen loosely in your hand – the modern equivalent being to turn on your computer – and allow it to move by itself. The other is to write down everything that passes through your mind. If you are a proficient typist, you can allow your hands to type without your thinking processes being involved. Initially the everyday mind tends to want to censor. If your mind insists on interfering, keep it occupied with a task such as counting backwards from a hundred down to one in threes or write in the dark or with a dim bulb.

Exercise: Writing automatically

Hold your pen loosely in your hand, poised over the paper. Consciously take your attention 'up' a step, lifting your awareness and opening your psychic gateways. Ask your gatekeeper to ensure that only genuine and true communication will be made. Either write the words that come into your mind or allow your hand to move rapidly over the paper – don't worry if it just looks like scribble at first.

When you have completed the writing, consciously and deliberately disconnect and bring your attention back 'down' a step, closing off your psychic gateways as you do so.

Further body awareness

If you let it, your body can be naturally psychic. Getting up when someone is approaching out of sight is natural for the body as it is an ancient defence mechanism. This can work for you if you allow it to. Whilst you are waiting for someone, tell yourself that you will step forward the minute they get to a certain point out of your sight line. Then allow your body to do this. Eventually you will never need to hang around waiting for anyone as you will instinctively know the right moment to arrive because your body will be in tune with the person you are meeting.

This ability of the body to know when someone draws near is useful if you have to walk in dark places. You can send your psychic awareness ahead to check out the energy of the place and to keep it safe. If you have to pass anyone about whom you feel uneasy, an ancient occult technique is to cloak your light so that you will not be noticed. As soon as you become aware of the approach, ask your gatekeeper 'make my light dim, make me invisible.' Remember to become visible again later.

14
Evidence for Psychic Ability?

There exists, already, sufficient evidence for the existence of [psi] phenomena which are incompatible with the known laws of physics.
John Beloff, Honorary Fellow of Department of Psychology, Edinburgh

Parapsychology tries to prove the existence of psi or esp (extrasensory perception) without necessarily acknowledging the existence of metaphysics or psychic abilities. The more research can 'prove' the existence of abilities beyond the normal senses, the more potential there is for acceptance by the scientific community of a psychic faculty. Unfortunately what scientists are looking for is a testable commodity with quantifiable, replicable results whereas an experience of expanded reality and psi states has been described as 'far more mutable, capacious, and capricious that we generally allow ourselves to imagine'. [42]

However, it might surprise you to know that the American nursing profession claims to have conducted more research into intuition than any other profession, other than psi researchers or parapsychologists, which is in itself evidence for a quiet revolution taking place within health care and the business world. [43] After Dr Melvin Morse, a paediatrician practising in Seattle, examined a significant number of accounts of near death experiences in the year 2000, he concluded:

> *NDEs and many other 'spiritual events' are real. We can, through scientific means, differentiate between mental illness, physical illness, substance-based altered consciousness, and legitimate spiritual experiences such as NDEs.*
>
> *Dr. Melvin Morse* [44]

Testing, testing

"Failure to reproduce an effect" does not demonstrate its absence.
Jessica Utts and Brian D. Josephson

When astronaut Edgar Mitchell went to the moon he took Zener cards with him. He used them to conduct telepathy experiments with earth. The results were such that, when he left the Space Program, he turned to the study of metaphysics and parapsychology, founding in 1973 the Institute for Noetic Sciences.

American Professor Charles Honorton, former director of the American Parapsychological Association, in an extensive review of fifty years research, pointed out that whilst psi research has consistently failed to find a physical basis for the phenomena, it has shown that, so far as can be ascertained in the light of current knowledge, it has a distinctly psychological basis. That is, it is a function of mind or consciousness.

At any given moment your brain is receiving and processing zillions of bits of information. If you paid attention to all of these, life would be an incomprehensible jumble. You would be in sensory overload. So, your perceptions are censored *before you become aware of them*. Your brain gives you the information it thinks you need. But your psychic mind is aware of much more – and passes this before your inner eye. It is this mind and inner eye (or ear) link that is part of what is called psychic awareness.

The corner of your eye may have noticed something. Say, for instance, it has seen a patch of wetness on your car tyre that looked as though a dog has sprayed against it. But your brain has not considered this important because it does not know that this could signify a problem with the brakes. But your mind is aware. So it gives you a dream in which your brakes fail. If you are wise, following such a dream, you check your brakes.

Major research work has been done on telepathy and remote viewing. Remote viewing, whilst strictly speaking not psychic, shows that consciousness can exist outside the body – and that it is not dependent on the brain. Consciousness is the part of human experience that science has been slow to catch onto but is now rapidly becoming one of the most talked about subjects. Researchers are, however, usually more concerned with proving that consciousness is a function of the brain or cell-life than exploring the enormous possibilities that consciousness beyond the brain opens up.

Statistics and replicability are a core issue for psi research. Scientists demand demonstrable, 'above chance', repeatable results. Stating that few psi experiments can be shown to demonstrate serious flaws, in a paper 'The paranormal: the evidence and its implications for consciousness' given at a symposium in 1996, Jessica Utts, a professor of statistics, and Brian D. Josephso, a Nobel Laureate professor of physics, pointed out an ordinary statistical analysis of 'the evidence' tended to discredit results but that significant discoveries often arise out of a results that do not fit expectations, saying:

It is possible to elicit psychic functioning in experiments with ordinary volunteers acting as subjects. Even more convincing results appear with specially selected subjects. [45]

They go on to suggest that sophisticated analysis is required, showing that a 1 in 3 success rate, above the 'by chance' rate of 1 in 4, is 'the hallmark of a genuine effect' within a 'growing collection of consistent results'. As is often the case with research, how the observer and analyser perceive the results can slew how research is reported and judged. Examining interviews with psychics, they point out that mediums claimed to be aware of a 'hierarchy of meaningful connections' but that:

Science has a poor handle on meaningful interconnections since they are alien to its usual ways of thinking. Perhaps it will need to overcome its current abhorrence of such concepts in order to arrive at the truth.

Parapsychology

People who believe in psi ("sheep") tend to score above chance, while those who do not believe in psi ("goats") show null results or psi-missing. This has became known as the "sheep-goat effect".

G. Schmeidler

Over the past few decades parapsychology and psi testing has been one of the fastest growing areas of university research, fuelled and funded in part by U.S. government interest.

Parapsychology definition:

'The study of interactions between living systems and their environment. The interactions are characterized by the acquisition of information from the outside world under conditions prohibiting involvement of known physiological receptors.'

(Professor Charles Honorton)

In 1982 it was said about psychical research:

'Although a variety of so-called psychic phenomena have attracted man's attention throughout recorded history, organized scholarly effort to comprehend such effects is just one century old, and systematic academic research roughly half that age. Over recent years, a sizeable spectrum of evidence has been brought forth from reputable laboratories in several disciplines to suggest that at times human consciousness can acquire information inaccessible by any known physical mechanism.'

R.G. Jahn, Dean of the School of Engineering/Applied Science at Princeton

And it has been pointed out:

> *There have been numerous replications of all the principal psi phenomena, as the many published meta-analyses testify. It remains true, nevertheless, that one can never depend on a particular psi effect showing up exactly when and where it may be required... Indeed, all our experience so far points to the fact that psi is, for whatever reason, inherently elusive and evasive...*
>
> *John Beloff* [46]

It is clear from research that:

> *The psi factor in nature is apparently not constrained by the laws of physics, chemistry, and biology, at least as they are understood today.*
>
> *Michael Grosso, Chair of Philosophy and Religion, New Jersey City University*

Nevertheless it is still true that:

> *We may safely predict that it will be the timidity of our hypotheses and not their extravagance, which will provoke the derision of posterity.*
>
> *Professor H.H. Price, Psychic Researcher (1950s)*

It may be that science has been asking the wrong questions, or looking at things from an erroneous perspective. As Michael Grosso puts it:

> *What's lacking, in my opinion, is knowledge that is immediate, intuitive.*

Scientists themselves would perhaps be better employed exploring their own psychic abilities, anomalous experiences and meaningful connections rather than seeking it in someone else. Then research would really leap ahead. It being quite some time since I wrote these words, I am delighted to say that it is now the case and enlightened scientists and medical professionals are bringing their research to our attention more and more readily.

Problems facing researchers

> *The experiencers of the reality are also the selectors*
>
> *Utts and Josephson*

Whilst there is an enormous body of evidence from such early pioneers as the Society for Psychical Research, J.B. Rhine and later researchers, much of the evidence for psi and psychic abilities is still anecdotal rather than empirical – that is, it is not repeatable in a laboratory under strict conditions. This may be because strict laboratory conditions induce an atmosphere that is antithetical to psychic functioning. Scientific criteria insists that experimental results be consistent and replicable with an incident of the phenomena above chance. Unfortunately the energy with which they are experimenting is temperamental and elusive, and far from replicable. It is also very susceptible to the effect of thought, especially those of sceptical researchers. It behaves strangely and does not follow any known scientific laws. It does not adhere to time, people exercising psi apparently move forwards and backwards in time, or out of it altogether

In more than one set of telepathy experiments, the person 'receiving' anticipated the object before it was 'sent' – precognition. At first the experimenters believed that way below chance had been scored. It was only when the results were reconsidered that the fact that the 'receiver' had been one symbol ahead of what was sent was recognised.

Professor R.G. Jahn, Dean of the School of Engineering and Applied Science at Princeton University in reporting his own interim results in 1982, and having surveyed over fifty years of psychical research by other highly respected institutions, commented that whilst metaphysical phenomena were difficult to replicate consistently, nevertheless in some cases results were far above random chance – particularly in the fields of remote viewing and psychokinesis (the ability to move objects by the power of the mind alone). His report summed up the difficulties facing researchers:

> *Once the illegitimate research and invalid criticism have been set aside, the remaining accumulated evidence of psychic phenomena comprises an array of experimental observations, obtained under reasonable protocols in a variety of scholarly disciplines, which compound to a philosophical dilemma. On one hand, effects inexplicable in terms of established scientific theory, yet having numerous common characteristics, are frequently and widely observed; on the other hand, these effects have so far proven qualitatively and quantitatively irreplicable, in the strict scientific sense, and appear to be sensitive to a variety of psychological and environmental factors that are difficult to specify, let alone control.*

Psychic awareness and metaphysical abilities are particularly susceptible to 'human factors'. The state of mind of a subject affects the outcome. The weather and other factors can affect state of mind. If the person is bored, too hot or too cold, or tired, the results will be poor. The British healer Matthew Manning was extensively tested in the 1970s. He says that if the testing involved healing, his enthusiasm and intention were engaged and the tests worked well. But if the test was on telepathy or psychokinesis, he quickly became bored, lost intention, and the results tailed off. For him, intention and expectation are two vital factors in successful metaphysical work. He intends and expects that something will occur, and it does.

There is another difficulty. Science has proved that observers interfere with the results of experiments by being there. In the metaphysical field, a cynical observer who does not believe that something is possible will adversely affect the outcome. In college, a fellow student and I were looking at the incidence of chance in a mathematics lecture. The experiment involved throwing two coins to see whether they would fall as heads or tails, matched or odd pairs. My fellow student and I happened to be sitting in a spiritual development group together at the time but we were in no way trying to influence the fall of the coins – at least not consciously. However, our first throw was two heads, so was our second, and our third.

By the time we got to our twenty-third-in-a-row throw of heads, the 'observer' who was recording the results was encouraging us, somewhat loudly, which brought the mathematics tutor over. "Impossible." she said firmly. "Throw again." We did, but for the rest of the session two heads did not appear together. Her assessment of the situation: "A fluke, sometimes it goes like that." Her mathematical mind put everything down to random chance. She could not comprehend psychic abilities and psi experiences. They existed outside her scientific framework.

15
Exceptional Human Experiences

We believe that by valuing these experiences in new ways, and sharing them we all gain meaningful insights into ourselves and our world. When these insights occur and we find a way to grow in a way that enables us to integrate and internalise them, what was an anomaly becomes an Exceptional Human Experience. [47]

Once I began to research this book the second time around I was delighted to find that NDEs, OOBEs, remote viewing and lucid dreaming were now, whilst still often labelled anomalous and regarded as rare being outside conventional experience and therefore somewhat strange, were nevertheless now called Exceptional Human Experiences (EHEs) – or Akashic experiences. They were recognised as life changing, life enhancing, enriching and worthy of study.

What particularly stirred my interest was a report that leading–edge researchers in the field of neurobiology have confirmed that, during NDEs, the neurochemical DMT (dimethyltryptamine) is naturally synthesised in the brain, probably in the pineal: a gland that has long been metaphysically associated with the 'third eye' and psychic experiences. DMT has been dubbed 'the Spirit molecule' and it has been hypothesized that it releases the soul at death for its journey to the post–death dimension. It could be that small amounts of endogenous, naturally occurring, DMT in the brain are what allows the soul to go travelling and return. DMT appears to be released when the Alta Major chakra is activated and this could be a fruitful area of research. Anecdotal evidence from my crystal workshops certainly suggests that crystals containing the chemical that forms 'brain sand' in the pineal, linked to DMT production, stimulate the opening of this chakra (see p.109) as do other new generation, high vibration crystals and some can be used to 'tune in' the metaphysical abilities of this chakra.

Naturally occurring DMT, in the form of ayahuasca and other etheobotanic substances (plant material), is what shamans have used for aeons of time to journey to other realms. DMT is officially classified as an hallucinogenic – and, therefore, to science is the stimulator of unreal, illusory experiences. But are they illusory? Or is it, as some scientists now believe, a stimulator for an Exceptional Human Experience that is a life altering moment, a stepping onto another path be it in this world or another. Is it that certain early humans (or even all of them under certain stimuli such as drumming, chanting, incantations and 'magical brews') naturally had the ability to journey out of their body? Their artwork and pictograms would certainly indicate this could be so.

And, after all most shamans were either chosen after a NDE or underwent a death as part of their initiation. I ask myself was it my own near death experience at the age of 5 that kept my psychic abilities alive, stimulated by another NDE in childbirth and then again at menopause? Did these replenish the supply of endogenous DMT in my system and give me access to dimensions of which other people are unaware? As a child I constantly had out–of–body experiences and psychic visions. Do I have within myself a natural neurochemical looking glass? [48] My psychic awareness tells me that the answer is a resounding yes.

Out–of–body experiences (OOBEs) and remote viewing

Time and space are modes by which we think and not conditions in which we live.
Albert Einstein

One of the best known ways in which consciousness can operate outside the body is through remote viewing. Remote viewing uses the ability of consciousness to leave the physical body behind and travel to a distant place, bringing back an accurate report of what is seen or heard. It is a subject that arouses great controversy. It is also known as journeying, out–of–body experience (OOBE) and etheric or astral travel. Strictly speaking it is a metaphysical ability rather than a psychic one, but it does help you to hone your psychic awareness and it certainly demonstrates that consciousness can operate away from the body.

From time immemorial psychics have used remote viewing to obtain information, it is an ancient shamanic tool but it happened in the west too. Queen Elizabeth the First of England's astrologer, Dr John Dee, described his journeys to other realms and times. His information was used to help the Queen negotiate the war with Spain.

A Victorian writer, Robert Young, described how his son introduced him to a Welshman named Davis – a man who had never left his own village. Young's son asked the entranced Davis to describe Young's home back in Dorset, which he did perfectly and included details of visitors whom Young was only able to confirm after his return home. As a test, Young then gave Davis a letter and asked him to locate the writer. Placing the letter on his forehead,

Davis was silent for five minutes and then said: 'I am in a strange country… I have found him'. He went on to describe the man and his daughter in great detail including his 'peculiar dress' and 'wonderful head' with its velvet cap. The description was an exact match with the Dorset poet William Barnes, writer of the letter. On several other evenings Davis viewed what was happening in Young's home – events which were again confirmed on his return. Sadly, Young said that while he had told his friends of the experience in great detail 'the general public would not believe it' and he, therefore, gave no further details in his book. [49] But the description is typical of a natural psychic using his power to travel beyond his body and view a scene as though it were happening in front of eyes – much as we would watch a news report today through the 'eye' of a television camera.

Until you experience a journey out of your body, it is possible to believe it is all a delusion. But once you have mastered it, you cannot doubt that it is real.

Many people who undergo NDEs report some degree of remote viewing. They correctly describe events that go on out of the sight or hearing of the body they leave behind as they 'die'. Such information is particularly significant when it comes from someone who, in life, was blind and could not under ordinary circumstances be able to know such things as the colour of a nurse's hair or what a doctor was wearing for instance and yet there have been detailed reports of such incidents. Complex surgical or resuscitation procedures are commonly described. People who have spontaneous out–of–body events frequently obtain information that they could not perceive in any other way.

A number of people have out–of–body experiences as part of their dreams – flying dreams may show an aptitude for remote viewing, for instance. The jolt felt immediately before waking can be caused by consciousness returning the body. It only takes a little effort to extend your awareness into recognition of being out of your body, and to direct your consciousness to view remote objects or places. Orthodox science has been attempting to satisfactorily – and repeatedly – replicate these experiences for the last fifty years or so with varying degrees of success.

Famous out–of–body journeys

I see myself as a tiny dot out of my physical body, which lies inert before me.

Edgar Cayce

As we have seen, remote viewing and out–of–body experiences are nothing new. Most of the great religious figures had at least one such experience. Christ was taken by the devil to the Holy City and set on the parapet of the temple as part of his temptation (Matthew 4:5), St Paul tells us in Corinthians II 12:2–4 that he knew:

> *a man [himself] in Christ who, fourteen years ago, was caught up – whether still in the body or out of the body, I do not know.. right into the third heaven, into paradise and heard words so secret that human lips may not repeat them.*

This was part of his conversion experience, his 'Road to Damascus'. Mohammed made his night journey to Jerusalem and from there to 'heaven' in a similar fashion. Much earlier, the Hindu Sutras of Patanjali taught the practice of projection out of the body, as did the practitioners whose wisdom is set out in the ancient Hermetic texts.

The American seer Edgar Cayce was able to induce out–of–body experiences at will through hypnosis. He used this ability not only to read the Akashic Record of people's past and present lives but also to explore the post–death realms and meet the Angel of Death. At a public lecture he explained:

> *As I went out, I realised that I had contacted Death, as a personality, as an individual or as a being. Realizing this, I remarked to Death:*
> *'You are not as ordinarily pictured – with a black mask or hood, or as a skeleton, or like Father Time with the sickle. Instead, you are fair, rose–checked, robust – and you have a pair of shears or scissors.' ...*
> *'Yes, Death is not what many seem to think. It's not the horrible thing which is often pictured. Just a change – just a visit. The shears or scissors are indeed the implements most representative of life and death to man. These indeed unite by dividing and divide by uniting.'*

Shamanic anchors

Shamans have long used a 'shamanic anchor' that connects the base of their spine deep into the centre of Mother Earth to keep them attached to their body when journeying. If you create for yourself anchors that connect you deep into the earth and into the centre of the galaxy you will have no problem returning to your body.

Exercise: Shamanic anchors

Sit comfortably with your feet on the floor. Be aware of the base chakra at the bottom of your spine. From this chakra picture cords going down each of your legs, out through your feet and into the earth where they meet at the earth chakra. Here the separate cords intertwine and continue on down through the earth passing through the soil, then through the rocks of the earth's mantle. The cord will then pass down through the molten magma of the inner earth until it reaches the huge ball of solidified iron that is the earth's core. Hook your anchor onto this ball. It will hold you gently yet firmly in incarnation. Whenever you need re–energising, the energy of the molten core will pass up the anchor and into your base chakra. From here you can pull it up your spine and into the dan ti'en, which is located just below your navel. This cord will always bring you back to your body when you are journeying on the earth plane.

Now take your attention to the top of your head. From the crown chakra, send out another cord. This one goes to the sun, picking up its energy and then it goes out through space to the centre of our galaxy in the middle of the Milky Way. Here you can hook your anchor onto the centaur's bow. Then, if you are taking a remote journey into interstellar space and multi–dimensions, you can return via the anchor.

Bring your awareness back to your body and feel how your body is suspended by your cosmic anchor from the crown chakra to the centre of the galaxy, and by your shamanic anchor to the centre of the earth. Know that these anchors will always allow you to return to your body no matter where you may journey.

***If you are kinaesthetic**, or a naturally 'floaty' person, you will find that holding or wearing Flint, Celestobarite, Elestial Smoky Quartz, Boji Stones, Faden Quartz and other earthing crystals will keep you anchored without closing off your psychic abilities.*

See also 'What to do when things go wrong' (Chapter 17) to assist you in dealing with an unexpected or unwelcome out of body experience.

A remote journey through space

There is a big planet with stripes, I hope it is Jupiter.
Ingo Swan

In the 1970s, the American Ingo Swann reported a remote viewing journey to Jupiter, to which a space probe was being sent. Swann began his description with the words quoted above. He described a thick hydrogen mantle and bands of glittering 'crystals' close into the atmosphere. However, the fact that he saw a ring *around* rather than the known bands on the planet made observers wonder if he had mistakenly targeted Saturn. But, when the space probe arrived six years later, it confirmed everything that Swann had seen. The rings were clearly visible on photographs and the atmosphere was largely liquid hydrogen. It also confirmed that the moons of Jupiter were as described by satirist Jonathan Swift, author of *Gulliver's Travels*, some two centuries earlier.

Ingo Swann's ability was a natural one. It manifested at the age of three. During a tonsillectomy, he was anaesthetized and apparently unconscious. However, when he recovered he was able to describe the operation in great detail. When he was older, he trained himself to leave his body at will. As an adult he was tested extensively by the Stanford Research Institute in California.

Developing your power to remote view

> *There is evidence that we are ultimately no more bound by space than we are by time.*
>
> *Michael Talbot*

Like most metaphysical abilities, remote viewing is a talent that can be developed with practice, although some people have a natural flair in the same way that great athletes or painters are born rather than made. It is these people who can make epic journeys to the planets or invisibly invade the Kremlin but you too can develop this ability through a simple exercise. You will need the assistance of a friend, at least in the initial stages.

Having worked through this book and developed control over your abilities and learned to shield yourself if necessary, you should now be ready to remote view. Holding a Shaman Quartz (a Quartz crystal that has canyons and mountains within it) can considerably enhance your ability to move your consciousness out of your body and journey to other realms.

The following exercise can be memorised or taped, but, in the initial stages at least, it is helpful to have a friend read the instructions, pausing to allow you to carry them out. This ensures that there is someone to guide you back to your body at the end of the exercise until this becomes an automatic process. With a little practice, you will be able to carry out the relaxation technique and maintain your alertness and awareness. If you find you fall asleep, you may prefer to do the exercise sitting up. The instructions suggest placing an object high up because most people find themselves below the ceiling when they take a remote–viewing journey. If your way is to be closer to the floor, adjust the placement the next time you do the experiment.

Remote Viewing Experiment

Ask your friend to place an object, unknown to you, in a room reasonably close to your bedroom, above head height – agree on the positioning before you start the experiment but make sure it is not somewhere you can accidentally glimpse the object. A locked room to which your friend holds the key is ideal but initially doors should be left open until you have learned to instantly bi–locate your consciousness – and to recognise that during remote viewing you can pass through apparently solid objects such as doors. The friend should, initially, choose something simple and colourful, like a ball or box but should not tell you what it is.

Exercise: Remote viewing

Lie down on your bed and allow yourself to relax. If you have a Shaman Quartz or Diaspore, hold this loosely in whichever hand feels right. Breathe deeply and evenly. As you breathe in, close your eyes. As you breathe out, open them. Do this ten times and then leave your eyes closed. By this time your eyelids will be feeling heavy and relaxed. Allow this feeling to spread all over your face. If you are aware of any tension, raise and lower your eyebrows two or three times. Let the feeling of relaxation flow down through your shoulders and arms. If the shoulders feel stiff, raise and lower each one in turn. If your hands are tense, clench them and then let them lie softly by your side. Allow the feeling to pass down through your chest, your abdomen and into your legs and feet. By this time, you will be feeling totally relaxed. Remind yourself to stay alert and aware. (If your body starts vibrating or feels like it is rolling from side to side, this is a very good sign that your consciousness is detaching.)

Ensure that your shamanic anchor is in place and your soma chakra open.

Slowly and gently withdraw your awareness from your body and let it focus on the centre of your forehead, between and above the eyebrows close to the hairline. Become aware that something is tugging gently at this point, let it pull your consciousness up and out. Soon you will find yourself floating above your body. You can turn and look down to see it lying on the bed below you. You will notice that there is a cord connecting your body with you as you float above the bed. This cord – which often shows itself as a pulsating silver line – goes from the forehead of your body to the subtle body acting as a vehicle for your awareness. You can use it to return to your physical body at any time by imagining yourself being 'reeled in' by your body. [If this is the first time you are aware of leaving your body, you might like to practice this by moving forward a little way and letting yourself by reeled back towards your body.]

Now make your way from the bed across to the door of your room. You will notice that in this unembodied form, you can pass through solid objects as easily as through the air. So, you will not need to open doors that are closed. Turn [right or left] out of the door and make your way down the hallway to the next room. Let your awareness pass through this door. Move over to where you know the object has been placed. Look at it, notice its shape and colour. Is there anything unusual about it? Is there anything else close to it?

Turn and make your way back to your room, letting the 'line' gently pull you back to your body. Let your consciousness flow back into your body. Settle yourself comfortably and become aware of your body once more.

Take your attention from the top of your head, down to your hands, through your chest and abdomen and down your legs to your feet, and back up again. Run your hands down your body to make sure that you are firmly anchored in your body. Give yourself a few moments to adjust and slowly sit up. Put your feet firmly on the floor and picture your grounding cord going deep into the earth.

Immediately write down what you saw in as much detail as possible – if you have been using a Shaman Quartz or other crystal hold this while writing as it will stimulate recall – and have a hot drink before you discuss the experiment with your friend.

Expanding your remote viewing technique

As you improve with practise, you can vary the placement and the object. Gradually move the object further away. Remote viewing 'hide and seek' entails your friend placing several objects all over the house and challenging you to find, and remember, them all.

When you are completely confident that you can return to your body at will and that you have complete control over the process, you can take longer journeys, programming in that the shift of awareness be instantaneous by saying as you leave your body, "I now instantly go to ..."

When you undertake any kind of remote viewing journey, remember that it is important to respect other people's privacy as otherwise the ability can rebound on you – no metaphysical power can be misused with impunity!

Always make a note of your remote viewing journeys in your metaphysical journal as this may build into a bigger picture over time.

Near death experiences (NDEs)

> *It was not the fact that I regained consciousness after so long a time that is remarkable but that fact that, while I was apparently dead, I was never so much alive in my life!*
>
> *John. C. Wheeler*

There are now many thousands of reports of near death experiences (NDEs) and considerable open–minded medical research into the subject. There is even a journal devoted to the subject and a professor at an American University has just been awarded a $5m research grant. [50]

But when I had my second NDE forty five years ago, I had no idea that I was entering into an experience reported throughout all cultures over thousands of years. [51] Indeed, it wasn't until almost ten years had passed that I learned my experience had a name. It took me into spiritual connection and regression work at a time when there were few people doing it and since then during my talks and workshops I heard many reports of NDEs, all of which contained several of the components of what I came to see as the classic NDE.

I have since found that eighty percent of people who have an NDE report that their psychic abilities are enhanced or abruptly switched on and it can take time to adjust. [52] The second experience did not so much trigger my psychic sensitivity as intensify it to a pitch I could not resist. As a child, I had quickly realised that I saw and heard things to which most of the adults around me were oblivious – and some that they preferred to keep hidden. My first NDE was so much a part of that experience that I didn't mention it to anyone. I had quickly learned, as so many children do, to keep quiet. I suppressed my abilities. My second NDE brought my repressed psychic abilities bursting to the surface again as it does for so many people (see Julie Chimes' story).

Classic Near Death Experience

- Consciousness leaves the body suddenly and without premeditation, the body is typically unconscious or 'dead' but may be in a heightened state of awareness
- Deep feeling of peace suffuses the soul
- Profound shift of consciousness away from identification with the physical body
- Soul passes up a tunnel of light
- Sense of moving into timelessness
- The soul is met by a being of light radiating love, often a religious figure
- Deceased relatives may appear
- Soul hears beautiful music, sees wondrous surroundings
- Soul undergoes a Life Review that is experienced intensely and with great feeling
- Soul identifies on–going lessons and processes
- Soul may be offered a choice or is told to return as it is not yet time

Most people who report an NDE say that it is a life changing event and for many it is an exceptionally pleasant experience although a few people do experience something much more horrific, or a combination of both – see http://iands.org/about–ndes/common–aftereffects.html for assistance after a distressing NDE.

A typical NDE case is that of John C. Wheeler who drowned and was certified dead by two physicians only to revive the next day. In his published account he said:

> *I could tell the persons around me everything that had happened when I was enabled to return… [he watched the recovery of his body]… In the fleeting moment between the conscious and the unconscious state, the thought of returning to life was repugnant, and I knew that I didn't want to live. But I was forced to and I returned.*

According to him death was delightful and, as with so many people, the effect of his N.D.E. was catalytic:

> *Up to the time of that experience I had been an agnostic, disbelieving in the hereafter, or a spiritual state of existence, but my whole outlook on life was changed. I never since have had a shadow of a doubt with regard to a spiritual state of existence. Man is dual and the physical body is the lesser part of him. I don't speak of a future state as a possibility, but as a fact. To me it is knowledge.*[53]

Science and NDEs

> *There is an invariant core to the Afterlife Hypothesis: the separation of spirit from body.*
>
> *Greg Stone*

There is huge controversy over whether an NDE is the product of a disordered brain or is a genuine spiritual experience. [54] Dr Peter Fenwick, a respected British consultant neuro–psychiatrist, and his wife Elizabeth investigated over three hundred NDEs. They wanted to establish whether an NDE was anything more than a 'trick played on us by a brain disordered by drugs, pain or sickness', and to explore *what* had the experience. Was it, as conventional science believed, purely a matter of brain? Or was it a process of consciousness?

As an expert in brain function, Peter Fenwick was aware of a paradox. Over 60% of his study sample of NDEs began when the patient was unconscious. And yet, according to conventional science, an unconscious person cannot use their brain to create or map a 'cognitive model' (an internal or external experience). Similarly, it was believed, memory does not function during unconsciousness. So, if unconscious people AND those who had been certified dead were having cohesive experiences of which they retained a vivid memory, it did not accord with conventional understanding of the brain.

In some of Fenwick's cases, not only were the people unconscious, or outwardly dead, but their brain had been severely damaged and so, according to the conventional view, they could not have been experiencing anything. And yet their reports were remarkably close to those of people who did not have brain damage.

If the brain was the cause, rather than the recorder, of an NDE, everything pointed to right brain involvement. Strong emotions and images are usually present in an NDE as are feelings of absolute reality, unity and 'knowingness'. Sense of time is lost, déjà vu occurs and psychic awareness is heightened. Beautiful music is often heard. All of which are functions of the right brain. Peter Fenwick reached the conclusion that, whilst there must be brain structures that mediate NDEs, mystical experiences and the like, at the same time, there was a transpersonal element to the experience that depended on *mind* rather than being inextricably linked to brain. Science is, of course, still arguing the brain **versus** mind or consciousness paradox – although it comes down heavily on the side of the brain–producing–mind theory. People who have had a NDE indisputably *know*: mind and consciousness continue without brain function. As Peter Fenwick points out:

> *If we have never personally had such an experience we can only theorise. And while theories are fine, and fun and even useful, I believe that we can learn more about its true significance by listening to the people who have been there, who have had first–hand experience of what the rest of us can only talk about.*

Split screen death

Whilst I was perfectly happy at the idea of being a mother with a child, the thought of being pregnant and especially of giving birth had from my earliest childhood given me a sinking feeling in my belly – right where my uterus sat. When I became pregnant in a land far from home and was depressed and nauseous before I even knew I had conceived, it seemed as though my foreboding was being played out all too graphically. I was living in the middle of a civil war zone and things were far from calm around me. The next seven months were hellish, my body seeming to mirror the turmoil in the outside world. Unlike my friends there who were also pregnant, my 'morning sickness' went on all day and every day. It didn't stop until I returned to England to have my child. And once it stopped, my blood pressure starting rising and I was soon diagnosed with pre–eclamptic toxaemia and hospitalised. The local cottage hospital was a cosy place and I didn't feel too bad but there was still that underlying 'premonition of doom'.

Eventually I was transferred to a large teaching hospital and the feeling of impending doom intensified. The doctors decided that labour must be induced as I couldn't stand an anaesthetic for a caesarean. I was alone in a small room, hovering somewhere around the ceiling when I saw a nurse walk in to see how I was doing. She ran from the room shouting for the resuss team. I meanwhile had met a being, it is probably easier to call 'him' a guide who showed me myself down on the immaculate hospital bed dying and then, beside that, me lying in filthy straw with a grimy old woman trying to deliver a baby that was stuck. Around me were a whole group of ragged children and I knew that I was their mother. I couldn't face living (I later learned that I was an umarried mother who was being impregnated at regular intervals by the son of the estate on which I was living, who was too scared of his mother to make our relationship legal). And so I died. (This picture was confirmed to me many years later by a guy who came up to me in a workshop and narrated the scene saying 'I was one of those children'.)

The whole experience was like watching split screen t.v. There were four sections, one of which I still cannot recall. But the guide also showed me what my life could be like if I returned, taking me to the interlife planning meeting to reconnect to my purpose as a healer – which seemed very far from that young woman lying on the hospital bed trying to give birth. He told me that I could give up, as I had in that other life I had been shown, but that I'd have to come back and do it all again to get to the point where I now was. The thought of having to go through what I'd already experienced in my deeply traumatic life was too much and I reluctantly decided to return to my body. I came to to find that I was about to be given a vacuum extraction, which would save the life of myself and my baby. It was a drastic measure but it worked. Life did indeed unfold as I was shown, and within a few years I was walking a totally different path that led to where I am today.

That near death experience reminded me of my life purpose and that guide has accompanied me throughout life and is always with me when I accompany other people through their death. It is what makes it possible for me to do my psychic work and to know beyond a shadow of a doubt that I will survive death. I didn't see the tunnel of light that most people talk about, I'm quite sure if I'd gone up that tunnel then I wouldn't have returned. But I have been up that tunnel since when sitting with dying friends and took them out into the light at the end, acting as a psychopomp for their soul. It is what makes me completely unafraid. I am always sad when I am turned back and they go on, but I know that that tunnel is waiting for me when the time is right.

16
Developing your Psychic Connection with Other Worlds

> *I lost track of time. It was all surreal. As I walked, I psychically saw row upon row of prisoners. The scenes were all [in] brown and white, marching beside me yet as if they were in another dimension. It was like I was with them but they didn't see me. I was awash in the creepy sensation.*
>
> *Jewelle St James,* Jude: My Reincarnation from Auschwitz

I know this section comes much later in the book that you would possibly have liked, and if you've turned to this section first I'd really appreciate it if you went back to the beginning and worked methodically through the book. Not so much fun, I know, but I do have good reasons. By following the preceding steps, you'll have gained full control over your psychic abilities and you'll be ready to make connections that take you much further with your psychic work – and you'll do so safely and sensibility without being prey to wild flights of fancy or getting caught up in something from which you cannot extricate yourself. I've spent a long time in the psychic world and I've seen the unfortunate results of unhoned abilities let loose. There are a lot of pranksters on the etheric levels close to the earth and if you don't learn to bypass them, what you'll kythe will most likely be absolute rubbish, no matter how impressive it may sound at first or how elevated the communicator claims to be. You may also find yourself playing host to an uninvited squatter for rather longer than you'd anticipated. I've also seen the results of an inflated ego and a lack of proper spiritual connection. So please, prepare yourself thoroughly for this part of the work, you will benefit in the end – and if you haven't listened and things do go wrong, you'll find a section that assists you deal with it later in the book.

I have always maintained that the best place to open up connections with other worlds is in a properly run psychic development circle, the kind you find at a Spiritualist church (not all circles are necessarily well run so you need to check them out) or at a psychic centre such as the College of Psychic Studies in London or Stanstead Hall in Essex. This is for two reasons. The first is that you have someone experienced who can keep an eye on you and ensure that whoever is communicating is beneficial and that they leave afterwards. The second reason is that the power generated by such a circle is immensely helpful when you are first opening up as you have to raise your vibrations and the spirit who is communicating has to lower theirs to reach you. Being boosted by the group energy can often take you up to a level of communication that you couldn't achieve alone. I still remember the late Maurice Barbanell, the medium for Silver Birch, telling the audience at a lecture he gave on trance mediumship, as it was called back then, that it was like a ladder stretching way up with one medium standing on the shoulders of another through many layers of vibration until the connection reached Silver Birch. As he said with his characteristic twinkle 'there are so many opportunities for misconceptions on the way down as the communication passes through so many minds'.

If you must develop alone for whatever reason, then there are steps and precautions that you can take not only to make the experience safer but also of more value – and rereading the downside of psychic connection and the section on psychic protection will be helpful as will opening your higher chakras. **Please don't kythe on your own until you are proficient.** Ask a friend to be present at the very least but try to join a properly supervised spiritual development group. (See the section below on kything as to how a friend can help and also 'what to do when something goes wrong')

Channelling (kything)

To me the word 'channel' suggests a one–way path, in which I would be like a radio receiver, tuning into a broadcast. When I say that I 'kythe' … it means that I open myself to who they are, and become intimate with them.'

Theolyn Cortyns

Psychic communication in the last quarter of the twentieth century and the beginning of the twenty first was characterised by 'channelling', that is obtaining messages from what was, often, seen as an extra–terrestrial or other–worldly source of spiritual wisdom and inspiration. (In earlier times mediumship, as it was then called, gave communications from 'guides' who had usually, but not always, lived on earth, or from spirits who had formerly lived on earth, or from the gods.) The quality of such channellings varies considerably and the best psychic protection is a sense of healthy scepticism and an open mind. A willingness to test out the advice given, rather than slavishly following it, gives a natural defence against its worst excesses. As does a questioning mind. But this can be difficult to maintain if you are the one doing the kything, which is why rigorous training is essential.

Unfortunately channelling appeals to the ego. Someone who otherwise feels rather insignificant can, in their eyes and those of beholders, gain kudos by channelling a great 'spiritual teacher' or Ascended Master. And there is always the added trap, which underlies all psychic sensitivity, of trying to please people by telling them what they want to hear – and sometimes to giving permission for something they would, under other circumstances, never consider, or offering unrealistic expectations of a miraculously changed life.

One of the first things that a metaphysical initiate used to learn was how to traverse – and bypass – the astral realms close to the earth. This is where entities and discarnate spirits who have not progressed far from the earth reside. Hardly the best place from which to obtain higher guidance – and its denizens delight in misleading the gullible 'channeller'. Years ago I went to visit some friends from the local Spiritualist church. As we sat down to lunch I was told excitedly to put down my knife and fork and listen carefully as 'Grey Horse was coming through'. 'Oh', I said, 'an Indian guide?' 'No' came the reply, 'he is the spirit of a horse. 'And does he appear at mealtimes very often?' I asked. 'Oh yes, all the time.' I picked up my knife and fork and began to eat. Grey Horse spouted some rubbish and I suggested – quietly, in my mind – that he move on and leave these gullible people alone. He took a bit of persuading but eventually moved on and wasn't heard from again. I feel sure that many other so–called channelled sources arise from the astral level. One of the best ways to ensure that you work beyond the astral is to have the intention that you aim for the highest vibration you can reach, that way you bypass the lower realms. Similarly if you kythe, that is are involved in an interactive process rather than being a passive channel that simply hands over their body to be used as the spirit wills, then you can retain 'quality control'.

Other 'channelling' pitfalls centre around the fact that, no matter how evolved the 'teacher' may be, the content of the communication has to pass through your own mind. The vocabulary, concepts and underlying prejudices you have can 'contaminate' even the best of material so that what comes out of a channeller's mouth may be a long way from what was originally intended.

I much prefer the word kything to channelling. This is an old English word which, as, Theolyn Cortyns suggests, has a much more multi–dimensional quality to it. She found the word had been used in a children's book in which it includes telepathy and picking up feelings and emotions from other people. As Theolyn says, it is a much more intimate concept than channelling. Neither she nor I give up our own thoughts when we communicate with other beings. We are not passive channels, we interact and we both work at a soul and higher self level. We have conversations and questions that go both ways and so can you. So, in this book I am using kything for what many people would call channelling. Kything is best taught under personal supervision as an enormous amount of rubbish can come through – some of it is part of the process as initially there is learning on both sides, but some of it can be deliberate misguidance or sheer drivel. Often you have no idea what will come out of your mouth until you actually say it so it takes courage to open your mouth and allow. If you are going to do this, you need an empathetic audience to assist you and, as with clairvoyance, it is better, initially, to have someone who is aware of who – or what – is communicating. If you find yourself kything, try to record what is said and assess the result carefully. To avoid unwanted kything, close your crown chakras tightly and always do the close down after a kything session.

If you can't have an experienced teacher present when you kythe, ask a friend who is blessed with ample common sense to assist you by carefully monitoring and keeping a record of all that you say and do – and questioning the entity that is supposedly communicating. It is vitally important to choose someone who wont be overwhelmed with who the entity claims to be rather than the quality of the communication. I've seen a great many kythers – many of them back in the time when it was still called trance – and I work in a light trance myself when reading the Akashic Record of past lives and when leading visionary journeys. I never allow an unknown source to kythe through me no matter how insistent they may be. Unless you work with someone you trust – which includes both your teacher or friend and the spirit who is communicating, you don't know what you're getting. Nevertheless, I've received some beautiful – and very practical – spiritual teaching from many sources as have many other people.

Some trance mediums or channellers go through horrible gruntings, groaning and writhings as their guide, allegedly, 'takes over'. Personally I never found this necessary. If I raised my vibrations to meet my higher self and that of the spirit, took a step back so they could use my voicebox and they communicated through my energy field without coming into my physical self, then the kything was effortless. (See below for how to kythe safely). This has the added advantage that I can monitor what is said and assess its usefulness as the kything proceeds – which is why I prefer to tape karmic readings rather than having someone face to face with me.

Channelling and walk–ins

If a communicator who has been involved in a channelling does not leave, or if a spirit takes over, then a 'walk in' is said to have taken place (something which seems to happen much more in the USA than in the UK). Some people willingly share their physical body with another soul or spirit and some happily move out and leave the squatter to it, but there are people who are taken over because their own protection is inadequate. In my view, walk–ins are highly undesirable and can be abusive. Good protection and sensible practice will prevent unwanted take–overs. Dealing with walk–ins is beyond the scope of this book and needs expert handling (see resources) but in an emergency apply Petaltone Plant Ally, Blast 'em off or Special 8 and Power Shield which should eject the squatter.

Questions to ask about kything

- Is this a safe space for kything to take place?
- Are my energies at their highest and most balanced?
- What is the source?
- Is this really an evolved being? (Content can be a clue!)
- Is this coming from my/their subconscious mind or ego?
- Is it imagination or fantasy?
- Is it coming from the astral level of being? (Tricksters abound at this level)
- Is this wishful thinking, grandiosity, disguised–lust or authoritarianism?
- Am I being told what I secretly want to hear?
- Am I in control of this process or am I being controlled or unduly influenced?
- Is this really of value?
- Do I trust those around me to help me if I get into trouble?
- Is this soul guidance at the highest level?

When not to kythe

If you have not been properly trained, then do not kythe. If your energy field is disturbed for any reason, it is unwise to kythe. If the place in which you are kything is 'unsafe' – that is, the energies are not clean and properly protected – it opens you up to psychic invasion. If you yourself are physically ill or low in energy, if you are mentally or emotionally disturbed, or psychically or psychologically unbalanced then you should not attempt to kythe. If you do not know your doorkeeper and guides, if your aura is weak and your psychic gateways wide open, and, most especially, if you do not know who is trying to communicate through you, then it would be sensible to desist. If you feel that someone is 'trying to take over', pull back.

If you have taken drugs or alcohol, it can create 'psychic overload' and blow your natural protection (the Aloha essence Kou when taken consistently discourages astral possession due to excessive alcohol consumption but alcohol and psychic work simply do not mix). If the group you are working in feels in any way inharmonious or the recipient is pulling on your energy, then it would not be wise to continue (in this case take steps to protect your spleen chakra). If you cannot distinguish between your own inner voices and that of a discarnate communicator, then do not kythe.

A group works at the level of its lowest common denominator. You cannot reach a high spiritual level if the group is pulling you down. Equally, if your own energies are under par, then, as like attracts like, you will not be able to reach the spiritual levels. Applying your common sense is the best possible protection for you in such circumstances.

Protection whilst kything

How much protection you will need during kything depends on how you work. It is essential to raise your vibrations to the highest level. This not only aids the communication but also ensures that you 'by–pass' the lower astral levels. This is where I find both Petaltone Plant Ally and Power Shield essences are invaluable and also the newer Special 8 or Heaven and Earth essences. It is also essential to close the link properly afterwards, separating your energy totally from that of the communicator (enclosing yourself in a light bubble helps here as does reapplying Power Shield).

Some people work at a light level of trance, others at a deeper level. Trance is a change in consciousness that enables the everyday mind to step aside and psychic communication to take place. It may also involve a spirit or being controlling your physical body to a greater or lesser degree such as where the voice or body posture changes dramatically – although even this is not a sign that the communicator is necessary external, internal figures can also communicate as a child for instance.

If you work at a light level of trance, then the communication will probably pass through your aura into your mental mind field and you will receive it and pass it on, consciously. You may hear it as a spoken voice or thought, have an intuition or 'get a feeling', or you may just have to relax your mouth, drop your jaw and trust something will come out. You may also find that you write or speak without thinking first what you will say. When working at this level, a strong aura and chakras in good working order will protect you, as will a guide or guardian of the psychic gateways on the other side. But you may need to work on receiving communications only when it is appropriate to do so – if you are 'stuck open' you will not be able to close down the communication. (There are crystals and flower essences that can help with this closing down, see p.39.) At this level of trance, working with a perceptive friend initially is sufficient to ensure you are protected.

If you are one of the people who literally step out of your body and hand it over to the communicator, then you need to know the communicator – and to trust your doorkeeper implicitly. You also need to ensure that all the communicator's energy leaves afterwards and that you have not picked up anything from the person or persons receiving the kything. This level of kything, certainly in the initial stages, needs a group of people one of whom at least is qualified to check out communicators and move them on when they have finished communicating.

When you have finished kything, closing down correctly is essential. (See grounding cord exercise and essences and crystals for auric close–down.) Bringing your vibrations back down to the earth level is vital – a cup of tea and a biscuit have a grounding effect as does doing something practical like gardening or washing up. The chakra shutters exercise will have helped you to control your chakras, but you can deliberately place your hand over a chakra or psychic gateway you feel is still open. Holding a Boji stone or a piece of Hematite stops you feeling 'floaty'. Flower essences will also aid in closing down properly.

How to kythe

It might be helpful to record this exercise and have a friend read it aloud while for you. In any case, do have another person present when you are learning to kythe.

Exercise: Kything

Sit comfortably in an upright chair in a room with low light (it is not necessary to sit in darkness). Breathe gently and relax. Make sure your grounding cord is in place and the base chakra open. Withdraw your attention from the outside world and ask your gatekeeper and/or guides to be present to assist and protect you.

Open your higher chakras and consciously and deliberately take your attention 'up' to the highest vibration you can reach – it helps to feel yourself ascending a ladder or going up in a lift. Ensure that you have made contact with your highest self and that your guardians are in place.

Drop your shoulders, lift your chin, and let your mouth hang loose and slightly open. Feel yourself take a step back, moving out of your body to stand behind yourself.

If you are entering light trance, listen for the thoughts or intuitions that pass into your mind and speak or record them no matter how silly they may sound.

If you are entering deep trance, keep breathing rhythmically allowing yourself to relax deeper and deeper whilst rising higher and higher until you feel as though you are standing behind and above your physical body. Give permission for whoever is appropriate to use your physical body to communicate and ask that your gatekeeper will check out the person who wants to communicate.

Keep out of the way as much as possible. Don't assume anything, try not to interfere by wanting things to go a certain way, focus on your spiritual self and bathing yourself in light (however, monitor from your higher perspective what is going on so that you can bring the session to an end if it is inappropriate, this teaches you 'quality control'.)

When the communicating spirit withdraws, consciously lower your vibrations and move back into your physical body. Close your higher chakras and your third eye and make sure you grounding cord is in place. Thank your gatekeeper and guides. Take a few moments to be sure you are grounded then move your fingers and toes, lift your arms and move your legs to ensure you are fully back in your body.

Take time to go over what was said and the impressions the other members of the group received. Do not be in awe of a spirit, objectively assess whether the kything was of benefit.

Protection against unwanted kything

- Close your psychic gateways
- Close and cover your crown chakra, using your hand.
- Call your gatekeeper in to protect your chakras including your spleen and soma chakra.
- If necessary, close all your chakras except the earth star.
- Take the Bush flower essences Fringed Violet and Flannel Flower or Red Clover (FES)

Crystals for kything: Golden Labradorite, Angelite, Apophyllite, Calcite, Channelling Quartz, Lemurian, Rhomboid Selenite.

Grounding: Boji stone, Hematite, Smoky Elestial, Mohawkite, Graphic Smoky Quartz, Flint.

Flower Essences for kything

Petaltone Heaven and Earth enables you to be grounded while kything.

Kything/Channelling Green Spider Orchid (Bush), Angelsword (Bush) – distinguishes between 'good' and 'bad' kythings. Red Clover (FES) – evicts an unwelcome communicator, Ti (Aloha and FES) – removes spiritual possession.

Close down: Fringed Violet and Flannel Flower (Bush), Power Shield (Petaltone)

Clairvoyance and Clairaudience

To give clairvoyance successfully, he or she will have had to absorb many lessons in communications. It is at such times that their earlier training with symbols, response to feelings and clear seeing, is put to use.

Paul Tandy [55]

Clairvoyance can be used to tune into guidance from discarnate entities and obtain messages from souls who have passed on through death. Although it is called 'clear sight', not all clairvoyants 'see'. Many *feel* or *know* the messages they receive or simply 'have an impression'. Some people 'see' objectively and others subjectively. If you are an objective seer, then it will be as though the spirit or an object is there in the room with you, a bit hazy maybe, but often as apparently solid as the incarnated people present. This can be disconcerting if it happens unexpectedly but spirit beings tend to have a kind of luminosity or dull light around them – but may disappear if you look too directly or screw up your eyes to get them into focus. Looking out of the corner of your eye is more effective. If you see subjectively, you see on an inner screen in your mind's eye. Obviously if you are an objective seer then you can work with your eyes open, if a subjective one then your eyes will need to be closed. To fully develop reliable clairvoyance you need to be under the mentorship of someone who has clear sight and who can discern who is trying to communicate with you until you have this ability yourself. Not all communicators have good intentions or are necessarily truthful. A wise teacher can also assist in recognising whether what you 'see' is symbolic or actual and advise on how to present the information. They can also teach you to 'work at interface'. That is, to work at the outer edges of your aura without allowing the spirit to move into your energy field.

If you do find that you are receiving 'messages', check with your gatekeeper that they are coming to you in truth and light before you proceed. Try to describe the person who is giving you the message but don't worry at this stage if you get details like hair or eye colour wrong, it will become clearer. Check who the message is for and be clear as to content. Simply throwing out names at random until someone 'picks them up' is often used as a means of connection but it is far better to make a point of asking your guides to show you very clearly who the message is for – a light over a person's head for example is very useful.

Say whatever you pick up or see in the way it is given. Initially it can feel quite challenging to say something silly without censoring or trying to make it mean something specific, but if you do this the message will eventually become clearer.

Exercise: To open the inner eye further

Fully open your third eye to 'see' who is communicating with you (if you cannot do this return to the section on opening your third eye). Then open your higher chakras and lift your consciousness 'up' and ask your higher self and your guides to be present. Try to feel where you end and the spirit begins and to work at the interface of your energies. If you are obtaining guidance for yourself, write it down or record it as you speak.

If you are receiving a message for another person, ask that the communicator be absolutely clear both in content and in who the spirit message is for. If you can see the communicator clearly, described them in as much detail as possible. Once you know to whom you are speaking, open your mouth and let the message come out. Avoid interpreting anything which you are given, if you 'see' a ring for instance, don't assume it means marriage. Say you see a ring. If necessary it can then be further clarified.

When the message is over, consciously disconnect from the person you have been speaking to and the communicator, bring your attention back to yourself and then ask for the next message to be given to you, having first identified the recipient.

When you have finished the sessions, thank the guides and communicators then carefully close all your chakras and make sure your grounding cord is in place before you move around.

A word of warning

Do be careful how you present the information you receive. What you are getting may not be the one and only indisputable truth, it may be a suggestion from the universe or your own mind interpreting incorrectly. Rather than saying 'this is how it is', say 'what I am getting is……' or 'my guidance is suggesting that ……..', 'I am seeing you as/doing….' and allow the receiver to comment. I say this because I have seen so many people confused and disturbed by ill–thought out interpretations or by messages from the lower level of the astral plane – the place where the bored, lost and malicious spirits hang out. The forcefullness with which you give 'messages' can also create a thought form or something more that brings it into being even if it wasn't intended. This can also happen when you give past life readings, telling someone about an injury for example can trigger the etheric memory and create a present life problem (just as it can when someone is regressed to another life unless it is sensitively handled).

I remember a woman who came to my early past life and astrology workshops. When anyone said something about an experience they had had or were discussing an aspect in their birthchart, she would suddenly butt in with 'that's because you were ....' and give them an extremely forceful past life reading, usually accompanied by a finger stabbing towards their third eye as if to ram it home. Despite my requests for her to desist or at least to gently offer it for consideration, she was adamant that what she saw was absolutely true. She did this to me on one occasion saying 'you were a young American G.I. who was killed very soon after the Yanks joined the war. You'd just come over here with your unit and were driving a jeep extremely fast down a country road when you overturned and were killed.'

As I was born in the middle of the war and it didn't have a ring of rightness to it, I didn't give much credence to this so called past life. When I brushed it off, her response was 'you'll see'. When I returned home I was amazed to find, parked on the grass outside my house, a large number of jeeps and other American WWII vehicles. They were on exhibition for the annual village fete. Glen Miller was blaring from a speaker and more trucks were arriving by the minute. A jeep came down the gravel truck, skidded and spun around blocking my gateway and just missing me and my car. I marched up the road and told the guys who were directing this unwanted traffic down my normally peaceful drive that there was no more room and it was an impossible situation. 'That's tough' said one of the guys. 'It's been decided by those above'. I cracked up laughing but couldn't explain what was funny. But for the next three days my ears rang with the sound of fake American accents, engines roaring and boogie–woogie blaring. My eighty something year old neighbour said to me 'It's just like being back in the war when the blighters were stationed up the road, you couldn't go anywhere without being in fear of life and limb'.

Was life imitating art, or art life? Was it 'truth' or did that woman's powerful mind create this situation? Be careful that you too do not create a similar chaotic acting out by your predictions or 'inner sights'.

Clairaudience

Clairaudience is another way that departed spirits or guides can communicate with you. Many people who are clairaudient 'hear' at a point behind and slightly to the left or right of them rather than through physical ears but they may tune into an inner ear.

Exercise: Practising clairaudience

Develop the habit of lightly listening whilst you are in a meditative or relaxed state – concentrating heavily is counter–productive. Initially it is rather like tuning in a radio with a lot of static and crackle to get past. Picture a dial tuning it in more clearly. When you do 'hear', try to ascertain whether the guidance or message is for you or for someone else. The 'hearing' often takes place behind one or other of your ears and if you have not yet opened your inner ear, return to that section.

I've already mentioned the 'Monty Python moment' when something is dropped into my head and I then have to disentangle it. Someone else described it as 'information just appears in your head – I feel like it is a kind of pressure in my head – almost like a mini adrenaline rush – then I have a thought about something that wasn't there before.' This is a modified form of clairaudience, a kind of cross between that and clairvoyance and it is fundamental to 'receiving impressions'. One moment you don't know, then you do. The secret is in learning to become aware, then to trust this process and your own knowing. The challenge is to disentangle it intelligently with clarity and without putting your own interpretation into it.

17
What To Do If Things Go Wrong

Then I realized that somehow the end of the tape had come and gone. I had no idea how to get back to my present life. I was trapped. I prayed and prayed for help. I managed to reverse the process that I had gone through to get there. That brought me back into my bedroom. I opened my eyes but to my horror I was still paralysed.

(Author withheld for confidentiality) [56]

In this section we're going to look at what to do if, in spite of all your precautions and the scrupulous attention you pay to your psychic well-being, things go wrong. It's not intended to fill you with foreboding, simply to show you why protection and safe working practices are so essential and to get you out of trouble in an emergency.

The above quotation comes from a workshop participant who had tried a 'do it yourself' past life tape. Her experience graphically illustrates why it can be unwise to do past life regression, kything or journeying on your own, especially when you are untrained. I know just how difficult it can be when things go wrong because I was thrown into the deep end with a woman who had been taken into regression by someone else as a demonstration and then abandoned there when the going got tough, so I had to find a way to bring her out. When I was starting out on the psychic path I also took part in Spiritualist seances where lost souls came for rescue but weren't recognised as such and I had to use my intuition and higher promptings to move them on. I believe I've had lives long training to do that kind of work so, fortunately, it came naturally to me. I can draw on that and a finely honed ability to think on my feet, to respond to every unexpected moment and to be creative in finding new ways if the old ones don't work. So let's go back to my workshop participant to see how she was extracted from her predicament. She began by telling us that:

I had put the tape on and lay on my bed. It took me on a journey and eventually into another life. Everything was going along fine until suddenly a tree fell on me. I was paralyzed, couldn't move. The pain was excruciating. [In the past life] I shouted and shouted for help until I was exhausted. No one came.

Although she managed to get herself out of that life and into conscious awarness of being in her bedroom, worse was to come.

> *But when I tried to move to my horror I was still paralysed. My chest hurt and I could not feel my legs at all.*
>
> *I lay there for hours and hours. Daylight faded. I cried and cried, and could not wipe the tears away.*
>
> *Suddenly there was a knock on the door. I realised it was a friend with whom I was supposed to be going out for the evening. I tried to shout but nothing came out. The house was in darkness. Would she think I had simply forgotten and gone out?*
>
> *Fortunately she had a sixth sense that something was wrong. She came in through the back door and shouted for me. She came up into my bedroom and saw me there on the bed. I managed to indicate the tape recorder with my eyes.*
>
> *She ran the tape back and played the end. It made no difference. So she talked me through it step by step. I had to go back into that life and tell her what was happening – while in the life I could speak. She told me to ask my guide to move the tree. But I was still paralyzed. She told me to leave that body behind, to let go of the sensations. To come back into my present life whole and healed. Gradually I was able to let go and the feeling began to come back into my body. She massaged me and then brought me a cup of tea.*
>
> *I sobbed as I told her how lonely and helpless I had felt stuck on the bed. It seemed like an eternity. I don't think I will ever forget that experience, it has scarred me for life.*

She was fortunate to have had that perceptive friend who had a basic knowledge of how to heal the situation. But she came to my workshop to see if there was any further work she needed to do and to reverse that sense of helpless loneliness which had stayed with her. As she suspected, there was more work to do in her past life when we had to reframe it so that someone found her and gave her the help she needed. In addition, we reframed it again so that she wasn't trapped under the tree at all, it missed her. We also needed to go into the between lives space – the interlife – to heal the etheric blueprint from which her new body would be made as otherwise the potential for problems in the present life was there. In that space we were able to bring her together with her higher self, guides and soul group so that she could see what she planned to do in her present life. Unsurprisingly perhaps the friend who had rescued her in her present life had been part of her present life plans for healing that other life.

It is not only people who do things alone who find that things go wrong though. Another workshop participant introduced herself by pointing to her neck and saying hoarsely:

> *I had a past life regression and had just had a knife stuck in my neck when the woman said 'that's it dear, your time's up, come back next week'.*

By the time she came to my workshop a couple of days later she could barely speak. Before the workshop could continue I had to have her go back to that point in the other life, take the knife out of her neck and heal not only the neck in the past life, but also in the present and on the etheric blueprint. It was a graphic illustration for the other workshop participants on how to do past life healing. By the time we'd done that her throat had healed and she could speak normally again. I've seen knee and back injuries reactivated in a similar way by people who seem to think that rerunning a past life is all that is needed, they don't consider the necessity of doing healing or reframing (which is why I recommend you go to an experienced, properly trained past life therapist).

It is really important not to panic when things go wrong, and especially not to precipitately yank someone out of trance or an altered state of consciousness. Take a breath and allow your intuition to speak before you take an action. And do the same if it's happening to you.

The most important thing to remember when anything goes wrong is:

Don't panic!

Take a deep calming breath

Ask for guidance and help

Close all your chakras and put yourself in a bubble of protection

Never shake or shout at someone who is in a trance or an altered state of consciousness. Speak quietly and warn them if you have to touch them - and do so gently. Getting them to slow or speed up their breathing, move out of the scene and look at it objectively as though it is being projected on a screen is the first step. Then ask their guide or higher self to come in with suggestions as to how to move on – the guide may speak directly to you or to the other person.

If someone is being influenced by someone else's mind or a spirit, or has been taken over by another spirit during kything and the like, see 'Dealing with spirit attachment' below.

Emergency measures

Sometimes, despite all your precautions, you find yourself picking up a negative atmosphere or tuning into someone else's misery or trauma and somehow you can't quite shake it off. The sensations go home with you. You may also come under ill-wishing from someone who is jealous of your abilities. There are effective 'first aid' measures you can take but the most sensible precaution is to familiarise yourself with the protective practices that will keep you safe: In the meantime:

To overcome negative vibes or toxic emotions you've picked up

- Imagine you are wrapped all around in white light
- Carry an Apache Tear or Black Tourmaline in your pocket
- Crystallise the edges of your aura
- Close and protect your chakras
- Call on your guardian angel or Archangel Michael and his sword

To deal with 'bad influences' or to clear negative energies

- Shower (in light if no water available) or bath in salt water
- Wear Amber or Black Tourmaline
- Wash your hands under running water
- Spray with Petaltone Clear 2 Light, Plant Ally, Blast 'em Off, Crystal Balance's Detachment and Light, Special 8 or Z14
- Comb the aura with Selenite, Angels Wing Calcite or Quartz

To ward off psychic attack

- Get into your purple pyramid
- Wear a Black Tourmaline
- Electrify the edges of your aura
- Place a mental (or actual) mirror between yourself and attacker facing towards the source

To prevent unwanted kything

- Close and protect your crown chakras, throat and third eye
- Ask your gatekeeper to keep your psychic doorways firmly closed

(see below for what to do if a spirit has attached and won't move out)

'Ghost busting'

- Don't panic!
- Put Astral Clear on a crystal and leave it in the room
- Wear a Black Tourmaline
- Burn Frankincense oil in a burner
- Invoke protection and the bubble of light
- Ask that the spirit be taken to the light

(See below if the spirit is resistant to moving on).

When people are deliberately blocking you

Sometimes things go wrong because someone else doesn't want you to see what they are up to – that someone may be in a physical body or an etheric one. Someone may also have blocked you through jealousy or by imposing a past life imperative not to see or to speak what you know.

If a past life edict was imposed, then Banded Agate placed over your third eye can help to release you (see below), especially if you follow this up with an Apophyllite Pyramid, Yellow Labradorite or Rhomboid Selenite with a purpose-made essence on it. This also works for most present life blocks.

If someone is deliberately blocking your psychic sight, picture yourself removing a blindfold and opening your third eye so that you can see again. Sometimes you may need to take chains, padlocks or gratings off the third eye. If you do, make sure they are dissolved and that your third eye is healed with light. Petaltone Greenway essence is helpful. Then ask your gatekeeper to be present and to guard your sight.

But if you are still blocked then you might to have to ask your higher self to talk to the other person's higher self and negotiate a release of the block or a dissolving of any soul contract that may be involved. I find that talking at a distance having wrapped myself in pink light and, separately, also wrapped the other person in pink light can be helpful. The higher selves or guides act as intermediaries. If all else fails, a technique I recently learned from an extremely intuitive Hungarian teacher is helpful:

Exercise: Remove a block

Write the person's name on a piece of paper. Around it write things like 'out of my space', 'leave me alone', 'unblock me', 'I reclaim my sight' and so on, whatever comes to mind but try to phrase it positively rather than saying 'don't'. Screw the paper up, put it in a plastic bag, add some water, tie up the top and put it in the freezer.

This can also work in extreme cases of energy depletion or ill-wishing. It literally freezes the other person out of your space.

Dealing with an unexpected OOBE

As you open up your metaphysical abilities you may find yourself having an unexpected out-of-body experience. This can occur during sleep, meditation or at any other moment. Once you know how to deal with this it is quite simple to return to your body. Unexpected out-of-body experiences are common with anaesthetics or the use of drugs such as ketamine but they can also occur if you wake up suddenly, or under shock or trauma.

Exercise: Dealing with an unexpected OOBE

Stay calm and do not panic.

Decide whether you want to continue the experience or return to your body.

Remind yourself you are having an Exceptional Human Experience and could take the opportunity to explore what that might mean for you.

Open the soma chakra in your forehead.

The easiest way to return to your body is to think yourself back. Give yourself the instruction: "Back to my body, now" and picture yourself melting back into your body. This usually works instantaneously. If it does not, 'reel yourself in' via the silver cord that connects your etheric body to the soma chakra on your forehead. Picture this cord retracting into your body and pulling you back at the same time.

Anchor your grounding cord deep in the earth.

If these experiences occur frequently and are not welcome, wearing a piece of Hematite, Smoky Quartz, Mahogany Obsidian or an Apache Tear helps you to stay in your body.

Sometimes, especially if you're under the influence of drink or drugs, even these measures won't return you to your body because you have picked up a hitch-hiker, who moves in with you. In which case you will need to know how to move it on. This usually needs expert help but the following pages will help you with emergency first aid.

To strengthen your silver cord, keep Faden Quartz with you at all times.

Picked up something nasty?

One group of earthbound spirits are trapped by their obstinate nature.
Wilma Davidson [57]

It is all too easy when you begin opening your psychic awareness, especially if you indulge in indiscriminate kything of any being who wants to communicate with or through you, to pick up something that is not to your benefit. A spirit may attach or to try to influence you. Similarly, not every guru or alleged master has reached a point of high spiritual evolution. Many so called masters are motivated by greed, control-freakery or other dubious intentions and, if you have been initiated by them, their tainted energy will have passed to you and will be lodged in your third eye or crown chakras. Many authorities insist that such tainted initiations cannot be reversed. Not so! Fortunately a banded Agate on your third eye and Smoky Elestial Quartz at your feet can clear the contamination and leave you a pure channel for the healing or spiritual energy to pass through or for you to receive psychic communications.

Physical signs of a spirit attaching or trying to take over or unduly influence are fairly easy to spot - you may feel these signals in your own body when working with someone else, so check out if it's 'yours' or 'theirs' as it can become a useful signal to watch out for in future.

Signals of spirit attachment or undue influence

- feeling of heaviness/suffocation in limbs or chest
- inability to move
- palpitations
- anxiety attacks
- nausea or extreme weakness
- difficulty in breathing
- icy chills
- goose pimples

- dreadful smells
- body distortion or bruising
- cravings – especially for drugs, nicotine, alcohol or sugar
- unease for no apparent reason
- extreme yawning
- constant repetition of thoughts that are not 'yours'

The first thing you need to do is to ascertain whether there is undue influence going on from someone living or 'dead' or from a thought form, or whether it is a more serious situation of spirit attachment. If the influence is from someone living or dead, then use protective measures to close your aura and the chakras through which they are linking in.

If it is a thought form that is causing the trouble the influence tends to be mental. You have thoughts that are not 'yours' or you find yourself acting in ways you didn't intend, hearing voices and so on. Also, although this is difficult to explain until you've encountered one, thought forms don't tend to have much life, they feel flat, one dimensional and repetitious even though they may seem to be very pushy or even malicious. If this is the case, use the light wand to zap them out:

Exercise: The light wand

Imagine that you are holding in your hand a long, slim wand of light. At the push of a button, the wand sends out a shaft of brilliant light that immediately and harmlessly dissolves all it comes into contact with. (Stibnite, Firework Obsidian, Lemurian or Lazer Quartz crystals are brilliant for zapping out a thought form, simply point and focus the energy to do its work).

If the undue influence is coming from someone who is still living, a cord cutting can be very helpful.

Undue influence and psychic vampirism

An incarnate spirit (i.e. someone living) who has hooked in to your aura and won't let go thereby depleting your energies, or a dodgy guru or 'spiritual' master who draws power from you in the guise of initiating you, may leave you with little will or energy of your own and therefore open to attachment or undue influence. Spirit attachment can only occur when an energy field is weak and depleted, and when you do not fully inhabit your body and your soul is not fully present so there is an energetic 'gap' or vacuum, so obviously being in control of your own psychic energies is the best prevention.

Exercise: *If someone is drawing energy or power from you*

- *Imagine or draw a green pyramid that goes from beneath your left armpit down to your waist front and back.*
- *Use the power of your mind or an Aventurine or Rainbow Mayanite crystal to pull out any hooks that may be lodged in your spleen chakra beneath your left armpit.*
- *Tape a green Aventurine or Jade over the site of your spleen chakra. (If you then get a pain under your right armpit protect that side with another pyramid or tape a Gaspeite crystal over the spot.)*
- *If the drawing of power is mental, close your third eye and protect it with an Amethyst pyramid. Be sure to remove any hooks that are locked into your third eye or crown chakras. Ask your gatekeeper to protect your chakras.*

To remove an undesirable initiation or a tie to a dodgy guru or master

This is best done by someone who has reached a higher state of initiation than the person who originally did the initiation or made the tie, but fortunately a Banded Agate can dissolve the tie or the initiation for you. As always seems to be the case, I intuitively found the way to clear the 'tie' during an emergency. I was asked late at night to clear a tie to a very dodgy self-styled master as the women was taking him to court the next day to regain money she had lent him. All I could find in my handbag (which always has a few crystals in it) was a Banded Agate – which I'd never seen before. We used this to tie cut from the master and clear her third eye and she took the stone with her to court. She won her case and avoided bankruptcy. You can do this yourself or ask a friend to assist:

Exercise: *Removing an undesirable tie or initiation*

If available, place a large Smoky Quartz or Smoky Elestial crystal at your feet to draw off negative energies.

Place a Banded or Botswana Agate over the third eye. If it feels appropriate, spiral the Agate out from the third eye, cleanse the stone and repeat until the tie or initiation is dissolved. Then heal and seal the third eye. Selenite, Apophyllite, Angels Wing Calcite or one of the high vibration Quartzes placed over the third eye for a few moments will assist the healing.

If the crown chakra appears to have been infected, place Selenite or one of the other stones over the chakra and ask that the infection be removed and divine light put in its place.

Note: if there was a heart opening at the same time as the dodgy connection was made, place a Rhodochrosite, Rhodonite, Tugtupeite or Danburite crystal over your heart to ensure that only divine love at its highest level is present in your heart. If it feels as though anything else might be lodged in your heart, ask the crystal to dissolve it and replace it with divine love.

Dealing with spirit attachment

> *Obsessive thoughts, 'psychic disturbance', the feeling that 'the lights are on but nobody is at home', or a deadness or glazed expression in the eyes can all be indications of 'possession'. Psychological trauma or extremely intense emotions are the usual causes.*
>
> *J.R. Worsley*

Spirit attachment used to be called possession, and often still is, but as it has particularly negative connotations and suggests that no freewill or autonomy is left at all, today we prefer the term spirit attachment. It means that a discarnate spirit or entity has entered or is affecting a living person's energy field – rather like a hitch-hiker piggy backing on the aura.

People often ask, how can this happen? Well, the answer is that there is a gap in the personal energy field into which the spirit can slip or there is a gap in the soul's energy field. Indeed, attachment can only occur when an energy field is weak and depleted, and when you do not fully inhabit your body and your soul is not fully present so there is a 'gap' or vacuum or when you voluntarily relinquish your body and move out. Although in the modern western world we are used to thinking of the soul as being all of a piece, the ancient Egyptians recognised seven layers to the soul. The soul is a vehicle for the eternal spirit that moves into and out of incarnation. Soul parts may remain in past lives, at previous deaths, in the between life state or earlier in the current life. This leaves you open to spirit attachment as you will have gaps in your aura. Soul retrieval and release is a specialised field and the scattered parts may be amenable to being called home by an experienced practitioner. It is rare to be able to do your own soul retrieval but it is essential that any gaps in the aura be shielded so that nothing else can attach.

Unfortunately spirit attachment can sometimes happen as you become more psychic because it is draws lost souls to you as you give off a signal, 'here I am, I can see you'. Spirits are attracted to your light – it also happens when you open to kythe. If your protection is strong then such spirits cannot attach but they may try to influence you and will do all they can to attract your attention. Fortunately your psychic awareness will help you to recognise that this is taking place and to help them on their way to the light.

Influence is a lighter, more intermittent form of attachment. It often arises out of momentary loss of energy containment such as in drink or drug taking, or the effects of anaesthetic, shock or trauma. Spirit attachment or influence is common in cases of depression or debilitating illnesses like M.E. and one of the best protections can be the desist from drug taking or from working psychically or in a healing way when your own energy is depleted or when your energy field has been breached.

Attachment can be seen in eyes, which are blank with 'no one home' most of the time or 'someone else' looks out from them. The attaching spirit usually seeks to experience something it was addicted to in life, or to control someone or to feel safe, or to complete unfinished business.

As the attaching spirit is, usually, an uninvited guest or the influence unsought, this is one occasion when it is not necessary to request the other person's permission to assist them as the spirit is usually breaching their autonomy (unless they've been deliberately invoked) and they negate a person's right to choice. However, once you have performed the release, let it go, do not go back to it. Some people want to hang onto their attachments, they make them feel important, wanted, needed and so on. If this is the case, you will never clear them so step right out of it.

Signs that a spirit is attached or over-influencing

- 'Blank' eyes
- Cannot make eye contact
- Someone else looks out from the eyes
- Behaviour out of character with normal persona
- Obsessive or addictive behaviour
- Unusual thought patterns
- Intense dreams or fantasies with a nightmarish quality
- Hears voices
- A feeling of being controlled by someone else
- Chronic fatigue, panic attacks, depression
- Overwhelming sugar cravings
- Person is vague, nebulous and insubstantial
- Sudden or extreme fatigue for no reason
- Constant lethargy and lack of enthusiasm

- Exhaustion that does not improve after sleep
- Disturbed sleep
- Irritability and over-sensitivity
- Depression and tearfulness
- Panic attacks or 'paranoia'
- Inability to concentrate and poor memory
- Loss of libido or exhaustion after sexual contact
- Over-excitement, hysteria or mania
- Being on an emotional or mental 'high'
- Rapid, constant and somewhat random chatter
- Crystals or other objects 'jumping' or shattering
- Stinking breath

Unless you are very experienced, it is wise not to attempt a release yourself as you may drive things deeper and if something is attaching to you then you need expert help but you can take emergency measures to prevent further damage. Calling on the Archangel Michael and his helpers to take the spirit to the light is a time honoured way of healing attachments. The spirit must be returned to the light not simply shooed away to go and bother someone else. Always call in an expert when dealing with someone else wherever possible. But there are times when an emergency measure is needed and the release below will get you out of trouble. Remember to dissolve the attachment and to fill the place where it was with light to seal and heal it. (Petaltone Astral Clear left on a clear Quartz and placed by the bed at night will often move the spirit on.)

If the person is not present you can either use a photograph or imagine them in the room with you, or use yourself as a surrogate by performing the healing on your own body (only do this if you are certain your own protection is strong and you have a good relationship with your gatekeeper). Once a clearing has been carried out, it may need to be followed up by soul retrieval and will certainly require bioenergetic repair and sealing. The advantage of using a crystal for this work is that it stands at the interface between you, the other person and the spirit, creating a barrier so the spirit does not attach to you after release. The crystal also calls in angelic helpers and divine light and amplifies it, facilitating the work.

Such clearing work has to be carried out with right intention, absolute integrity and a total absence of fear. If you cannot bring these qualities to the work or if you feel vulnerable, desist as you will do more harm than good. You should not carry out clearing – or indeed any psychic work - if you yourself are carrying entities, attachments or negative energies, or if your soul is fragmented or your aura breached. Knowing your limitations is essential and it is also essential to know how to check yourself to be sure you haven't unknowingly taken anything on (see checking the aura pp.95-98).

Remember, not all attaching or influencing spirits have left their physical body (i.e. they're still 'alive' rather than 'dead') and such spirits need to be returned to their own physical body rather than sent off to the light. Attachments can arise from the thoughts and feelings of others who try to influence or control or who try to clutch onto your strength – a common experience for intuitive healers, readers and counsellors. It's as though they 'have their hooks into you' (see the disconnection above). Attachments can arise to objects in addition to people – these can be cleared quite easily with Petaltone Z14 and Clear2Light and Crystal Balance Detachment. Follow up with Crystal Balance Light spray..

Remember too, it's not always external attachment that is the problem *although it will feel like it is*. It may be your own projected or repressed qualities or obsessive/compulsive thoughts, desires and toxic emotions manifesting, apparently externally.

Petaltone Astral Clear, Z14, Plant Ally or Clear Tone essences or a dedicated Aventurine or Candle Quartz can be effective clearers, as can burning a candle in a church and asking that the soul will be forgiven and taken home to the light.

Exercise: Releasing spirit attachment with crystals

1. *As soon as you even begin to think about this process, immediately place a bubble of protection around yourself and mentally throw out a wide energetic net around the spirit to trap the attachment so that it cannot slip away.*
2. *Lay out a protective Selenite, Black Tourmaline or other protective pentagram (five pointed star) on which you can sprinkle Astral Clear or Clear2Light, or to grid the corners of the room. (Burning Frankincense can also assist.) If the person is present, lay Selenite around them. (If the crystals aren't available see the alternative method below).*
3. *Holding a Brandenberg or a Smoky Amethyst (use one of each if combined stone not available), place Selenite or Labradorite on your third eye or on the person with the attaching spirit. Ask that the spirit will make itself known to you and tell you why it has chosen to stay close to the earth.*
4. *Gently ascertain whether the spirit knows it has passed to another plane of being – or indeed whether it is still on the earth plane.*

5. *Talk to the spirit as appropriate, addressing his or her concerns and offering unconditional love, reassurance and understanding. Then ask if the spirit is ready to move into the light for healing. If the answer is yes, remove the energetic net.*
6. *Place your Brandenberg over the soma, heart and solar plexus chakras. Visualise hands reaching down to help the spirit move into the light. If the spirit is reluctant, ask that his or her guardian angel and higher self will assist the process and hand the energetic net over to them.*
7. *Ask if the person who had the attachment needs to call any part of his or her own energy or soul back. If so, call it back with the Brandenberg and place it over the heart. Allow that energy to be reabsorbed. [If there is reluctance, further soul retrieval work may be called for, Tugtupite on the heart seed chakra can assist with this.]*
8. *Invoke Archangel Michael and put one drop of Z14 on the floor at the person's feet. Stand back and wait for it to do its work.*
9. *Now take the Brandenberg all the way around and under the body, sides, front and back, to heal and seal the aura. (Petaltone Plant Ally can be extremely useful at this point).*

It is essential when any kind of release has taken place that the aura be healed and sealed to prevent further incidents and any crystals used be cleansed thoroughly so that the etheric levels are also purified and sealed.

Exercise: Alternative release method

Sit quietly and focus your attention on calling in higher helpers and guides to assist you. Ask that the spirit be taken to the light by his or her guardian angel. This works if the spirit has simply lost the way home. Sometimes simply knowing that he or she is in the post death state is all a spirit needs to move on of its own accord but you may need to do more.

If you can actually communicate with the spirit, ask if there is anything you can do to assist, what he or she needs. Surprisingly perhaps the requests are usually simple and easy to arrange, and often relate to unfinished business. (You may need to use your creativity here, asking that other spirits be present or writing an etheric letter that can be handed to a guide for delivery). One you have agreed to do or offer whatever is required, the spirit usually moves on.

If the spirit is deeply entrenched, or is still of the opinion that their advice and assistance is crucial for the well-being of someone still on earth, calling in an expert is your best course of action, but do choose someone who moves them on to an appropriate place rather than just banishing them elsewhere to bother someone else. Your local spiritualist church, shamanic practitioner or metaphysical centre or the Spirit Release Foundation or the School of Intuition and Healing after Spirit Release Foundation will be able to help. In the meantime, keep your own energy high to ensure you are protected.

Crystals for assisting lost souls: Nirvana Quartz, Smoky Amethyst, Smoky or Amethyst Brandenberg, Candle Quartz, Aegerine, Spirit Quartz, Rose Quartz, Super 7, Shattukite, Jet.

Essences for assisting lost souls: Bush Boab made into a spray with Angelsword, Fringed Violet and Lichen. Petaltone Astral Clear on a clear Quartz , Z14 on Amphibole Quartz (remember to invoke Archangel Michael to assist), Plant Ally.

Crystals for ascertaining where or what the attachment is (place on your third eye or 'comb' around the body): Chrysolite, Quartz with Mica, Celestobarite, Apophyllite.

Crystals for releasing spirit attachment (place over the soma chakra, solar plexus or heart): Brandenberg Amethyst, Smoky Amethyst, Nirvana Quartz, Halite, Spirit Quartz, Smoky Elestial, Marcasite, Stibnite, Datolite, Smoky Phantom Quartz, Yellow Phantom Quartz, Avalonite, Fluorite, Selenite wand, Larimar, Laser Quartz, Petalite, Labradorite, Aegerine, Iolite, Clear Kunzite, Blue Selenite, Herkimer Diamond, Smoky Citrine, Brown Jasper, Pyrolusite. Celestobarite, Larimar, Shattuckite.

Crystals for releasing mental attachments (place over the person with the attachment's third eye): Smoky Amethyst, Blue Halite, Yellow Phantom Quartz, Limonite, Pyrolusite, Aegerine.

Crystal for calling home soul fragments: Faden Quartz, Spirit Quartz.

Crystals for releasing disembodied spirits attached to places (leave in the room or site): Quartz, Marcasite, Smoky Amethyst, Larimar (enhanced if you add Astral Clear).

Crystals traditionally used for 'demonic' possession: Jet, Smoky Amethyst, Dravide (Brown) Tourmaline.

Crystals for removing disembodied spirits after kything or other metaphysical activity (place over the third eye or crown chakras): Banded Agate, Botswanna Agate, Shattuckite.

Crystals for repairing the aura after removal of disembodied spirits: Aegerine, Quartz, Stibnite, Selenite, Faden Quartz, Laser Quartz, Phantom Quartzes, Angels Wing Calcite, Rainbow Mayanite.

The chakras and spirit attachment

> *With our chakras blocked we cannot ingest the nourishment stored in the Luminous Energy Field.*
>
> *Alberto Villoldo* [58]

Attachments frequently take hold through the chakras and you should check out the chakras carefully for attachments if you are experiencing any kind of psychic disruption or blockage of your psychic abilities – place your hand over the chakra and notice if it feels cold and energyless or if it squirms beneath your fingers. If you are visual, you may be able to see smoky wisps or tendrils, black spots, hooks and ties. Crystals often jump at the site of attachments.

It's not only discarnate spirits that can attach. Anyone you have ever had sex with can have left some of their energy field in your lower chakras, for instance, but strong thoughts of lust can lodge there even if there has been no physical contact, and it is common to find that miscarriages or still births have left behind some of the energy of the soul who would have been born. You will find emotional attachment hooks into the sacral and solar plexus, thought forms in the third eye, ancestral hooks in the soma or higher chakras and so on. You may also find that someone who is blocking your psychic sight has sealed your third eye shut (this can be released with a Rhomboid Selenite, Rhomboid Calcite, Auralite 23 or Banded Agate placed over the third eye).

Chakric attachments:

Earth Star (below the feet)

Attachments: spirits of place, stuck spirits. If permanently open, you easily pick up negative energies from the ground or 'spirits of place', either as attachments or as events that have taken place.

Base (bottom of the spine)

Attachments: lovers, mothers. Anyone you've had sex with can attach, but you can also have attachment to your mother who can manipulate through the chakra and you may suffer from projection of your own feelings.

Sacral (below the navel)
Attachments: anyone you've ever had sex with, needy people, thought forms, unborn children, parents. 'Emotional hooks' that drain your energy and you are vulnerable to another person through sexual contact or powerful feelings such as lust or possessiveness that create attached thought forms.

Solar Plexus (between waist and heart)
Attachments: previous relationships, relatives, needy people. The solar plexus takes on other people's thoughts and feelings. An emotional linkage point, it is where you store your emotional baggage and other people dump theirs. Invasion and energy leeching take place. With a 'stuck-open' solar plexus you take on other people's feelings too easily.

Spleen (under left arm)
Attachments: psychic vampires, needy people, ex-partners. Psychic vampires leach your energy, as do past partners, children or parents. (Releasing attachments from the spleen chakra may then trigger anger which tends to be felt under the right arm which will also need protection.)

Heart seed (base of breastbone)
Attachments: parts of your soul left in other lives or dimensions. If you left parts of yourself at past life deaths or traumatic or deeply emotional experiences, these parts attach and try to influence you to complete unfinished business. You may need to call them back or send them to your higher self.

Heart
Attachments: anyone you have ever loved. This chakra can be the site of a great many hooks. You may have given away parts of your heart and need to reclaim them or made promises that tie you to others.

Higher Heart (above the heart)
Attachments: guides, gurus or masters, mentors. Opening the higher heart chakra can tie you to an initiator and not all masters or gurus have clean energy or the best of intentions.

Throat (over throat)
Attachments: teachers, mentors, gurus or masters, thought forms. Other people's thoughts and beliefs attach to the throat chakra.

Third eye (slightly above and between the eyebrows)
Attachments: thought forms, ancestors or relatives, lost souls. Strong beliefs block this chakra and may be caused by undue influence or thought form attachment. If stuck open, you are vulnerable to the thoughts, feelings and influences not only of people on the earth level, but also on the etheric. You are constantly bombarded with thoughts and feelings that are not your own.

Soma (above the third eye, at the hairline)
Attachments: 'lost souls', walk-ins. When this chakra is stuck open it is all too easy for spirits to attach.

Past life (behind the ears)
Attachments: past life personas, soul fragments, thought forms from previous beliefs.
If stuck open, you feel unsafe and overwhelmed by past life memories of trauma and violent death and fears. Past life personas and thought forms attach or re-manifest.

Crown (top of the head)
Attachments: spiritual entities, lost souls, mentors. If stuck open, you are prey to illusions and false communicators, thought forms, spirit attachment or undue influence.

Soul star chakra (a foot above your head)
Attachments: ancestral spirits, E.Ts, 'lost souls'. Stuck open or blocked, it leads to soul fragmentation, spirit attachment, ET invasion, or overwhelm by ancestral spirits.

Stellar Gateway (above the Soul Star)
Attachments: so-called enlightened beings that are anything but. When stuck open, a source of cosmic disinformation, illusion, delusion, deception and disintegration that leaves you totally unable to function in the everyday world.

Note: This chakra cleansing can be amplified by putting a drop of Petaltone Clear2Light, or spray the crystal with Crystal Balance detachment, Z14 or Plant Ally before use and placing a drop of Z14 (remember to invoke Archangel Michael) on the ground or, preferably, on an Amphibole Quartz to close the proceedings.

Exercise: To clear and check the chakras for attachments

Beginning with the Stellar Gateway about a foot and a half above the top of the head (or as high as your arm can reach) and using a clear Quartz, Brandenberg, Smoky Quartz, Flint, Rainbow Mayanite or Selenite crystal – or a Stibnite wand if the attachment is extraterrestrial – 'unwind' the chakra (this is usually done in an anti-clockwise direction but do it in the way that feels right to you as not all chakras rotate in the same direction). Wind out in a spiral at least a foot away from the body.

When you are sure the chakra is clear and has no attachments, cleanse the crystal by spraying with Clear2Light and/or Z14 and then wind it back in in the opposite direction.

Work down each chakra in turn not forgetting the earth chakra beneath your feet.

Then wrap yourself – and the person you are working on if you are doing the cleanse for someone else - in a cloak of light. Sweeping Anandalite through the aura is excellent for this.

Then check out the aura with your mind or the crystal to ensure there is no attachment or influence elsewhere. If there is, disperse it with the crystal and call in light to heal and seal it.

Chakra disconnection can also take place by using the power of your mind:

Exercise: Chakra cleansing using your mind

Close your eyes and relax, turning your attention inward.

Take your mind to each of your chakras in turn and check whether there is a connection to another person or if there is any energy from another person left in the chakra. If so, use a laser light to detach the connection from yourself and the other person and to completely dissolve the connection in whatever form it took.

Remember to check the higher chakras and to enlist the help of your higher self if the connection is being maintained because of a vow or promise to another person.

If it is, ask if it still appropriate to carry it on, if so then ask for help to complete the task. If it is not, then rescind the promise, dissolve the ties it made, and let go with love.

18
Groups and Intuitive Organisations

If organizations can get logic, rationality and goal orientation working in tandem with intuition, then they will be positioned to generate unexpected solutions and creative yet feasible ideas – potentially opening up a wellspring of human capacity for the 21st century.

Bill Overend [59]

A huge shift is taking place throughout the business world. The role of intuition in organisations is rapidly being recognised with Henry Mintzberg suggesting that intuitive or 'strategic thinking' delivers better and more relevant results than lengthy, analytical planning. Many MBA and PhD facilities now offer Intuition in Management courses. Intuition operates three ways within an organisation: personal, interpersonal and collectively. The personal relates to how you function within the organisation and within your chosen field: how and on what basis you make decisions, suggestions and innovations and how much foresight you can bring to your work. The interpersonal comes into play when you react or respond to colleagues and other group members, how you perceive their feelings, and how the group dynamic functions. The collective operates when an organisation itself functions intuitively and employees are encouraged to think creatively:

> *Man, unlike any other things organic or inorganic in the universe, grows beyond his work, walks up the stairs of his concepts, emerges ahead of his accomplishments.*
>
> *John Steinbeck*

The same kind of dynamics operate in any group and so the exercises and suggestions in this section can be applied both to your work life and your spiritual and psychic expansion.

Intuition at work

Successful entrepreneurs are innovators and risk–takers who appear to have an extraordinary ability to know where future business opportunities will eventuate and how to profitably actualize these ventures. The patterns of thought and action displayed by entrepreneurs are thus informed by an unusually high degree of both creativity and intuition.

Dana Tomasino [60]

In a study made by Harvard University, 13,000 executives reported that they relied on left and right brain skills equally – and yet credited 80% of their successes to intuition [61] Intuition works across all classes and ranks in an organisation from the CEO to the post boy, from the most experienced member to the newcomer. However, it has been identified that intuitive thinkers rise faster through an organisation with more intuitives being found in the higher levels of management. Research conducted by Shell amongst the Fortune 500 companies that concluded that:

> *Intuitive information processing strategies are most often found at the highest levels of an organisation and in specific functions like research and development.* [62]

Intuition is increasingly being taught as a skilful strategy for middle management and newcomers are encouraged to keep an intuition journal to develop their skill. It has been identified that intuitive thinking is encouraged in businesses encompassing a high degree of risk and ambiguity such as financial planning and the computer industry, and those concerned with research and development, policy decisions and forward planning. Fund administrators were also likely to be intuitive, instinctively picking their way through complex situations. Intuitives were deemed to be most helpful in situations with:

- Time constraints
- A high level of pressure
- Several plausible alternatives
- A high level of uncertainty
- Non–predictable variables
- No precedent
- Limited information available
- Unstable market or industry

Employees using intuition reported that they knew instinctively once the right decision had been reached because they felt physically and mentally calm, totally confident and committed to the outcome whereas prior to the decision they felt physically and mentally edgy and experienced bodily discomfort.

It is not only employees and management who are intuitive – organisations themselves are now starting to function intuitively. Organisations that function intuitively are people orientated and concerned with the environment. Roles and responsibilities are being re–evaluated within the global scheme of things rather than the global market. Ethics and integrity are becoming increasingly important as solutions to humanity's problems become more pressing. Intuitive organisations recognise the interconnectedness of all life and, like leavening in bread, their vision is spreading.

Intuitive organisations:

- Think globally
- Are people centred
- Are highly creative
- Treat everyone as of equal value
- Are ethical
- Look for innovative solutions
- Capitalise on individual creativity for the benefit of the whole
- Are elastic: flexible and forward looking
- Respond to and create change

Your intuition at work

Organisations don't innovate, people do.
Tesolin

Using your intuition can sharpen up your working day and improve your relationships with colleagues. Once you are in the flow of using your intuition the day to day struggle falls away leaving far more time to be creative and fulfilled in your work:

- You act with total appropriateness. Freed from knee jerk reactions you find creative responses.
- You have more creative energy available.
- You are intuitively aware of what is required from you in advance and therefore more prepared and open to possibilities.
- You are more creative and innovative.
- You are a better listener because you hear the whole story: said and unsaid.
- You are able to 'think on your feet', dealing quickly and spontaneously with whatever comes your way.
- You recognise when pieces are missing or the information doesn't add up.
- You ask the right questions.

- You use your intuition to create contacts, setting up an intention in advance.
- You do not waste time trying to contact someone who is out, your intuition tells you when they return and suggests positive steps to take in the meantime.
- Rehearsing the outcome you want, through visualisation, prepares the way to easy acceptance of plans and suggestions. It revolutionises sales techniques and people management.
- Trusting to your own perceptions gets the job done far more efficiently and innovatively than relying on 'experts'.
- Problems are exacerbated by what we think we know – knowledge, preconceptions and expectations get in the way. When you change to what is actually perceived there are far less misunderstandings. Communication is clear and action brisk.
- You find new ways of looking at things. Henry Ford asked the question: 'How can we get the work to the people' and the assembly line was born.
- You understand your fellow workers more acutely and your people skills improve. You are aware when someone's mood or energy is low or high – and act accordingly. Taking time for an empathetic word revolutionises relationships with colleagues.
- You think the unthinkable and do the impossible – and take the necessary risks to achieve that.
- Group skills become more cooperative and you find joy in teamwork.
- Empathetic and intuitive managers allow rather than trying to control the situation or other people. They are aware of problems and potentials before they occur and take appropriate steps.
- You know yourself and your colleagues very well indeed.
- You rise effortlessly to the top of your profession.
- Your job satisfaction is higher than your unintuitive peers.

Benefits to businesses:

- Stronger motivation for staff urged to take calculated risks
- More effective leadership
- Better decision–making
- Better sales performance or targets met
- Higher profit margins
- Better hiring decisions are made

- Innovation is optimised
- Strategies and forward planning are effective
- Industry trends are identified in advance

Exercise: Empathetic communication

When speaking to a colleague you want to be more in tune with, hold the phone to your left ear or cover your right ear with your hand. There is evidence to suggest that the impulses received by that ear go to the right brain, which is far more empathetic than the left. (If you want to detach yourself and be more objective, use your right ear.)

Embracing difference

If you have a colleague with whom you have difficulties, the following exercise will help.

Exercise: Embracing difference

Sit quietly for a moment or two, bringing your attention deep into yourself. When you feel ready, allow your awareness to rise up to the highest possible level until you reach the point where all is one.

From this place, look at your colleague. Identify what irks and irritates you, what you dislike, what makes it difficult for you to get on together. As all is one, you will see that this merely an extension of the things that irk and irritate you about yourself. Thank your colleague for being a mirror for you and embrace these traits within yourself. They have a positive gift for you. Take the time to allow your intuition to tell you what it is. When you know, resolve to put it into practice.

Now find within that oneness all the positive aspects of yourself and your colleague. Embrace these and resolve to manifest them more strongly in your own life and to recognise them within your colleague.

Feel how much love and respect there is between you in this place of oneness and bring this back with you as you slowly return your awareness to the everyday world.

Stand up and make contact with the earth beneath your feet to ground yourself.

Intuitive leadership

Leadership is not an affair of the head. It's not something you do by thinking about it hard. You do it from the heart, and when your heart is in your business and your business is in your heart, when your heart is with your family or your community or the people who work there, you get extraordinary things done.

James M. Kouzes

People who are strongly intuitive become leaders. They may not set out to do so, but people follow them instinctively, especially as their people skills and management style are empathetic and personally motivating rather than coercive and authoritarian. Other people respect an intuitive leader's judgement, their creativity, appropriateness and integrity, and they honour their courage and risk taking – what seems like a risk to non–intuitive people is the obvious solution for an intuitive person.

Intuitive people are 'inner led'. Listening to their inner voice, they do not need an outer authority to get them to act. They are fearless and certain without being arrogant. They have passion that they are not afraid to express. And yet they care about the people they lead, they show understanding. They communicate with regard to people's concerns and objectives as well as those of the organisation.

Within an intuitively led organisation, everyone benefits. Work becomes more meaningful. There is unity of purpose and people are inspired to produce their best work. Because intuitive people are connected into the whole, in the organisation everyone looks out for, and appreciates, everyone else.

Group creativity

The perception of separateness of an individual from other persons (or from the universe) is an illusion.

Willis K. Harman (Professor of Engineering–Economic Systems, Stanford University)

In an intuitive organisation, the sum of the parts is much greater than the individual members as group energy is heightened and enhanced by intuitive teamwork. At the same time, individual input is stimulated.

Research suggests that the brainstorming sessions that became fashionable in organisations during the 1980s and 90s may not be as conducive to group creativity as was first thought. There is evidence that certain individuals within the group will be more than happy to offer their contributions – in order to be noticed and for their own glory rather than the good of the group – and other, more introverted people who dislike taking risks and who fear the judgement of the group, will hold back. A situation that can lead to deep lack of trust within the group. In addition, as one of the major factors in creative intuition is that, initially, the idea comes as a picture that has to be translated into words, an intuitive idea can be difficult to express fully immediately.

It may be more conducive to hold anonymous creative sessions in which everyone makes their contribution from their computer terminal. This removes fear of group judgement and the cult of personality from the equation. One of the best ways for this to work is for the group to convene, intuitively rather than physically, at a fixed time and to spend twenty minutes in quiet contemplation, consciously linking to the group mind and intention. Images and half–formed ideas can be entered onto the computer so that the whole group can explore them whilst the group mind is united.

Building the group mind

A group that links together becomes far more creative. One person should be chosen from the group to lead the exercise, and the topic and goal decided in advance by the group as a whole:

Exercise: Building a group mind

Close your eyes and breathe gently. Raising your eyes and looking up to the point above and between your eyebrows, picture a yellow ribbon going from this point up towards the ceiling where it meets the ribbon of everyone else in the room. This is where our group mind is situated, it is the interface of all your individual minds. Picture a bright light shining at this point and sending beams down into each individual mind as a linkage point.

Now take your mind to the topic we are addressing today. Think about it, setting out its problems, its potential and its possible solutions. Look at the goals and how they can be achieved. As you think, let the light take your thoughts into the group mind.

It would be useful to have an advisory committee to help us so ask that everyone who has expertise in this field will mentally unite with us and give their input. Be receptive to their advice as you listen to your inner voice and to the group mind.

[Allow 5–15 minutes of quiet reflection time].

Take a moment or two to finish what you are doing and go over the solutions that have occurred to you.

Now take your mind up to the joining point of the ribbons and detach your ribbon, bringing it back into yourself with your own individual mind but know that you can access the group mind whenever it is appropriate. When you are ready, open your eyes. Feel your feet firmly on the ground.

Appoint a group scribe who can record what is said on a large white board. Then go round the group sharing the insights and solutions that arose for each person and use them as a spring board for a group discussion.

Group practice

Intuition can be enhanced through group practice – and psychic awareness can strongly affect group interaction. Some groups come together specially to enhance their psychic connection but all groups including those within an organisation can benefit from intuitive exercises. It raises creativity and opens the way to risk taking.

There is more interaction between a group than is apparent at surface level. At a very deep level, our minds are one. At a more superficial level, however, group dynamics can be disharmonious. Groups operate at the lowest common denominator. In a group who come together with a spiritual purpose, jealousy and dissent can be rife if the highest connection has not been made. Groups interact at a subtle level and if someone does not trust a member of the group at gut level that group will not function coherently – and the lack of trust may be an intuition that should be listened to.

Group trust

Group trust can be enhanced by a few moments of silence, focused thought, or meditation, before commencing the business of the group. Sitting together in silence for a few moments melds the group together and opens the way to trust.

If you are taking part in a brainstorming session to generate ideas or solutions, you could focus on the thought: 'solutions'. Develop this further with a meditation to create a space within the centre of the group that attracts solutions into it, which make themselves known with clarity and ease to the group.

It is also possible to programme a crystal to aid the group. Amphibole, Cathedral and Spirit Quartz works for this as they absorb the group's intention, and transmit it back as clear thought. They also link into the universal mind and so help to focus intuitive solutions.

The overall energy can be lifted if one or two people within the group are able to intentionally hold a higher energy for the others and gently lead them upward. Such an upliftment occurs naturally when the group mind is harmonized. If the brainwaves of the group are synchronized, not only will intuition or psychic abilities be enhanced but the overall consciousness of the group will be raised.

Exercise: Breathing together

Rhythmic breathing harmonizes group brain waves:

As a group, breathe in for a count of 4,
hold it for 3,
and out for 5.
Repeat 10 times.

Group protection

Group protection is important whether you are brainstorming in an intuitive session or whether you are working within a group with a more spiritual or metaphysical intention. When you work in a metaphysical group, protection is as important as when you work alone. If you feel uncomfortable with someone in the group, it may be that you need to protect yourself from their energies. This is especially so if they are angry or disruptive. It is not a matter of shutting them *out*. It is more a matter of not allowing them to disturb your serenity. If you hold your own space, crystallize the edges of your aura, and put them into a loving energy, their attitude may change – and you will be able to intuit what is bothering them and find ways to address this.

It may also be that you need to explore exactly what makes you feel uncomfortable – this can be done through group discussion or between the two of you, perhaps with a third person present as mediator. Remember that unresolved issues of any kind between group members are not conducive to group harmony. However, it may be that your psychic perception is working and the person about whom you feel doubtful does not have the welfare of the group at heart. If this is the case, paying attention to your psychic intuitions could be a timely warning.

Setting up the space

The purple pyramid meditation is excellent for setting up a group space. The colour of the pyramid can vary in accordance with the purpose of the group. The pyramid could be set up by the group leader before the group assemble, but it will work much better if the whole group are involved in creating the safe space. Adding in extra steps after bringing amethyst light down into the pyramid greatly enhances group cohesion:

Exercise: Setting up the space

Feel the light activating the crown of your head. You will feel this open up. From your crown, your own light will shine. It will go up in a beam to the apex of the pyramid to interface with the light of all others in the group.

This is the point where we all meet. It is where we become one mind. Our joint light goes up from the pyramid to meet the universal mind from which we can draw inspiration and intuition.

When the group is ready to disband, disconnect all the beams of light, ensuring that no one is taking anyone else's energy away with them, close the pyramid down and send its healing energies out to the world wherever they are needed.

As a symbol of the safe space you have created, you may like to place a piece of Hematite in the centre of the group. Hematite enhances group trust, keeps it grounded and focused, and helps to maintain a safe space.

Closing the group

It is essential a group is closed down properly and that people do not allow their energy to go home with anyone else or take anyone else's with them. A few words to close the group are useful, perhaps suggesting that they put on a cloak of protection to see them safely home. If the group is metaphysical in nature, reminding people to pull their auras in around themselves, releasing any energy that is not theirs and letting it go back to where it belongs, and taking back any of their own energy from anyone else to whom it has gone is essential. Some groups like to send out the energy that they have generated to wherever it is needed in the world for healing or any other purpose that is appropriate.

Sound

Sound is useful harmonizer of group energy, bringing the group's brainwaves into alignment. Some groups use chanting – such as Om – whilst others find focusing on the sound of a Tibetan bowl, cymbals or a bell helpful. Monks and nuns used plainsong to induce a meditative state and appropriate background music played as the group come together, or whilst setting up the safe space, will generate group harmony at many levels. Many organisations or groups intuitively used tools such as a school song or a slogan to harmonize the brainwaves without consciously realising the effect it would have.

Development groups

The remarks above apply in particular if you are sitting in a meditation or development group. It must be harmonious if it is to work for the highest good. It is sensible to appoint a group leader who can keep the sessions on track, sensitively stopping idle chatter in its tracks and encouraging the shyer members of the group to come forward. If the leader has common senses combined with finely honed psychic abilities, so much the better. He or she can keep an eye on any spirit who may want to communicate, and can recognise when 'messages' are mere wishful thinking reflecting back what someone wants to hear or when 'channelling' is a load of codswallop (believe me, I've heard an awful lot of that in groups and from the platform of spiritualist churches!) The leader of such a group cannot afford to people please in an effort to be liked. They must be able to keep discipline without being overly authoritarian and can break up cliques or alliances not for the group's highest good. The leader should also be responsible for ensuring that the space is safe and clean before the session comments, and for opening and closing the session in an appropriate way and ensuring that every member is in a fit state, fully grounded, shut down and wholly present, before leaving. Once the group has been opened, the group should be fully focused on the task at hand and other concerns should be left outside the room until it has been closed again.

Group exercises

Exercises quickly bring a group together and open up psychic abilities. These exercises will be as useful to a meditation or psychic development group as to a working group as they strengthen group cohesion and intuitive communication. Decide who will lead the group. The group should sit in a circle, preferably within arms reach but having some space round each person. The leader has the task of speaking the preliminary instructions, setting the exercise in motion and closing the exercise. When the group leader is attuned to the group, he or she will know how long the pauses should be and when to commence leading once more – and when to gently encourage a group participant who may lack confidence to speak out.

What colour am I?

The leader starts off by explaining to the group what will happen. That first of all, they will be attuning to their own colour. Then they will look at the colours of the group. And finally, they will go round the circle, each in turn, to pick up their neighbour's colour. Suggest that, when it comes to their turn, they should try to project their colour to their neighbour and that their neighbour should keep an open mind to receive the colour. When the neighbour knows the colour, it is spoken aloud. The person projecting the colour answers: 'Yes' or 'No'. The neighbour can try again, or can open it to the group. The leader can suggest that anyone who does not pick up the correct colour might like to put their hand out to the person projecting the colour to see how they feel. (Kinaesthetic people may pick up the colour red as 'hot', blue as 'wet' or 'cool' and so on.) Remind the group that some people are better at transmitting and others at receiving but that, with practice, both are possible. As leader and as a group, encourage anyone who holds back to express what they feel – either what they are picking up or their own inner emotions. This will help them to trust the group and builds group cohesion.

Exercise: What colour are you?

Sit with your eyes closed, feet on the floor and your hands resting loosely on your thighs. Breathe gently and easily. Breathe in for the count of five: one, two, three, four, five. Hold the breath for the count of three: [slowly] one, two three. And breathe out for the count of six: one, two, three, four, five, six. And again: In: one, two, three, four, five. Hold: one, two, three. And out: one, two, three, four, five, six. And again. In: one, two, three, four, five. Hold: one, two, three. And out: one, two, three, four, five, six. Let that rhythm continue without having to give more attention to it.

Think of a colour. See that colour as a light above your head. The colour will come down from the light, filling your whole body and suffusing your aura. Take the colour into the centre of your being. [Wait]

Look around the circle – with your eyes open or closed. There will be a rainbow all around you, each colour connected to a member of the group. What colours do you see? [wait]

*Now bring your attention back to yourself and attune to your own colour once more. We are now going to go around the circle. ***[Name of the person on your right hand side] What colour am I?*

[The person on the right of the leader names the colour. If it is not correct, another opportunity is given or it is thrown open to the group. When that colour has been established, move on]

*"*** it is your turn"*

**** turns to the person on her right and asks: "xxx, What colour am I?"*

[Each member of the group takes a turn.] When everyone has completed their turn, bring your attention back to yourself. Let your colour return to the light above your head. As it switches off, close your third eye shield, and bring your attention back into the room.

Throwing the ball

Throwing the ball also uses colour. It is particularly helpful in a new group as it also establishes names in peoples' minds.

Exercise: Throwing the ball

When the exercise begins, the ball goes around the circle but as it progresses, it is tossed across the circle at random. The person throwing the ball calls the name of the person to whom it is going and visualises the coloured ball – the colour changes at random at it moves around the group. The person receiving it calls out the colour they saw. The person who threw it says: 'Yes' or 'No' and names the colour. Giving the colour enables other members of the group to see if their own telepathic receptivity is correct.

Identifying transmitters

It may be that one, or more, members of the group are particularly strong transmitters. This can interfere with group exercises. If a group consistently seems to be getting the colours wrong, the leader should ask if anyone in the group is getting them all, or most, right. Ask that person to throw the ball and check how many people in the group picked up the colour. If most do, this is a person with a strong sending ability. That being the case, ask that person if they would mind stepping outside the room for a few moments and to refrain from thinking about the exercise. If the group gets more correct hits, the person who is out of the room, by apparently picking up a colour, is in fact sending it more strongly than the person who is throwing the ball. It would be helpful for the group if, during an exercise, that the strong sender deliberately refrained from naming or seeing a colour in their mind unless it was their turn to be the sender.

However, if you do have a strong sender in your midst, you have an enormous asset. You can expand your telepathy games by asking that person to send from another room or a distant place while the group are together. You could also utilise the ability while the group is separate. Arrange a specific time when the group can all tune into the sender and have the sender transmit twenty colours which individual members of the group pick up, everyone keeping a list. Next time the group meets, compare lists.

19
Living Psychically

We know more than we know we know.
Michael Polanyi

Your psychic ability is not something apart from your daily life, it underpins it. Allow it to and it will transform your life. Coming from a place of intuitive trust totally changes your approach. You will no longer be defensive, aggressive, suspicious or self-orientated. You can be open with people and allow your life to flow effortlessly. This is not a passive process, however. It is dynamic. You need to act when appropriate. Following authentic psychic guidance, you instinctively know what is needed, the actions to take, the decisions to make. You will be in the right place at the right time. People will be drawn into your orbit to facilitate your path. The right job will come along or the old one will open out. Life becomes harmonious, your well-being is enhanced, your abundance assured.

The psychic life

> *Once you awaken your psychic connection and get in the habit of listening to and acting on it, every decision in your life will become reflective of your inner truth.*
> *Gabrielle Roth*

A life that runs smoothly is far less stressful and much more is achieved with far less effort expended when you are in touch with your psychic guidance. Before you begin a project, make a phone call, or start a conversation with someone, take a moment to tune in. Check that you are on the right path, that this action is beneficial (using the finger pull method of dowsing can be helpful here until knowing becomes instantaneous). Empathising at a psychic level makes contact far easier and deeper and creates a cooperative atmosphere. If you have to point something out, or complain, for instance, take the time to mentally rehearse. See yourself making your point and it being received and dealt with constructively. Visualise a successful outcome to anything and it will manifest.

If you want to make contact with someone but don't know where they are, send a message out into the ether. When I urgently needed my house-sitter and he was uncontactable by phone, I sent him a psychic email. I pictured him in my mind, told him the day I needed to leave, and mentally asked him to arrive in time. He walked in with an hour to spare. But I knew he would be there as we had a strong psychic connection. When I wondered what had happened to a friend I hadn't heard from in ten years, within a day she had telephoned saying 'I heard your call on the ether'. As it turned out she had just had her third diagnosis of cancer and I had clearly picked that up over the ether too.

I use this same principle to find a parking space, to get to the train or airport at exactly the right time, and to attract the particular person I need to make contact with in a big gathering – whether I am aware of their identity or not. I allow myself to be in a receptive space that draws to me what I need. Note that I say what I need rather than what I would like. I have found that what I think I would like is not always what I really need. Sometimes this brings apparent difficulties, delays or sidetracks into my life. Trusting that this is still right can be difficult, but it inevitably proves to be so although sometimes my psychic awareness works without telling me what is going on! Holding trust and the right intention is essential.

Living psychically can even save your life. Perceiving that a car is coming moments before it comes round the corner on the wrong side of the road can avoid accidents, as can instinctively recognising that a car is about to pull out in front of you or that someone is going to brake suddenly. Use the finger pull method of dowsing to check if it is safe to pull out when you are at a place with a restricted view.

Perfect timing

As your psychic sensitivity to ensure that you arrive in perfect time. This means that if you are late, the person you are meeting will also be late. If your train is delayed, you will still be in perfect time, and so on.

Finding a parking place

It is possible to send your psychic awareness ahead of you to spot a parking place, automatically guiding you in the right direction. But you can go further than this. Your psychic ability can create that parking spot.

Picture an empty space waiting for you exactly where you need it. Trust the picture, and there it will be.

Last time I did this there was one parking space in the whole of a crowded station car park, right where I wanted it, and there was also a daily parking ticket waiting for me in the machine. That was an unexpected bonus for which I was truly grateful.

Clear the way

An ancient Sufi chant to clear the way is *Ya fa tah*. It is exceedingly useful when stuck in traffic jams or behind a slow moving vehicle. As you chant, use your psychic awareness to check whether the vehicle will turn off right or left. You can also extend this by psychically hoovering up any objects that are blocking the way so that you have a smooth journey – extremely useful if you have to travel by an unreliable train service. This is a subtle use of psychokinetic energy.

Instant access

Whilst you can use your psychic perception to tell you when someone is available, you can also use it to ensure that they are there when you need them.

Exercise: Instant access

Take a few moments to bring your attention into yourself. Picture the person you want to speak to, whether in person or by telephone, and picture them available, helpful and ready to give you their full attention and cooperation.

Psychic awareness and creativity

> *The poet is a light and winged and holy thing and there is no invention in him until he's been inspired and is out of his senses, and the mind is no longer in him.*
>
> *Socrates*

There is enormous evidence, mostly anecdotal and experiential but nonetheless indisputable, that creativity is an intuitive process. Great thinkers, artists and scientists throughout the ages have all relied on intuition:

> *It should not be hard for you to stop sometimes and look into the stains of walls, or ashes of a fire, or clouds, or mud, or like places in which you may find really marvellous ideas.*
>
> *Leonardo Da Vinci (Notebooks)*

> *[the pioneer scientist must have] a vivid intuitive imagination for new ideas are not generated by deduction, but by artistically creative imagination.*
>
> *Max Planck*

Invention is not the product of logical thought.
Albert Einstein

Intuition and creativity go hand in hand. As artist David Whyte explains:

> *You feed your longing and desires and they do the work. My whole life has been following my intuition and strange beckonings.*

Artists and inventors have learned to pay attention to the elusive thought, the inspiration that slips unseen from other minds. Niels Bohr, the atomic physicist, confessed that he had not worked out his complex atomic models by classical mechanics but rather by intuition. He dreamt he was on a giant gas sun around which planets whirled, whistling as they passed, each attached to the sun by a filament. The dream represented events within the atom. As Ralph Waldo Emerson perceptively said:

> *In every work of genius we recognize our own rejected thoughts.*

And, as Einstein pointed out:

> *the formulation of a problem is often more essential than its solution, which may be merely a matter of mathematical or experimental skill. To raise new questions, new possibilities, to regard old questions from a new angle, requires creative imagination and marks real advances in science.*

Overcoming creative blocks

You have only to work up imagination to the state of vision and the thing is done.
William Blake

"I chip away everything that is not elephant" a sculptor replied when asked how he created a statue from a block of stone. Further questioning revealed that he was able to discern the form of the elephant within the stone and reveal it.

Many people find themselves confronted with creative blocks. You don't have to be a great artist or writer to create. Decorating your home or landscaping your garden are creative acts. So too is living your life to the full. Making the most of your talents and potential is creative. If you feel blocked in any area of your life, a simple exercise can reveal the way forward.

Exercise: Overcoming creative blocks

In your mind's eye, take yourself into your favourite place. Spend a few moments enjoying this beautiful space. Feel it, smell it and see it.

Then, if you walk a little way to one side, you will find that a large block of stone or wood has been left for you, along with a mallet, chisels and smoothing materials.

Walk around your block. Look at it from all sides. Feel its texture, its warmth or coolness. Allow an image of what this block might hold to come into your mind.

Pick up the tools, weigh them in your hand. See how each one is specially shaped for the task it performs.

Using these tools, allow your hands to begin chipping away at the block to reveal the image at its centre. Hear the sound of the hammer, feel the flakes as they chip off. Look at how the colour changes. If you are working on wood, it will release its own special smell.

When your image is revealed, use the smoothing and polishing materials to bring out its full beauty.

When it is complete, make your way back to the centre of your favourite place. Think about your creation, what did it mean to you? What did it signify? How did you feel about it?

Then bring your attention back into the room and write up your experience in your metaphysical journal.

Problem solving

It is by the logic that we prove, but by the intuition that we discover.

Poincare

Allowing your psychic awareness to solve problems makes life flow more smoothly. If you have a problem to which you cannot find a solution try the following:

Post up your solution where you will be sure to see it – over the washbasin, on the fridge door and so. This way your subconscious will cooperate with you in bringing the solution into concrete manifestation.

Exercise: Problem solving

Spend a few minutes writing out your problem, list the ways you have tried to solve it, and the difficulties you have had, the blocks you have come up against. Be as specific and detailed as possible but avoid excuses.

Put your pen away and close your eyes.

Breathe gently and easily. Now think about your problem and why you would like to find a solution. Be as succinct and positive as possible.

Take your attention away from your problem and leave it in the hands of your psychic awareness. Meanwhile, take yourself to your favourite place. Explore it, see the sights, hear the sounds, and smell its perfumes. Take as long as you like.

Then when you are ready, look around. You will see a building away to one side. Make your way over there, feeling the ground beneath your feet and the pull of your muscles as you walk.

When you reach the building, stand by the door. Put out your hand and touch the door. Feel its texture beneath your fingers. Notice how it feels. Then find the door handle. Open it, and go inside.

There you will find the solution to your problem. Remember to ask how you will implement the solution to bring about an optimum result.

When you have learnt all you need, come back through the door bringing the solution with you. Make your way back to your favourite place and return your attention into the room.

Write down your solution and how you will implement it as fully as possible using the present tense.

At least once a day, read aloud your solution. Put in motion any action required. Your psychic awareness can show you how to solve a problem but it needs action on your part to manifest an outcome.

Psychic abilities and self-healing

People can train themselves to listen carefully to the messages and needs of their own bodies. [63]

Asking yourself some basic questions about your well-being in an intuitive way can give deep insights into your state of mind and body. The following questions are apposite to many health issues and are best asked while sitting quietly with a minimum of distractions. Hopefully by this stage of the book you will be able to answer yes to most of these questions immediately but reminding yourself is useful:

- Do I regularly talk – and listen – to my body?
- Am I getting the exercise, rest and relaxation my body needs?
- Am I overlooking indications of stress, pain or dis-ease?
- Is my body trying to tell me something?
- Is the food I am eating beneficial for me?
- Does the food I eat have the right nutrition or lifeforce in it?
- How will I feel an hour after eating this food?
- What does my body want me to do right now?

Some psychics merely have to look at someone to diagnose an internal illness or emotional dis-ease. Whilst ability at this level is rare, it is easy to develop your healing abilities, especially as it applies to your own body. If you get into the habit of regularly scanning your body, and checking on your emotional equilibrium, you can maintain health and well-being – try to time this for one of your ultradian rest periods to maximise the effect.

Exercise: The body wellness scan

Sit down, close your eyes, relax and breathe easily. Take your attention to the top of your head and down to your sinus passages. Check that they are unobstructed. Then move to your eyes. Check out how they feel and how they are functioning. Do the same for your ears. Notice if anything feels out of balance, and place healing light there if needed.

Begin to move your attention down through your brain. Check out each part as you come to it including the pituitary and pineal glands, make sure the blood and chemical mix is flowing well, the neural connections are all firing in sequence, and the endocrine system properly regulated. If any part is blocked or malfunctioning picture healing light flowing through it.

Move your attention into your neck and shoulders, checking out your thyroid gland and voice box (if your thyroid feels 'fast' or 'slow', picture the control mechanism as a scale and bring the pointer back to normal), and down your arms to your finger tips and back up again. Bathe any areas of stiffness in light.

Bring your awareness down through your body, checking out each organ in turn and putting in healing light where necessary. Look at your lungs, thymus gland and heart. Then check out your oesophagus, stomach, liver and pancreas. Follow your intestinal system through to its end. Return your attention to the spleen, kidneys, ladder and into the reproductive organs. Check that the organs of elimination are removing toxins efficiently and put in a 'cleaning team' to help if they are not.

Take your attention to the blood circulating through your body. Check the arteries and veins that carry it, clearing any blockages with light.

Now take your attention to your lymphatic system, let your mind follow its channels making sure that the lymph is flowing freely. Clear any blockages. Ensure that your immune system is working at full capacity.

Let your attention go on down through your thighs, knees and into your feet, checking as you go.

Take your attention back to the top of your head. Picture a shaft of healing light coming down to envelop and pass through your body. Let a feeling of well-being flow through your whole body, energising and healing as it goes.

If you become aware of any area that does not return to balance and good health, be sure to check it out with your physician or natural healer.

By taking your attention into your solar plexus, you can check out your emotional health and dowse for appropriate methods to gently release and rebalance your emotions.

You can use the *Crystal Wisdom Oracle* cards to bring you back to a sense of well-being. Simply lay the appropriate card over an area of dis-ease or your chakras and allow the energies to rebalance themselves. Instructions are in the pack, or you could use my *Crystal Healing* pack which comes complete with healing crystals to lay out on your chakras to return body, emotions, mind and spirit back into harmony.

Incorporating your higher self

We are not trying to change reality.... We are letting reality change.

Dr Andrea Kary

By now you should be used to consulting your higher self and incorporating the intuitions that come to you in this way into your life. Dr Andrea Kary uses her higher self to give her a different perspective on the things that happen in her life. As she explains:

> *I've been trying to take 100% responsibility for what is being manifest in my life. So whenever something happens that I'm not too happy with, I ask "If this is my higher self manifesting this, why? or what would be the lesson?" I've been amazed at how quickly the answer, or AN answer pops into my brain. And interestingly enough, if I take that answer to heart and act on it, in whatever form I am able, the situation usually resolves itself quicker than I was expecting.*
>
> *Here's an example: I started my irrigation pump 2 weekends ago and discovered that I had not done a good enough job winterizing the pumphouse and the 4 inch valve had frozen and cracked. So I spent an hour flogging myself for my carelessness, since this time of year, it usually takes 2-3 weeks to get someone out for repairs and my pastures were already dry. Then I took a deep breath and asked: "If this was my higher self manifesting this broken pipe, why would it do that?" The immediate answer was that I have been thinking about how to influence weather patterns, particularly rain, but I'm basically lazy and it's easier to just order up irrigation water and turn on the pump, so better start now.*
>
> *It was a partially cloudy afternoon and the main rain clouds were too far north and too far east for them to be blown my way with the current winds. But I dropped into my heart space and into my right brain and did like the Hopi Indians: I smelled the rain,*

I saw the rain, I heard the rain, I felt the rain, I tasted the rain. Then I climbed into bed for a nap. An hour later, it was pouring rain (remember I live in the desert). And when I called the repair man the following day, they were able to fix it by the end of the week.

So, I guess this is what I am thinking about, when you talk about bringing forth what is inside you. By asking the higher self for the lesson, it can be shifted if only by the virtue of a different perspective of the problem.

You too can use 'weather magic' to assist your life in exactly the way that Dr Kary sets out – or to do the reverse. When I was about to walk the twelve mile Preseli mountain trail to the source of the healing Bluestones of Stonehenge I took a bus with the friend who was showing me the way. We'd left the car at the end of the walk and were about to get off the bus at the start when the bus driver said "the tourist office are recommending people don't do that walk it's too boggy – and look at those rainclouds". There were huge towering thunderclouds all around. "Oh", I said flippantly "I'll just have to keep an umbrella over us" and thought no more about it.

It was an amazing walk with stunningly wild scenery and incredible earth energies, with rays of the sun streaking down through the clouds and not a drop of rain until we reached our car which was waiting at the other end - when the heavens opened and five hours worth of rain came down in a few minutes, or so it seemed.

Another moment of living psychically had come when we reached the bluestones and were sitting down to meditate. "I think I'd better tell you," said my friend, "I left the GPS behind and I don't actually know how to get down from here, every time I've been before I've landed up in a deep bog". "Not to worry", I said, a little less flippantly this time, "I'll ask for someone to come and show us the way – look that flock of sheep coming down the track might know". "I think we'd better follow the walkers behind them," Chris grinned. "They'll know". And so they did. It was worth missing the meditation, we'd have been in deep trouble without them.

There is one thing you can be certain of when you live a psychic life; it will never be dull or boring!

Conclusion
The Spiritual Psychic

I didn't realize how sharing my journey through life helped people, until I started to get comments and emails telling me how my blogs have changed their life, and that what I was going through was everything that they were going through. How I handled situations gave people a different outlook in life.

Lisa Williams (www.lisawilliams.com)

Let me state something here that I should perhaps have said way back at the beginning. Being psychic doesn't necessarily mean you are spiritual. I once sent a workshop participant off to a well–known teaching venue to see what she could learn. She came back saying exactly that. She'd sat at the feet of mediums, healers and channellers but, as she said, it didn't help her one iota with her soul pathway. Her whole focus in life was to develop her spirituality and the question she had brought to me was how to give service to others. She had thought that maybe that meant that she should become a healer or a medium. But no, her way was different. She was here to develop and then radiate her spirituality out to the world. She was to be the antithesis to the 'doom and gloom merchants' and those who simply wanted to prove survival of death or to demonstrate psychic powers without thinking of the deeper implications. She was to rise above ego and ambition and work quietly in the background. A spiritual presence on the earth, but one who wouldn't be recognised. Celebrity had no part in her soulplan. Don't get me wrong, some psychics are extremely spiritual people and we need them to be out there showing the way. Others, sadly, are not. We've examined the all too common pitfalls on the psychic path.

To me being psychic is a tool in your spiritual armoury. It expands your awareness, opens up your consciousness, guides your life and gives you access to higher knowledge and a sense of being connected to all things. It can help you give other people insight into their pathway and possibilities. Witnessing psychic phenomena can prize open people's minds, receiving a message can set them on a new road. But it isn't a cop out. It doesn't help you to avoid the necessary learnings and lessons in life, to bypass your own karma, or to go against the agenda that your soul had when it set out on its long incarnatory path. It can, however, assist you in putting your skills and abilities, the fruits of the lessons learned, into practice more easily. But beyond that, to my mind we are here primarily to make spiritual progress. As William Bloom puts it:

> *As I progressed, I began to realise that the ability to manipulate energy or work with imagery did not mean that I or someone else was spiritual. I began to understand that clairvoyance, psychism and energy manipulation were skills and tools like plumbing, embroidery, mechanics or banking. Being expert at them or having a natural talent for them was meaningless when related to spirituality. Spirituality, for me and I dare say for most people, is about a deepening connection with the wonder and spirit of life; is about wisdom, compassion and expanding consciousness; is about harmoniously serving the community.* [64]

So, why did I take the trouble to write this book? Well, I happen to believe that, if you train your intuition and hone your psychic abilities, you then have the possibility of rising above the mundane world, of transcending consensual reality and moving into All That Is. From there, the view of our earth and our earthly lives is very different. You realise that it is purposeful, fair and just, and that there is so much more to experience. Judgement drops away, insight and compassion increase, and unconditional love becomes a core part of the process of your being. As with crystal work, you gain access to the multi–dimensions of consciousness that take you far away from what you thought you knew. You are able to travel effortlessly through the myriad dimensions that surround us. This is where the future of humanity lies. But it's also where many of the pitfalls lie, the deceivers and the downright mischievous lurk, the inner turmoil that trips you up lingers so you need your psychic discernment and an ability to get right to the heart of the matter instantly. This is why, although I honour and value the assistance of guides and wise beings, I would urge you to have immediate experience of those other worlds. To move beyond being merely psychic into a metaphysical awareness that is both spiritual and experiential. To truly know. To become all that you are.

Let me close with a quote from a celebrity psychic who travels the world bringing words of inspiration and comfort to others and who is, in my experience of her, totally authentic and honest with herself and who epitomises the process of soul–searching and sharing that makes her truly spiritual:

> ***Determined to stay present***
>
> *I am so aware that I haven't blogged for some time, in fact I have actually hidden a little – no let's be honest Lisa, you've hidden a lot! I have wallowed in self pity and drama,*

become consumed with emotions that I didn't want to deal with, and saw a great deal of fear within me, I never wanted to admit it, but I have had too.

How was I supposed to motivate and inspire others if I couldn't drag myself out of this? How could I write when I just didn't feel like it? The truth was I couldn't. So why I am telling you this when this is supposed to be inspirational – well – I wanted you to see that we are all human and that we all have issues even people like me who inspire others to lead a spiritual life.

Letting go of controlling things and being vulnerable, opening yourself up to possibilities and allowing life to unfold in the way that it's supposed to, and you know what I have done this and I am happy beyond words. I have amazing people in my life and I am grateful... No ego, just me feeling good about where I have been, and knowing what I have gone through and where I am now.

I have seen the light, it's about being present. Years ago I wanted to leave this world by choice, but now life is a gift and I am going to live it...

It's been an incredible journey and one that I have to embrace and look back on with love, because it's made me who I am. Yes it was painful, yes it was hard, but I am happy, and I know I am loved and that is all that I can ask for.

Lisa Williams
(http://www.lisawilliams.com/blog/Posted – Wednesday, May 16, 2012)

Acknowledgements

To all my mentors and everyone from whom I have learned, my gratitude and thanks. I have enjoyed so many stimulating conversations and experiences over the years but particularly with Dr Andrea Kary, Kyrin Moreton, Diane Conway, Sylvia Ghent and Zsuzsanah Griga, so thank you all and everyone else who has contributed in any way to this book. And to Margaret Cahill, editor extraordinare, friend, all round amazing person and a very wise woman for taking the trouble to work through each exercise in this book and check it out before publishing. It has always been a pleasure and a privilege to work with you and this book was no exception.

Resources and Further Reading

Karmic readings

For details of Judy Hall's work see her website www.judyhall.co.uk

Crystal suppliers

Judy Hall's personally charged crystals: www.angeladditions.co.uk
Crystal Course: 21 Days to Understand Crystals Judy Hall, E-Book (Hay House) from Amazon.co.uk and Amazon.com
www.exquisitecrystals.com

Resources

British Society of Dowsers www.britishdowsers.org
Institute of Heartmath http:/www.hearthmath.org
Petaltone Essences www.petaltone.co.uk
School of Intuition and Healing www.intuitionandhealing.co.uk/
Simon Lilly Drum Journeys www.greenmanessences.com
Spirit rescue and detachment: The Spirit Release Foundation at www.spiritrelease.com
Crystal Balance Company Essences: Detachment and Light www.crystalbalance.net
Steven Halpern *Initiation and Ancient Echoes* (CD). Available from Google and Amazon

Bibliography

Carr-Gomm, Philip and Stephanie. *The Druid Animal Oracle*, Connections Book Publishing, 1996.

Davidson, Wilma. *Dowsing for Answers*, Green Magic, 2007.

____ *Spirit Rescue*, Llewellyn, 2007.

Griffn, Joe and Tyrrell, Ivan. *Dreaming Reality: How Dreaming Keeps Us Sane, or Can Drive Us Mad*, HG Publishing, 2006.

Gunn, Celia M. *Simply Totem Animals*, Zambezi, 2010.

Guiley, Rosemary Ellen. *Harper's Encyclopedia of Mystical and Paranormal Experience*, HarperCollins, 1991.

Hall, Judy. *The Soulmate Myth*, Flying Horse Books, 2010.

____ *21 Days to Understand Crystals* (Hay House) from Amazon.co.uk and Amazon.com

____ *The Book of Why*, Flying Horse Books, 2011.

____ *Good Vibrations*, Flying Horse Books, 2008.

____ *The Crystal Wisdom Oracle*, Watkins/DB Books, 2013.

____ *101 Power Crystals*, Fair Winds, 2011.

____ *Crystals and Sacred Sites*, Fair Winds, 2012.

____ *Crystal Healing Pack*, (Godsfield), 2011.

____ *Earth Healing*, Watkins, 2014.

Hawkins, David R. *Power vs. Force: The Hidden Determinants of Human Behaviour*, Hay House Inc., 1995.

Jung, C.G. *Memories, Dreams, Reflections*, Fountain Books, Glasgow, 1977.

Lawton, Ian. *Your Holographic Soul*, Rational Spirituality Press, 2010.

____ *The Big Book of the Soul*, Rational Spirituality Press, 2008.

Lilly, Sue and Simon. *The Essential Crystal Handbook*, Duncan Baird, London, 2006.

Laszlo, Ervin. *The Akashic Experience: science and the cosmic memory field*, Inner Traditions, 2009.

Lucas, Winafred Blake. *Regression Therapy: A Handbook for Professionals*. Deep Forest Press, 1993.

Morse, Melvin.*Where God Lives*, HarperCollins, 2001.

Pinchbeck, Daniel. *Breaking open the Head*, Flamingo, 2004.

Ritchie, George. *Return from Tomorrow*¸ Chosen Book Publishing, 1978.

Skafte, Diane. *When Oracles Speak*, Thorsons, 1997.

Spezzano, Chuck. *The Enlightenment Pack*, Rider, 1996.

Villoldo, Alberto. *Shaman, Healer, Sage*. Bantam Books, 2000.

Endnotes

1. Laszlo, Ervin. *The Akashic Experience: science and the cosmic memory field*, Inner Traditions (Vermont 2009), p.6 (hereinafter Laszlo). I recommend this book for its fascinating fusion of experience and scientific explanation with ancient wisdom.
2. 'Solutions for Stress: developing your intuition', Institute of Heartmath on http://www.heartmath.org/index2.php?option=com_content&task=view&id=154&Itemid, consulted 24.09.2008
3. Carr-Gomm, Philip and Stephanie, *The Druid Animal Oracle Connections*, Book Publishing 1996 p.150.
4. Personal conversation with the late Professor Alan Bennett shortly before his death.
5. Davidson, Wilma. *Dowsing for Answers*, Green Magic, 2007, p.13 [hereinafter Davidson].
6. Taggart, Bill. 'Using an Psychic development journal: Dimensions of Intuitive Experience', *The News* Vol.4 No.1, March 1997.
7. Skafte, Diane. *When Oracles Speak*, Thorsons, London, 1997, p.240 [hereinafter Skafte].
8. Hall, Judy. *Good Vibrations*, Flying Horse Books, 2008 p.7.
9. Davidson, Wilma. *Spirit Rescue*, Llewellyn, 2007, p.142 [hereinafter Davidson 2].
10. Tighe, James. 'Relaxation' http://www.bbc.co.uk/health/conditions/mental_health/coping_relaxation.shtml.
11. Rossi, Ernest. *The Psychobiology of Mind/Body Healing*, W. W. Norton & Company, 1994.
12. Spezzano, Chuck. *The Enlightenment Pack*, Rider, London, 1996.
13. Ritchie, George. *Return from Tomorrow*, Chosen Book Publishing, 1978.
14. Brunton, Paul. title mislaid.
15. Ramachandran, V.S. 'Mirror Neurons and the brain in a vat' in *Edge, The Third Culture*, on http://www.edge.org/3rd_culture/ramachandran06/ramachandran06_index.html, consulted 13.10.2009.
16. See for instance the Society for Psychical Research ESP and Neural Activity – EEG and MRI studies on http://www.spr.ac.uk/expcms where you can download:
    Charman, R.A. (2006). 'Has direct brain to brain communication been demonstrated?' *Journal of the Society for Psychical Research*, 70, 1-24.
    Charman, R.A. (2006). 'Direct brain to brain communication - further evidence from EEG and fMRI studies.' *Paranormal Review*, 40, 3-9.
    Charman, R.A. (2006). 'Correspondence: Something really is going on.' *Journal of the Society for Psychical Research*, 70, 249-251.
17. Institute of Heartmath on http:/www.hearthmath.org/index2.php?option=_com_contents&task=view&id=154&Itemid
18. Lilly, Sue and Simon. *The Essential Crystal Handbook*, Duncan Baird, London, 2006.

19. This information was passed to me during a personal conversation. I do not yet have further details.
20. See www.heartmath.org for details of ongoing research programmes and the results of studies.
21. See www.heartmath.org 'Emotional energetics research'.
22. Sadly the excellent site http://www.animalspirits.com/indexlist.html seems to have disappeared but see:
    Farmer, Steven D. *Power Animal Oracle Cards*, Hay House 2005.
    Sams, Jamie and Carson, David. *Medicine Cards*, Bear & Co. Santa Fe 1988.
    Carr-Gomm , Philip and Stephanie. *The Druid Animal Oracle*, Connections Book Publishing, London, 1994, and the excellent:
    Gunn, Celia, M. *Simply Totem Animals*, Zambezi, Plymouth, 2010.
23. Bloom, William. *Feeling Safe*, p.71.
24. Lipton, Bruce. *The Biology of Belief* and Emoto, Masaru *Messages from Water*, Vols 1-3. This work still has to be replicated by the scientific community as Emoto is apparently reluctant to reveal his process and the percentage of photographs he rejects as against those he publishes but it still gives considerable food for thought. (see Also http://www.is-masaru-emoto-for-real.com for a scientific criticism and analysis of his work.)
25. Guiley, Rosemary Ellen. *Harper's Encyclopedia of Mystical and Paranormal Experience*, New York: HarperCollins, 1991, pp. 463-464 quoted on http://www.themystica.com/mystica/articles/p/precognition.html.
26. http://www.williambloom.com/writings/memories-atlantis-84.htm.
27. Lawton, Ian. *Your Holographic Soul*, Rational Spirituality Press, 2010.
28. Grof, Stanislav. Personal notes taken at 'Beyond the Brain', New Avenues in Consciousness Research Conference, August 24-27 1995, St. John's College, Cambridge, England.
29. Morse, Melvin. *Where God Lives*, HarperCollins, 2001.
30. Lecture given by Peter Fenwick on near death experiences and their impact on consciousness studies. Date mislaid. A précis of the lecture can be found on http://www.thepsychictimes.com/articles/fenwick.htm.
31. Lucas, Winafred Blake. *Regression Therapy: A Handbook for Professionals*, Deep Forest Press, Crest Park, CA 1993, Vol.1 p.65ff.
32. See for instance the Heartmath site and the work of Hemi-sync.
33. Ramachandran 'Mirror Neurons and imitation learning as the driving force behind "the great leap forward" in human evolution', *Edge* no.69, May 29, 2000.
34. See, for instance, the work of Nobel Prize winner Roger Sperry and the 'split-brain experiments'.
35. I am grateful to Dr Kary for allowing me to quote extensively from our correspondence and for the insights she has facilitated in me.

36. Eden, Dan. 'Left Brain, Right Brain', Turn on your brain http://www.viewzone.com/bicam.html
37. You can follow this research on the Heartmath.org website but it is summarized on the Vital Source blog.
38. Unfortunately I have mislaid the source of this information.
39. Davidson.
40. See Hawkins, David R. *Power vs. Force: The Hidden Determinants of Human Behaviour,* Hay House Inc., USA,1995/2002 p.30.
41. Jung, C.G. *Memories, Dreams, Reflections.*
42. Pinchbeck, Daniel. *Breaking open the Head,* Flamingo, 2004 p.6.
43. Anon. 'Intuition's Role in Health and Healing', http://www.lifesciencefoundation.org/inmain.html
44. Morse, Melvin with Perry, Paul. *Where God Lives,* HarperSanFrancisco, 2000.
45. Utts, Jessica and Josephenson, Brian D. 'The Paranormal: the evidence and its implications for consciousness on http://www.temp.phy.cam.ac.uk/-bdj10/psi/tuscon.psi cibsykted 18.9.08.
46. Beloff, John. See footnote 28.
47. Exceptional Human Experience Network, http://www.ehe.org/display/splash.html
48. The phrase 'neurochemical looking glass' is taken from p.3, *Breaking Open the Head* by Daniel Pinchbeck (Flamingo, London 2004). Pinchbeck experimented with just about every psychedelic drug and etheobotanic substance known to ancient and modern man, not a research method I'd personally recommend, but his book makes fascinating reading for those who quite naturally visit the realms he describes and who can compare their experience with his. My thanks to the lovely Stephen Gawtry of Watkins Books for the introduction to this book.
49. Young, Robert. (ed. Alan Chedzoy) *Early Years: Recollections of Life in Sturminister Newton in the Early 19th Century,* Dorset County Museum. I am indebted to Roger Gutteridge for bringing my attention to this incident.
50. The International Association for Near-Death Studies, *Anabiosis,* The Journal for Near-Death Studies and see http://iands.org/research/research-news.html
51. For a full historical account see http://www.near-death.com/medieval.html
52. 'Increase in Psychic Phenomena Following Near-DeathExperiences', Bruce Greyson http://www.medicine.virginia.edu/clinical/departments/psychiatry/sections/cspp/dops/greyson-publications/NDE10.pdf.
53. Wheeler, John C. 'Death Was Delightful', *Psychic Observer,* Michigan date unknown cited in Muldoon and Carrington *The Phenomena of Astral Projection,* Rider & Co. first published 1951, 1984 reprint, p.218.

54. See for example Susan Blackmore *Dying to Live* and Greg Stone's reply 'A Critique of Susan Blackmore's Dying Brain Hypothesis' on http://www.near-death.com/experiences/articles001.html. The website www.near-death.com has a wealth of useful articles and case histories. See also:
   Fenwick, Peter and Elizabeth. *The Truth In The Light*, BCA, England, 1995.
55. Tandy, Paul. *Cause and Effect*, Volume 1.
56. Hall, Judy. *Principles of Past Life Therapy*, Harper Collins, London, 1996, page125ff.
57. Davidson 2.
58. Villoldo, Alberto. *Shaman, Healer, Sage*, Bantam Books, London, 2000, p.75.
59. Overend, Bill, 'Right brain meets left: applying intuition to business'. www.banffleadership.com [hereinafter Overend].
60. Tomasino, Dana, 'The psychophysiological basis of creativity and intuition: accessing 'the zone' of entrepreneurship. Abstract of a paper given at the Third AGSE International Entrepreneurship Research Exchange, February 8-10 2006, Auckland, New Zealand.
61. Study by Jagdish Parkh, Harvard University.
62. Overend.
63. 'Intuitions role in health and healing' http://www.lifesciencefoundation.org/inmain.html consulted 24.0.2008
64. William Bloom: Psychic or Spiritual Powers?
   http://www.williambloom.com/writings/psychic-or-spiritual-powers-82.htm

Titles from The Wessex Astrologer
www.wessexastrologer.com

Martin Davis — **Astrolocality Astrology**; **From Here to There**

Wanda Sellar — **The Consultation Chart**; **An Introduction to Medical Astrology**; **Decumbiture**

Geoffrey Cornelius — **The Moment of Astrology**

Darrelyn Gunzburg — **Life After Grief**; **AstroGraphology: The Hidden Link between your Horoscope and your Handwriting**

Paul F. Newman — **You're not a Person - Just a Birthchart**; **Declination: The Steps of the Sun**; **Luna: The Book of the Moon**

Jamie Macphail — **Astrology and the Causes of War**

Deborah Houlding — **The Houses: Temples of the Sky**

Dorian Geiseler Greenbaum — **Temperament: Astrology's Forgotten Key**

Howard Sasportas — **The Gods of Change**

Patricia L. Walsh — **Understanding Karmic Complexes**

M. Kelly Hunter — **Living Lilith**

Barbara Dunn — **Horary Astrology Re-Examined**

Deva Green — **Evolutionary Astrology**

Jeff Green — **Pluto 1**; **Pluto 2**; **Essays on Evolutionary Astrology (edited by Deva Green)**

Dolores Ashcroft-Nowicki and Stephanie V. Norris — **The Door Unlocked: An Astrological Insight into Initiation**

Martha Betz — **The Betz Placidus Table of Houses**

Greg Bogart — **Astrology and Meditation**

Kim Farnell — **Flirting with the Zodiac**

Joseph Crane — **Astrological Roots: The Hellenistic Legacy**; **Between Fortune and Providence**

Komilla Sutton — **The Essentials of Vedic Astrology**; **The Lunar Nodes**; **Personal Panchanga**; **The Nakshatras**

Anthony Louis — **The Art of Forecasting using Solar Returns**

Lorna Green — **Your Horoscope in Your Hands**

Martin Gansten — **Primary Directions**

Reina James — **All the Sun Goes Round**

Oscar Hofman — **Classical Medical Astrology**

Bernadette Brady — **Astrology, A Place in Chaos**; **Star and Planet Combinations**

Richard Idemon — **The Magic Thread**; **Through the Looking Glass**

Nick Campion — **The Book of World Horoscopes**

Judy Hall — **Patterns of the Past**; **Karmic Connections**; **Good Vibrations**; **The Soulmate Myth**; **The Book of Why**; **Book of Psychic Development**

John Gadbury — **The Nativity of the Late King Charles**

Neil D. Paris — **Surfing your Solar Cycles**

Michele Finey — **The Sacred Dance of Venus and Mars**

David Hamblin — **The Spirit of Numbers**

Dennis Elwell — **Cosmic Loom**

Gillian Helfgott — **The Insightful Turtle**

Christina Rose — **The Tapestry of Planetary Phases**

Lightning Source UK Ltd.
Milton Keynes UK
UKOW03f2130130115

244419UK00001B/19/P